D0454442

ROGUE NATION

ALSO BY PETER SCOWEN

Trahison tranquille

ROGUE NATION

The America the Rest of the World Knows

PETER SCOWEN

M&S

National Library of Canada Cataloguing in Publication

Scowen, Peter
    Rogue nation : the America the rest of the world knows / Peter Scowen.

Translation of: Le livre noir des États-Unis.
Includes index.
ISBN 0-7710-8005-0

    1. September 11 Terrorist Attacks, 2001.   2. Anti-Americanism.
3. United States – Foreign relations – 20th century.   4. United States –
Foreign public opinion.   I. Title.

E744.S4613 2003   327.73'009'045   C2003-900326-4

We acknowledge the financial support of the Government of Canada
through the Book Publishing Industry Development Program and that of
the Government of Ontario through the Ontario Media Development
Corporation's Ontario Book Initiative. We further acknowledge the
support of the Canada Council for the Arts and the Ontario Arts Council
for our publishing program.

Excerpts from *Blowback: The Costs and Consequences of American Empire* by
Chalmers Johnson, © 2000 by Chalmers Johnson. Reprinted by permission
of Henry Holt and Company, LLC.

Typeset in Janson by M&S, Toronto
Printed and bound in Canada

McClelland & Stewart Ltd.
The Canadian Publishers
481 University Avenue
Toronto, Ontario
M5G 2E9
www.mcclelland.com

1 2 3 4 5   07 06 05 04 03

CONTENTS

ACKNOWLEDGEMENTS

The bulk of this book was researched and written over the space of twelve weeks in the spring of 2002 – a period that included visits to New York City and Paris. Anything written this quickly cannot call itself a history book without doing a grave injustice to the work of historians who spend a lifetime on a subject. This is an exercise in journalism that owes a great debt to real historians, most notably Chalmers Johnson, Robert Jay Lifton, Greg Mitchell, Gar Alperovitz, and Henry Kissinger, as well as to the authors and editors of the *Oxford Companion to the History of the United States* and the *Penguin History of the United States of America*. I also relied heavily on the research of political scientist Benjamin R. Barber and nutrition expert Marion Nestle. Their words and facts pushed me in all the important directions, and I hope that I have amply credited them in the body of the text and in the footnotes. As well, I owe a debt to the National Security Archives, whose tireless efforts have forced various departments and agencies of the United States government to cough up invaluable documents and make them available on the Internet. If anything, this book is a testament to the reliability of a high-speed home Internet connection combined with the power of

Google. Through Internet searches, I found numerous leads that I was able to narrow down to their original sources. As often as possible, I went back to the original document; where expediency required it, I used newspaper reports and books as second-hand sources. The Internet archives of the *Baltimore Sun* and the *New York Times* were invaluable, as were those of the *National Post* in Toronto. The chapter on the Florida recount of the November 7, 2000, presidential election is based almost entirely on the reporting of the *Los Angeles Times'* "America Waits" coverage. Other valuable sources include the Amnesty International and Human Rights Watch Web sites. The Toronto Reference Library is also an excellent source of hard-to-find material.

Readers should note that all dollar figures provided are in American currency.

On a personal note, I need to thank Ken Whyte and Doug Kelly of the *National Post* for giving me leave to write this book. My wife, Lee-Anne Goodman, was, as always, 100 per cent behind me. I also want to thank her for turning me on to great American alternative bands like Wilco and the Dandy Warhols. Sorry about the mess around my desk.

Above all, my endless gratitude to my sister for surviving the World Trade Center attack on September 11, 2001. This book would have been unimaginable without her courage and inspiration.

INTRODUCTION

Toronto, Tuesday, April 2, 2002
My oldest sister spent this past weekend with my wife and me
at our home in Toronto. It was an honour to be in her presence.

Amy, an executive with an American management consulting firm, was in her office on the fifty-fourth floor of the
south tower of the World Trade Center by 8:30 a.m. on
September 11, 2001. She later recalled having an inexplicable
desire to reach out to faraway friends by e-mail when she got
to work that morning. When the first plane sent by Osama
bin Laden struck the north tower at 8:48, she knew right away
something terrible had occurred; her immediate guess was
that New York's tallest office buildings had been bombed
again, as they had been in 1993. From her window, she could
see thousands of sheets of paper drifting slowly in the air cur-
rents between the twin structures; above them, part of the
north tower was engulfed in an enormous wall of fire. For
reasons that are still largely mysterious to them, Amy and her
staff decided to leave their still-untouched building immediately. It just felt like the right thing to do. She and about
twenty-five colleagues slowly made their way down, at first in
the elevators and then in the emergency stairwell. They were

descending by foot and were at about the thirtieth floor when the second hijacked plane hit their building fifty storeys above with a force that lifted some of them into the air. They regrouped and started walking more quickly, making their way to the subway level and eventually outside, where instinct told them to head north, away from the towers. They still had no idea what had happened and would only learn of the cause of pandemonium, and how close they came to being killed, later in the day. Amy found out when she went to a friend's home in Greenwich Village seeking refuge and saw the footage of the planes, one after the other in a deliberate and precise attack, smashing into the two towers.

For her family, it was a morning of anguish. Dispersed in Montreal, Toronto, and Silver Springs, Maryland, and with phone lines jammed, our parents, Amy's husband, Chris, me, and my two other sisters spent three hours in that awful limbo between hope and dread. We knew Amy was resourceful and that, if she could get out, she would. But we did not know which tower she worked in or on what floor. Was she on the floors that were struck or, worse, above them? Her husband returned from walking their son to school to a voice message from Amy telling him that the north tower had been bombed but that she was all right and was leaving her building. He climbed to the roof of their house in Brooklyn and watched as the south tower – her tower – collapsed at 9:59 a.m. He retched at the sight.

This is all we knew in the first hours. My youngest sister and I watched the television coverage in her bedroom in Toronto. I was overwrought, an unhelpful reaction that ironically served to calm my sister. She was reassuring me about Amy's resourcefulness when the second tower fell before our eyes. Kate stopped her comforting banter abruptly and then said, deadpan, "That can't be good." Our feelings of helplessness increased when we learned of the explosion at the Pentagon and of the hijacked plane that had crashed in a Pennsylvania field. A resignation began to overtake us. We started to feel guilty worrying about one single person when it was now clear so many had died. We did not know which way to turn. Every phone call provided a moment's hope, but no relief. A friend in Toronto called to tell us Amy had e-mailed him that she was safe and to get word to us, but he could not determine whether she had sent the message from inside her office or from a location away from the havoc (she told us later she had sent the e-mail from an art gallery in Soho). I cannot imagine what our parents were going through, or Amy's husband, but for a brief moment that still haunts me, I was sure she was gone.

Finally, at about 11:30 a.m., Amy's husband got through to our mother in Montreal to tell her that her daughter, our sister, his wife, was safe. She had reached him by phone from her friend's home in Greenwich Village and was heading to Brooklyn to be with her family. I called her in Brooklyn from my office late that day and recorded an interview with her for the *National Post*. Amy described, in the emotionless monotone of a person in shock, her inexplicable and instant conclusion, based on nothing other than instinct, that she should get the hell out of her office. "It was an unbelievable decision," she said without enthusiasm. (A transcript of the interview with Amy appears at the back of this book.)

Her visit this past weekend was happy but difficult. Amy had come to Toronto for the funeral of her best friend's sister. While here, she visited another friend whose young husband had died suddenly a year earlier, and with a third friend whose mother had recently died as well. She cried frequently, and laughed a lot, too, when my wife nicknamed her Calamity Amy. When a taxicab Amy was in that weekend ran a Stop sign and was nearly creamed by another car, the adrenalin rush triggered memories that caused her to break down and sob. She was clearly still suffering from what she had gone through six and a half months earlier, a fact she acknowledged. Among the things that most troubled her was the way so large and life-altering an event had been able to sneak up on her. She wrote in a diary of "thinking back on how we were innocently moving toward being participants in a cataclysmic event. The day before – Monday – sitting in a meeting with senior people and then seeing them afterward – Thursday – with our whole universe changed forever."

I, too, was still struggling to come to terms with the events of September 11. My first reaction had been anger. I liked it when George W. Bush, the United States president, announced this was to be a battle between good and evil. I wanted not justice, but revenge. It felt right to me when the U.S. government rounded up Muslims and made no bones about its intention to retaliate with all its impressive military might. I also joined the mainstream of thought in saying no one ought to seek explanations for the attacks in American policy, because to do so would be to blame the victims indirectly. It seemed heartless in the face of such loss, and my family's near tragedy, to ask the victims and their loved ones to accept partial responsibility for what had been inflicted on them, or even to entertain the idea.

But even in moments of anger, reason still lurks in the back of the mind, looking for an opening. I felt an odd and disconcerting ambivalence about the fact that terrorism, which until that moment had been a remote reality – something that happened on television to U.S. embassies in Africa, or to men and women in Northern Ireland and the Middle East – was suddenly a local horror. Having worked in the media for eighteen years, a third of that in the alternative press, I knew the United States had committed atrocities of its own and was on thin ice when its president divided the world into good and evil. Above all, I simply could not reach a useful conclusion about why my sister and her workmates had become the target of a terrorist organization. What had innocent Americans from all walks of life done that possibly merited them being blown out of the sky on a beautiful late-summer morning?

This book is my investigation into the country where my sister was almost killed. I wrote it to answer nagging questions – notably, whether the United States government, through its foreign policies and past deeds, put its citizens in the line of fire, and whether it can truly claim the moral high ground in its new war on terrorism.

Back in the early months after September 11, these were questions that were not being asked. A period of grace had settled over America during which it became politically unfashionable, even treasonous, to suggest there was the slightest causal link between the policies of the United States and the terror attacks. The government, rather remarkably, announced itself to be as innocent as bin Laden's victims – a bystander chosen as a random target by an irrational force. The government's leaders and spokesmen, from the president down, insisted bluntly that the attacks were not a geopolitical event related to America's overseas interests. Many, including myself, bought this line out of sympathy and fear; for many others, I now realize, it was an imposed and largely artificial patriotism created by the joint efforts of the American government and a mainstream media overcome by fits of jingoistic overkill.

This book, then, is a belated examination of recent American history in light of its post–September 11 pretensions to moral clarity and innocent intentions. It is an attempt to arm readers with information to challenge the United States government's received wisdom about what happened.

Because, underneath their horror and patriotism, how can Americans *not* suspect there is a link between their government's foreign policies and the September 11 attacks? There *has* to be. How else do you explain it in a fashion that bears scrutiny? It is a laughable notion to suggest otherwise, that recent American foreign policy is somehow unlinkable to September 11. It is equally foolish to pretend the United States is a virtuous, innocent nation. There is no such thing as a virtuous nation. Not only is it foolish, but also self-defeating. For, in the strict black-and-white terms demanded by George W. Bush and others in their speeches after September 11 – where evil is evil and good is good, and nothing is relative – the United States of America in the past fifty years has been led by governments that have been as cruel and inhumane as any that have ever existed. When nuance is outlawed from a world filled with war and death, there can be no good guys, an irony apparently lost on the American leadership.

Americans see themselves as the citizens of a good, as opposed to evil, nation. The struggling citizens of other countries do not have the luxury of being so simplistic. They acknowledge America's good qualities, but they also know America to be a sponsor of state terrorism and backer of murderous dictatorships. They know a country that has happily participated in, or even undertaken, the extermination of inconvenient peoples in foreign nations when its interests demanded it. They dodge, or sometimes they don't, the trillions of dollars' worth of bullets and missiles American arms manufacturers have exported with a near complete disregard for who is buying them and for what purposes. They must scrape before a superpower that threatens to cut humanitarian aid to developing nations that do not embrace American democratic values, while at home it makes a mockery of those values. They marvel at a government that denounces human-rights abuses in other countries while condoning a justice system in which people are sentenced to hundreds of years in prison for minor drug possession, and which executes people who commit capital crimes as children. They watch as that country exports food and a lifestyle so unhealthy as to warrant being labelled in the same gruesome fashion as a pack of cigarettes. More than anything else, they see a government, purportedly on behalf of its wounded people, accusing other governments on grounds on which it does not stand perpendicular itself, as Mark Twain would have put it.

My sister was not bin Laden's target. Neither was the American way of life, nor civilization as a whole. Bin Laden's target was the United States government; the activities of that government in the Middle East were his addled justification. He may also have been targeting, though this may be giving him too much credit, American exceptionalism – the messianic conceit that allows America to believe itself exempt from the clichés of geopolitics. But terrorists never kill policies or beliefs. They kill innocent people – Israelis out for a pizza dinner in Haifa, embassy workers in Africa, employees in a New York office tower, tourists in a Balinese nightclub. No country should give in to the demands of terrorists, but no country can afford to ignore the grievances behind a terrorist's demands, for they are sometimes valid complaints shared by reasonable people. If Americans took a moment to see their country the way people of other nations do, they would learn of the callous horrors their government is capable of perpetrating and better understand the need for a nuanced view of the world. They would understand why other nations are a jaded audience for America's sermons about democracy and freedom. And they would finally get something the people in other countries grasped a long time ago, much to their sorrow – that a government is not innocent just because its murdered citizens are.

ONE

RIGHT AND WRONG

Everything is not O.K. And this was not Pearl Harbor.
– SUSAN SONTAG, *NEW YORKER*, SEPTEMBER 24, 2001

On September 11, 2001, the United States of America was attacked on its home soil for the first time since the War of 1812. On September 12, George W. Bush, the president, proclaimed America to be an innocent victim of evil. And so began a concerted and largely successful attempt to silence dissent in the land of the free.

As Bush put it the day after the attacks, America was "strong"; its government and businesses would continue without interruption; and its military would avenge the destruction, which was carried out by terrorists who targeted America because it was "the brightest beacon for freedom and opportunity in the world." The U.S. was not attacked, a point Bush made very clear, because of anything it had done or was doing; it was targeted only because it stood out among freedom-loving nations – as if France, Sweden, or Belgium were less free or could just have easily been the target of terrorists embittered by America's military presence in Saudi Arabia. This, in turn, meant there was no need to examine

American foreign policy as provocation. In another statement the same day, Bush said the attacks were an "act of war" and described America's coming days as "a monumental struggle of good versus evil." On September 14, administration officials began warning Americans that the war on terrorism would be a "long struggle" and reiterated the message that any freedom-loving nation could have been the target. One senior administration official said leaders of other nations had called President Bush to say, "It could have been us." On September 16, Bush confirmed that Osama bin Laden was the prime suspect.[1]

In the media, meanwhile, September 11 became a "day of infamy," an echo of the term used by President Franklin Delano Roosevelt to describe the Japanese sneak attack on Pearl Harbor in 1941.[2] As was the case then, the American government was held to be an innocent, well-meaning bystander of an unprovoked atrocity. During the first forty-eight hours after the September 11 attacks, this unsubstantiated claim became, through repetition by media commentators and politicians, the prevailing wisdom. Within three weeks, it had become gospel, preached by political leaders who made it clear that anyone who doubted was tantamount to being a terrorist himself. Rudolph Giuliani, the mayor of New York whose credibility was unassailable because of his heroic leadership in the aftermath of the attacks, summed up this new order in a speech to the United Nations on October 1, 2001:

> This was not just an attack on the City of New York or on the United States of America. It was an attack on the very idea of a free, inclusive, and civil society. . . . On one side is democracy, the rule of law, and respect for human life; on the other is tyranny, arbitrary executions, and mass murder. We're right and they're

wrong. It's as simple as that. . . . The era of moral relativism between those who practice or condone terrorism, and those who stand up against it, must end. Moral relativism does not have a place in this discussion and this debate.

President Bush reinforced this view in a speech at the White House a week later.

In this conflict, there is no neutral ground. If any government sponsors the outlaws and killers of innocents, they have become outlaws and murderers themselves. And they will take that lonely path at their own peril.

Commentators invited to opine on television and in newspapers joined in, adding their voices and weight to the idea that America was an innocent victim, and that, as Bush said on November 7, 2001, you were either "with us or with the terrorists." Of particular note was a column by Sherry Cooper in the *National Post* on September 28, 2001, in which she stated in black-and-white terms anyone could understand that America was, beyond question, in the right: "The United States has become the scapegoat, much like the Jews were scapegoats in Nazi Germany."[3]

American television networks, meanwhile, adopted a solemn, self-righteous, and sycophantic tone, reducing the larger tragedy and the thousands of smaller personal ones inside it into emotionally manipulative headlines and graphics. John Powers, writing in *LA Weekly*, an alternative newspaper, noted:

Suddenly, we were being told how to be patriotic and how to mourn. CNN shifted its slogan from "America Attacked" to "America's New War." CBS's became

"America Rising." ABC's Web site offered download-able American flags, while Kmart printed a full-page version of Old Glory in Sunday's *New York Times*. When volunteers did something to help a victim, the TV story was accompanied by an explanatory logo: "Quiet Acts of Heroism."[4]

Anyone in the mainstream media who preached a contrary gospel, or searched for a middle ground, was given all the respect reserved for accused witches in Salem. Among the few who tried was Susan Sontag, a highly regarded essayist and novelist who spent those first terrible forty-eight hours glued to CNN in Berlin, where she was at the time, and then filed a thousand-word piece to the *New Yorker*.[5] What she produced was a passionate and angrily contrarian response to the endless and unquestioning coverage, accusing American politicians and the media of leading a campaign "to infantilize the public." Sontag wrote, "Where is the acknowledgment that this was not a 'cowardly' attack on 'civilization' or 'liberty' or 'humanity' or 'the free world' but an attack on the world's self-proclaimed superpower, undertaken as a conse-quence of specific American alliances and actions?"

By writing those words, Sontag had defied the president. She had asked Americans to examine their government's past and current policies for clues as to why their innocent fellow citizens had been targeted.

The backlash was swift and savage. Sontag was called an "America-hater," a "moral idiot," and a "traitor."[6] In the *New York Post*, David Talbot wanted her "drawn and quartered," in her words.[7] A television commentator said she should be "disgraced for her crazy views."[8] In the minds of her critics, such as Charles Krauthammer, a syndicated columnist for the *Washington Post*, her greatest sin was that she was unwilling to be black and white about the attacks, that she asked questions at a time when the nation's leadership was insisting on a nodding silence.

> This is no time for obfuscation. Or agonized relativism. Or, obscenely, for blaming America first. This is a time for clarity. At a time like this, those who search for shades of evil, for root causes, for extenuations are, to borrow from Lance Morrow [another American columnist], "too philosophical for decent company."9

"Moral relativism" and "equivocation" were out; gung-ho, follow-the-leader patriotism was in. Questioning America and its government, or examining root causes, was somehow a lack of "clarity"; insisting on America's near-holy status was considered clear thinking. An unrepentant Sontag subsequently told an interviewer her *New Yorker* piece had prompted "lots of very nasty letters" that accused her of being a traitor.10 She was furthermore accused of having condoned the attacks, an impression that was unfair and wrong, and to which she felt obliged, however reluctantly, to respond.

> I'll take the American empire any day over the empire of . . . "Islamic fascism." I'm not against fighting this enemy – it is an enemy and I'm not a pacifist. I think what happened on September 11 was an appalling crime, and I'm astonished that I even have to say that, to reassure people that I feel that way.11

Sontag also made it clear she did not believe "the September 11 attacks were the pursuit of legitimate grievances by illegitimate means."12 She saw them for what they were: the mass murder of civilians, an act that is never justifiable, regardless of where it occurs or whether it is supported by legitimate, democratic governments such as the United States and Israel, or by rogue regimes such as the Taliban in Afghanistan. As a historian, Sontag knows of the many such killings sponsored or perpetrated by the United States government and its agencies around the globe (and discussed in later chapters of this book). She was only suggesting that Americans, now suddenly and painfully aware of the horrible human costs of such acts, question the alleged moral superiority of their country and re-examine its "alliances and actions."

(It needs to be mentioned that there were other writers producing material that questioned the United States' reaction to the attacks and pointed out that the country was not an immaculately conceived terror victim. The *New York Review of Books* published seriously intelligent analyses of the events, some of which are quoted in this and other chapters; weekly alternative newspapers, America's final resting-place of the left, were also publishing thoughtful contrarian pieces.)

For daring to think in a way government preferred she didn't, an admired writer was marginalized and treated like an intellectual leper. Sontag got off lucky. Bill Maher, the comedian/host of the ABC television show *Politically Incorrect*, ultimately lost his job for doing just what Sontag had urged: questioning America. During a show in the days following September 11, he, like Sontag, took issue with the idea that the terrorists were cowards. "We [the United States] have been the cowards lobbing cruise missiles from 2,000 miles away," he said on-air, referring to a 1998 U.S. cruise-missile strike on bin Laden's camps in Afghanistan. "That's cowardly." It was a glib line that, before September 11, would have drawn no attention and required the Applause sign to elicit a response from the studio audience. Instead, advertisers, such as FedEx (a major contractor to the U.S. military[13]), threatened to boycott

ABC, while affiliated stations across the country dropped the show. Pundits called for Maher's head. Even the government weighed in. Ari Fleischer, the White House press secretary, warned in a Colonel Klink moment captured on television that "Americans need to watch what they say, watch what they do, and this is not a time for remarks like that." Maher was forced to apologize in order to prevent his immediate sacking. His show was dropped by ABC eight months later, in May 2002, after his ratings purportedly fell below acceptable levels.

Maher's fate was similar to that of two American print journalists who were summarily canned for saying the wrong thing. Dan Guthrie, a columnist for the *Daily Courier* in Grants Pass, Oregon, and Tom Gutting, city editor of the *Texas City Sun*, were fired for the innocuous sin of making fun of the president. Both wrote columns ridiculing Bush for not returning immediately to Washington from Florida, where he was giving a speech the morning of September 11, upon hearing of the attacks. Because of fears the president was also a target, the Secret Service obliged him to remain in the air on the presidential jet, Air Force One, and later hole up in a military bunker in Nebraska for most of the day. Giuliani, meanwhile, was at ground zero in New York and taking charge of the difficult moment. Bush was then not nearly as popular a president as he would later become; both columnists thought he looked silly and even cowardly, and said so. When readers and advertisers complained, the journalists' publishers caved in to pressure and fired them. Les Daughtry Jr., the publisher of the *Texas City Sun*, explained it was "not appropriate to publish [the column] during this time our country and leaders find ourselves in."[14]

One would have thought that the firing of a journalist for criticizing the president would become a *cause célèbre* in the United States, a natural for a national media so steeped in the importance of its own freedom, but that was not the case after September 11. There was no outrage in the media, no warnings of slippery slopes ahead.

Authors also came under fire. Michael Moore, a left-wing American filmmaker and writer, was set to release his latest book, *Stupid White Men and Other Excuses for the Sorry State of the Nation*, on October 2, 2001, but was suddenly informed by his publisher the book was being held back. The publisher, HarperCollins, demanded he rewrite sections that were especially critical of the president, or they would destroy the fifty thousand copies ready for sale. According to Moore, his editor told him, "It's not the dissent we disagree with, it's the tone of your dissent. You can't question the President about his past felonies or alcohol abuse right now."[15] The book was released unchanged in March 2002 after a grassroots protest started by librarians became too large to contain. It immediately became a bestseller.

University professors, a stubbornly left-wing bunch in the United States, found themselves the subject of a particularly vexatious offensive. Two months to the day after the attacks, as the United States government was gearing up for what it considered its rightful retaliatory strikes on Afghanistan, an organization called the American Council of Trustees and Alumni posted a report on its Web site in which it questioned the patriotism of American academics. The Council was founded by Lynne Cheney, the wife of Dick Cheney, the vice president of the United States, and she was a member of its board. The document, called "Defending Civilization: How Our Universities Are Failing America and What Can Be Done About It," was not so much a report as it was a sensationalized list of 115 quotations and incidents in which students and professors questioned the government's desire to go to war. The list named names, prompting those on it to be pilloried in the press and become the subject of intimidation and threats of dismissal. It created such a furor that the report was subsequently revised and the names edited out, although the offending quotes were often still attributed in precise terms, such as to the dean of Woodrow Wilson College at Princeton University, making the removal of the dean's name an empty gesture.[16]

A history professor at the University of New Mexico, Richard Berthold, was quoted as making the intemperate and distasteful observation, "Anyone who can blow up the Pentagon gets my vote." He apologized and was reprimanded by the university after the New Mexico state legislature insisted he be fired, and threatened to cut the university's funding. To be fair, the terrorist attacks did expose a left-wing political correctness in American universities. The report cited cases of censorship of professors and students who tried to speak up in favour of military retaliation for the attacks. At one university, the administration permitted students to hold an anti-war demonstration but refused the same right to students who wanted to hold a pro-war counter-demonstration. At the College of the Holy Cross, the chairman of the department of sociology demanded that a secretary remove an American flag from her desk.[17]

However, the vast majority of the quotations the Council took offence with were simple expressions of opinion about American foreign policy; their sole fault was that they deviated from the mantra that the United States was an innocent victim. They were not "with us," as Bush put it, so they were "with the terrorists." A sampling:

"Imagine the real suffering and grief of people in other countries. The best way to begin a war on terrorism might be to look in the mirror."
– A Massachusetts Institute of Technology (MIT) professor of anthropology.

"There is a terrible and understandable desire to find and punish whoever was responsible for this. But as we think about it, it's very important for Americans to think about our own history, what we did in World War II to Japanese citizens by interning them."
– Dean of Woodrow Wilson School, Princeton University.

"This war can end only to the extent that we relinquish our role as world leader, overhaul our lifestyle and achieve political neutrality. . . . Perhaps our best options now are to search for the origins of this new war, draw strength from understanding our own weaknesses, and make changes within ourselves and within our relationship to others. Many wonder if we are paying an accumulated debt for centuries of dominance and intervention far from home, retribution for our culture of consumption and exploitation. . . . We must reexamine our place in the world and begin to imagine a world without superpowers."
– Brown University School of Medicine anthropology professor.

"If I were the president, I would first apologize to all the widows and orphans, the tortured and impoverished, and all the millions of other victims of American imperialism. . . . There are few if any nations in the world that have harbored more terrorists than the United States."
– Credited to a student journalist at a University of North Carolina teach-in.

"[The American flag is] a symbol of terrorism and death and fear and destruction and oppression."
– Professor of physics, University of Massachusetts at Amherst.

"[The terrorist attack] was no more despicable than the massive acts of terrorism . . . that the U.S. government has committed during my lifetime."
– Professor of journalism, University of Texas at Austin.

Even tame demands for moderation and warmed-over anti-war chants from the Vietnam era were singled out as dangerous and un-American:

"We should build bridges and relationships, not simply bombs and walls."
– Speaker at Harvard Law School.

"What do we want? Peace! When do we want it? Now!"
– Chant at Harvard rally, September 20, 2001.

"An eye for an eye leaves the world blind."
– Student sign at same rally [quoting Gandhi].

"We need to hear more than one perspective on how we can make the world a safer place. We need to understand the reasons behind the terrifying hatred directed against the United States and find ways to act that will not foment more hatred for generations to come."
– Professor emerita of women's studies, University of Oregon.

"It is ridiculous for us to go and kill more people because of what bin Laden did."
– Student, Columbia University.

Lynne Cheney's Council was angered that academics refused to comply with Bush's demand for total support, a compliance that was apparently a requirement of all citizens after September 11. "While America's elected officials from both parties and media commentators from across the spectrum condemned the attacks and followed the President in calling evil by its rightful name, many faculty demurred," the report said. "Some refused to make judgments. Many invoked tolerance and diversity as antidotes to evil. Some even pointed accusatory fingers, not at the terrorists, but at America itself."

The Council concluded that universities were not doing a proper job of educating students about the values the administration insisted had been the real target of the terrorists.

Rarely did professors mention heroism, rarely did they discuss the difference between good and evil, the nature of Western political order or the virtue of a free society. Indeed, the message of many in academe was clear: BLAME AMERICA FIRST.

The report, as well as the firings of journalists and the pillorying of Susan Sontag, seemed to spread a chill across the United States that prevented, or at least postponed, any examination of the Bush administration's ambitions. It became next to impossible to discuss the government's not inconceivable role in provoking the attacks, or Bush's belligerent response to them, without being branded a coddler of terrorists or a traitor. The left, in particular, became a regular target of vilification at the hands of editorialists, such as this from the *National Post*:

> When a person says the United States "had it coming," what he or she means is that murder is a morally appropriate rejoinder to a perceived slight or injustice. The annihilation of innocent civilians is thereby cast as a legitimate means to promote one's political or theological ends. This is familiar territory for the radical left: Since the time of Lenin, Marxists have preached the virtues of exterminating inconvenient classes of individuals in order to bring those still living into a state of equality.[18]

One American columnist, Aaron Lukas, made a direct link between left-wing anti-globalization demonstrators and the terrorists:

> Like terrorists, the anti-globalization movement is disdainful of democratic institutions. When elections don't go your way, then maybe hurling a fire extinguisher at a policeman will get your message across.
>
> In the struggle between civilization and barbarism, those who torch a McDonald's and those who ram airplanes through skyscrapers are releasing their destructive energies in a common cause.[19]

In such a climate, when Americans permitted themselves to question their country and its values in the wake of the attacks, it was in the form of New Year's Eve introspection. Searching desperately for answers, and getting only bromides from their leaders, they examined their personal habits for evidence of behaviour that might have made them deserving of such pain: *Do we watch too much television? Are we polite enough to each other? Are our movies and TV shows too violent? Do we read enough books? Should we embrace religion?* Americans, suddenly faced with their own mortality, resolved to be better people. Their newspapers and TV news shows produced numerous touching stories about "the new civility," "the fragility of life," and other post–September 11 revelations. Television talk shows such as *Late Night with David Letterman* and *The Tonight Show with Jay Leno* went off the air, because no one felt like laughing in public. When the shows returned more than a week later, the hosts, formerly known for their routine sending-up of American culture, instead adopted tones of sombre patriotism. Leno returned to the air to stand before the huge image of the American flag and weep openly. Letterman had to console Dan Rather, the CBS news anchor, as he, too, cried on-air. Hollywood film studios, meanwhile, held back the releases of films (*Swordfish*, *Collateral Damage*) deemed too violent and having terrorism-related plots; *Men in Black II* and *Spider-Man* were re-edited to remove scenes that involved the World Trade Center. Oprah Winfrey, the daytime TV talk-show host who has become America's confessor, hosted a teary television prayer meeting broadcast from the Bronx. Sales of bibles went through the roof. Americans rushed to give blood and made billions of dollars' worth of donations to the victims of the attacks. Not permitted to question their government, they turned their gaze upon themselves, a phenomenon President Bush mentioned in his State of the Union address on January 29, 2002:

> After America was attacked, it was as if our entire country looked into a mirror and saw our better selves.

We were reminded that we are citizens, with obligations to each other, to our country, and to history. We began to think less of the goods we can accumulate, and more about the good we can do. For too long our culture has said, "If it feels good, do it." Now America is embracing a new ethic . . .

This sudden fit of introspection officially ended on March 13, 2002, when Fox television broadcast *Celebrity Boxing*, a show in which pudgy, washed-up television actors and lowlife personalities made infamous by scandal fought each other in live bouts. In one match, Paula Jones, who alleged she had been propositioned by former president Bill Clinton while he was wearing no pants, was chased around the ring by Tonya Harding, who was convicted of conspiring to have her competitor in a figure-skating championship kneecapped with a lead pipe. The gaudy show was so popular it was rebroadcast, and new fights were taped and aired, as well.

When you think about it, Americans were probably all too happy not to question their government. For the first time since the Second World War and the Japanese attack on Pearl Harbor, their country clearly seemed to be on the side of right. After decades of doubt created by the atomic bombing of Nagasaki and Hiroshima; by Vietnam and the Gulf War; by questionable government actions in Chile, Nicaragua, Malaysia, and elsewhere; by domestic scandals such as Watergate and Zippergate, it felt good to be able to claim the moral high ground. Commentators went further, using the occasion to announce piously there was no more need for America to play the game of cultural relativism or feel shy about being the *greatest damn nation in the world*. The age of American self-flagellation was over; pundits gloated that theirs was a culture and democracy superior to that of any other land,

and certainly better than anything available in bin Laden's native Saudi Arabia and his current address, Afghanistan.

It was a sentiment that spilled over the border into Canada. On December 29, 2001, in a front-page column in the *National Post* entitled "Why Deny the Obvious? West Is Best," Robert Fulford was blunt about the West's superiority. "Islamic political life remains a scandal," he wrote. "Islam has spawned no democracies, and no Islamic countries have joined the developed world. Half a century ago, South Korea and Egypt had the same standard of living. Today, South Korea's is roughly five times Egypt's. South Korea accepted the methods of the West while Egypt rejected them."

That South Korea had the "methods of the West" imposed by the United States, that during most of the half-century after the Second World War it was run by puppet governments propped up by the U.S., and that the Korean standard of living only began to catch up with the rest of the Western world's in the 1980s, not fifty years ago, seemed not to matter any more. All that anyone cared about was that it had "Western" values, however delivered, and was better off economically for it.

More nuanced commentators made it clear that even if America did have its faults, it was still the best country on the planet, one for whose continued existence the rest of the world should be grateful. They contended, without referring to them directly, that America's past slaughters – Hiroshima, Vietnam, Nicaragua, Chile, the Gulf War – were beyond reproach because they had helped secure the American way of life, now more highly prized than ever, and anyway were risible inconveniences compared to the inhumane monstrosities of September 11. Two such commentaries were included in the American Council of Trustees and Alumni report, "Defending Civilization."

The United States is an imperfect nation, but it is also the last, best exemplar of a democratic republic. To suggest the U.S. is the primary source of the world's ills – as many professors do – is simply misguided.[20]

The attacks in New York and at the Pentagon rekindled respect for our country. Academics who ignore this risk becoming as irrelevant as yesterday's Sovietologists . . . America is more than the sum of its problems. Some of the nation's intellectuals may have been lacking this perspective on September 11, but it's a precious piece of wisdom we can take away from ground zero."[21]

America is, indeed, "more than the sum of its problems." Of that there can be no question. It is a country founded on principles that are universally admired, if not always lived up to: freedom of the individual in all its forms, the protection of human rights, unfettered markets. By the late nineteenth century, when Europe was largely still ruled by aristocracies, the U.S. had been a democracy for a hundred years. Alexis de Tocqueville, the French nobleman who visited the United States in 1831 and wrote *Democracy in America*, marvelled at the nation's revolutionary politics. "The people," he wrote, "reign in the American political world as the Deity does in the universe. They are the cause and the aim of all things; everything comes from them, and everything is absorbed in them." Thanks to books like de Tocqueville's, America became the Old World's symbol of modernity; the place where a new society was created and a new chapter of history written. It was a young country whose brashness was charming enough not to be offensive. It remains a country that affords most of its citizens an enviable lifestyle, and one to which people everywhere still dream of emigrating. Its inventors produced many of the twentieth century's most significant scientific and industrial innovations. Jazz music, cutting-edge films, groundbreaking novels, awe-inspiring architecture, and revolutionary modern art have all sprung from American imaginations. Cities like New York and Los Angeles are peerless international centres of culture and finance. As well, in some of its foreign policy, the United States has shown kindness and mercy to other nations, and generosity to its defeated enemies when it was stirred up enough to battle Fascism in Europe.

At least, that is the way it used to be. Ever since it dropped atomic bombs on two Japanese cities in 1945 and emerged from the Second World War as a superpower, the United States has become something else. In the Old World from which it sprang, America has become less a symbol of new possibilities than one of dangerous self-absorption. As a superpower, it is vulgar and venal in its popular tastes, blithely unconcerned with the effects of its cultural domination on foreign peoples, brutally self-serving in its foreign policy, unmerciful toward its enemies, and indiscriminate in its use of the massive weaponry at its disposal. As even American observers have noted, the United States, "in its foreign dealings, is often arrogant: it asserts a preemptive right to be where it chooses, to do as it sees fit, with scant attention to the consequences of others."[22]

Richard Armitage, the deputy secretary of state, was asked on television, on October 11, about bin Laden's reiterated obsession with the presence of U.S. troops near Muslim holy places. Should we not pay attention to Muslim sensibilities in this matter? Armitage ignored the question – we're there, he asserted, to protect Persian Gulf oil sites against the threat from Iraq, and we are staying. If you even raise the issue, he warned the

[American] interviewer, you are playing in bin Laden's ballgame. His reply will doubtlessly be run and rerun on al-Jazeera television [a prominent network in Arab countries through which bin Laden frequently issues statements and videos] – it will make fine recruiting material for the next generation of terrorists.[23]

These are the United States' "problems"; its new, self-appointed role as the defender of the free world against terrorism only serves to make the "problems" more noticeable; the fact that its superpower status allows it to avoid paying compensation or facing retribution for its misdeeds in turn makes them even more galling to the rest of the world. And everything is further exacerbated by the United States' position as the only superpower left standing after the Cold War; there is no competitor for top spot, whose evildoings serve as a mollifying counterpart to U.S. arrogance.

American politicians and media commentators after September 11 have been unable or unwilling to face these realities, preferring to bathe cozily in jingoistic platitudes. They have nodded in silent, unquestioning approval when their president turned their introduction to terrorism into a new era of American world dominance, declaring that he was henceforth reserving the right to invade any country deemed to be a harbourer of terrorism. They failed to notice that he was, in a sense, restarting the Cold War, using not communism but terrorism as the justification for rearming despotic regimes and carrying out other questionable U.S. activities overseas. They supported to an almost unanimous degree the idea that America had the right to bomb Afghanistan, and perhaps invade Iraq, because the targets were terrorists. They took it on faith that terrorism exists solely as an evil entity, without relation to the world in which it operates.

Susan Sontag, in her *New Yorker* piece, wrote of the "disconnect" in the American psyche between the September 11 tragedies and the country's role in the world. Like their leaders, Americans simply would rather not examine their country's past and current actions for possible explanations of the terrorism delivered upon their homeland. They prefer to take it on faith that every covert and overt military operation undertaken by their armed forces and intelligence services overseas since the Second World War has been, and will be, carried out to further America's highest ideals and spread democracy across the globe, thus making them immune from criticism or justifiable counterattack. If only that were true.

TWO

THE AL-SHIFA ERROR

This is no time for obfuscation. Or agonized relativism.
— CHARLES KRAUTHAMMER, *WASHINGTON POST*

Speaking to a reporter from a London newspaper three weeks after September 11, Khatim Mahadi, a Sudanese journalist, said his people were not "crowing over America's misfortunes," as the English reporter put it, "because, unlike Westerners, Africans are used to distinguishing between bad governments and innocent victims."[1]

"We have more experience of suffering than you," Mahadi said. "We know what brutality is."

Indeed the Sudanese do, and not just at the hands of their government but those of America, too. Sudan, Africa's largest country, lies in the northeast corner of the continent, the southern neighbour to Egypt and directly across the Red Sea from Saudi Arabia. Civil war broke out there in 1983 between the Muslim government (Sudan is about 75 per cent Muslim) and U.S.-backed Christian rebels in the southern part of the huge, and mostly poor, nation. The war has claimed thousands of lives and kept the country mired in poverty and violence. So it didn't help that, on August 20, 1998, the American government under Bill Clinton used cruise missiles to destroy a crucial pharmaceutical plant in the capital city of Khartoum.

The attack was part of a two-pronged retaliation for the bombing of U.S. embassies in Kenya and Tanzania on August 7 of that year. Two hundred and twenty-three people were killed in the two embassy explosions, and thousands more were injured. An angry Clinton administration felt a military action, rather than diplomacy, was the required response to such outrageous atrocities. The administration quickly identified bin Laden as the terrorist behind the bombings and sent cruise missiles into his campsites in Afghanistan. The pharmaceutical plant in Khartoum was also chosen as a target because the government believed the facility was manufacturing nerve gas to be used by bin Laden operatives on American targets.

An American submarine in the Red Sea launched sixteen Tomahawk cruise missiles that struck the Al-Shifa pharmaceutical plant with terrifying precision. The plant was utterly destroyed, while neighbouring facilities across the street only suffered minor damage. An undetermined but small number of people were killed and injured, mostly watchmen, because the attack came in the middle of the night.

Clinton, vacationing on the island of Martha's Vineyard when the strikes occurred, told the media that his administration had incontrovertible evidence that the Al-Shifa plant was producing nerve gas, or was at least preparing "precursor" chemicals that, mixed with other chemicals, create a dreaded variety of nerve gas called VX. The gas, he said, was destined for bin Laden's use. VX nerve gas was developed by the U.S. military in the 1960s for use in Cambodia during the Vietnam War (it was never deployed); a single drop on a person's skin will kill them within minutes. Its accidental release in Utah in 1968 killed thousands of sheep, including some as far as sixty-five kilometres (forty miles) away. There was good reason for the United States to be worried about the possibility of a radical madman like bin Laden getting his hands on such a poisonous brew, especially since its intelligence agencies were saying that bin Laden was planning more lethal attacks against U.S. targets.

Within days of the destruction of the Al-Shifa plant, the Clinton administration's story had begun to unravel. Two Britons, a documentary filmmaker and an engineer, told various London media that the Americans "got this completely wrong."[2] The engineer, Tom Carnaffin, said he worked at the factory as plant manager from 1992-96 and that it was not suited for producing nerve gas. Among other things, the plant did not have the airlocking doors required to prevent accidental gas escapes. That prompted American journalists to start asking an obvious question: If the plant was indeed a nerve-gas facility, would it not have been grossly irresponsible to bomb it and possibly release poisons into the winds of Khartoum?

When TV crews arrived on the site, they found no evidence that this was a highly secure facility under the protection of the Sudanese military, as the Clinton administration claimed. Nor was there any evidence of nerve-gas production. What they found was a ruined factory around which thousands of painkiller and malaria-treatment pills littered the ground. Pressed to explain itself, the White House said it had soil samples from the plant that contained above-average traces of Empta, a VX-nerve-gas precursor chemical. Officials also claimed the plant was owned by bin Laden or by people linked to him. Those claims, too, fell apart over the course of the following months.

Clinton and his team were ultimately forced to admit they did not know who owned the Al-Shifa plant. When it subsequently came to light that the owner was a Saudi businessman named Salih Idris, the administration quickly claimed the man had links to bin Laden and froze his assets at the Bank of America; it later backed down and quietly released the $24 million. Chemical experts hired by Idris did their own examination of the soil around the Al-Shifa plant and found no evidence of Empta.[3] The lead scientist was Professor Thomas D. Tullius, chairman of the chemistry department at Boston University. Tullius's team examined thirteen carefully collected samples from around the ruined plant and found no traces of Empta or the substance it breaks down to, Empa. His team of scientists discovered that the plant's septic tank was intact, allowing them to search for every chemical that had ever been flushed out of the factory. Still no Empta or Empa.

Idris also hired a respected international security company, Kroll Associates, to investigate his alleged links to bin Laden. The investigators determined he had no direct links to bin Laden but may have unknowingly done business with some of the Al-Qaeda leader's many companies.[4] The White House refused to acknowledge or respond to this information; it stuck to its position that the strike against the Al-Shifa plant was a necessary deterrent to terrorism and it stood by its evidence for carrying out the strike.

An investigation by the *New York Times* published on October 27, 1999, told another story.[5] The newspaper's reporter, James Risen, wrote that the Clinton team was unsure of the evidence provided to it by its intelligence agencies in the days before the retaliatory missile strike. Even the intelligence people, including George J. Tenet, the director of the CIA, had doubts. The administration later suppressed a report that said the bombing was unjustified, Risen discovered. He learned that the soil sample supposedly taken from the Al-Shifa plant actually came from land sixty feet away that may not have been part of the facility. And he pointed out that the CIA and the U.S. embassy had pulled out of Khartoum in 1996 because of alleged terrorist threats, leaving the Americans with limited intelligence-gathering resources in the Sudan.

It is not that the U.S. had no reason to suspect Sudan of terrorist links. On the contrary, in 1991 the country's Muslim government announced a policy under which all Arab nationals could settle there without a visa. Overnight, the country became the real-life version of the Mos Eisley spaceport in *Star Wars*, a seedy outpost of outlaws and terrorists who operated their illegal activities with impunity. One such terrorist was bin Laden, whose radical Islamic fervour had made him unwelcome in his homeland. Risen notes:

> At about the same time [1991], Mr. bin Laden moved to Sudan after his exile from Saudi Arabia and began to invest heavily in commercial enterprises, often through joint ventures with the Government, while using Sudan as a base for his loosely knit international terrorist organization, Al Qaeda, American intelligence officials said. The CIA received intelligence reports indicating that in 1995, Mr. bin Laden won tentative approval from Sudanese leaders to begin developing chemical weapons for use against American troops in Saudi Arabia. But in 1996 the Sudanese, responding to pressure from the United States and Saudi Arabia, forced Mr. bin Laden to leave, prompting him and many of his supporters to retreat to Afghanistan.[6]

Subsequent CIA intelligence raised more alarms about chemical weapons being developed in Sudan and bin Laden's desire to use them on Americans. But the only solid link to

Al-Shifa came from an informant in 1997 who said two sites in Khartoum "might be involved in chemical weapons production. The informant also mentioned a third site – Al-Shifa – on which he had less information, but which seemed suspicious to the informant because it had high fences and stringent security."[7]

On August 6, 1998, the day before the embassy bombings, the U.S. State Department said in a memorandum that the CIA's evidence that Al-Shifa was linked to bin Laden and chemical weapons was "weak."[8] That did not prevent Al-Shifa from being on a list of twenty possible targets once the U.S. decided to retaliate for the bombings with force. The list was pared down to bin Laden's camps in Afghanistan and two sites in Sudan: Al-Shifa and, because it was thought to be owned by Al-Qaeda, a Khartoum tannery.[9] The tannery was dropped from the list at the last moment, and there were those in Clinton's administration as well as in the CIA who felt Al-Shifa should be spared because of a lack of evidence, but it was too late. The United States felt it had to strike back hard and that it would be a public-relations disaster not to destroy Al-Shifa if American interests were subsequently attacked with chemical weapons, as they believed bin Laden was preparing to do.

Ultimately, the decision to destroy Al-Shifa came down to the Clinton administration's desire to show terrorists that America could strike back against them from remote locations and hit multiple targets. There was less concern about the legitimacy of the Sudan target than there was about the message Clinton wanted to send; and there was no concern about what the strike would do to the Sudanese people. As it turned out, American missiles destroyed a legitimate and vital business – one of three pharmaceutical plants in an impoverished country, and the only one making much-needed tuberculosis drugs at a minimal monthly cost for a hundred thousand patients, according to the *Guardian*.

> Costlier imported ones [TB pills] are not an option for most of them – or for their husbands, wives and children, who will have been infected since. Al Shifa was also the only factory making veterinary drugs in the vast, mostly pastoralist, country. Its specialty was drugs to kill parasites which pass from herds to herders, one of Sudan's principal causes of infant mortality.[10]

Other reports indicated the Al-Shifa plant produced malaria drugs for southern Sudan, causing humanitarian aid groups to worry that as many as 10,000 children would die as a direct result of the bombing. Sudan, with a population of 35 million, has an average of 7.5 million malaria cases, and 35,000 deaths related to the disease, every year. It is a disease that kills slowly and painfully, and doesn't discriminate between adults and children. A treatable ailment, it only kills those who lack access to the lifesaving drugs Al-Shifa made. One relief agency, Medical Emergency Relief International (MERLIN) in London, said Sudan suffered its worst malaria epidemic in forty years in 1998, making the destruction of the only plant in the country producing malaria drugs not much less than a crime against humanity.

The bombing also prompted many of those humanitarian aid workers to leave the country, putting Sudan's population at greater risk of starvation and disease. Writer and activist Noam Chomsky, quoting from various sources in his book *9-11*, said the attack also shattered a "slowly evolving move toward compromise between Sudan's warring factions." The

European Sudanese Public Affairs Council in London reported in September 1998 that over the previous year,

> the Sudanese government had been involved in repairing the image of Sudan. . . .
> The government has introduced a federal system, a long-standing southern Sudan demand, negotiated the 1997 Khartoum peace agreement with several rebel factions, and has agreed to an internationally-supervised referendum in four years time whereby the people of southern Sudan would be able for the first time ever to opt for unity or separation. . . . Only a few months ago, the government drafted a new constitution, which was accepted by referendum. This constitution guaranteed a multi-party dispensation. It extradited the international terrorist known as "Carlos" and expelled Osama bin Laden at the request of the United States. It has also introduced visas, thereby ending previously unhindered travel to Sudan by Arab nationals. It has vigorously adhered to the adjustment programmes of the International Monetary Fund.[11]

In short, Sudan had everything to lose by harbouring a terrorist nerve-gas plant at the displeasure of the United States. The country appeared to be moving itself out of a period of lawlessness and civil war when the United States bombed the Al-Shifa plant. In March 2002, three and a half years later, the civil war continued apace. There were reports of civilians being gunned down by government helicopters as they waited in line for food, and of entire villages being wiped out by the U.S.-armed rebel forces. The country was in a government-declared state of emergency and the United States continued to impose sanctions on Sudan for its human-rights violations and "suspected ties to Islamic terrorists."[12] The U.N. lifted its economic sanctions in 2002, allowing oil companies to move back for the first time since 1996, which brought new money into the government for its war on the rebels. The U.S. has never acknowledged an error on its part in the bombing of the Al-Shifa plant.

For the United States, Al-Shifa was a symbol of its ability to strike at its enemies from afar and hit more than one target. For the Sudan and Arab countries, it was proof of the United States' indifference to the well-being of anything and anybody that does not work in its interests; proof that America will kill innocent people simply to make a point about its might. Osama Bin Laden used the Al-Shifa disaster to gain support in Muslim countries; he used it to turn moderates into radicals, or at least to get moderates to be a little more likely to turn a blind eye to his activities. "Overnight, the man has been transformed from an outlawed criminal on the run into a national hero standing against a hated superpower . . . which has come to our region and wreaked its own havoc here," wrote Sanaa Al-Said, a columnist for the Egyptian newspaper *Al-Wafd*. "Changes are on the way. U.S. hegemony will, one day, come to an end, and then the world will breathe more freely."[13]

The attacks may even have given bin Laden, or whoever came up with the idea, the impetus to mastermind the September 11 horrors. If Americans could strike at innocent victims in multiple targets from remote locations, so could Al-Qaeda. There is something eerie about the fact the radical Islamic press (www.muslimedia.com) referred to the missile attacks on Al-Shifa and bin Laden's camps in Afghanistan as the "twin attacks"; the World Trade Center is often referred to as the "twin towers."[14] It is also noteworthy that the Al-Shifa and Al-Qaeda camp attacks came on August 20; it is not out of the realm of reason to ask whether bin Laden was trying to strike on the anniversary of those dates but had to settle, for logistical reasons, on a date three weeks later.

That, of course, is speculation. There is no doubt, though, that fallout from the Al-Shifa attack was also damaging to the United States government and the people who live under it. Bill Clinton, the president who at the time of the bombing had been exposed as a bald-faced liar for saying he had not had sexual relations with Monica Lewinsky, suffered further blows to his credibility when it was demonstrated that his administration had struck the wrong target. Pundits speculated that the hasty and violent retaliation was prompted by the president's desire to shift the media's focus off his philandering and onto something that might inspire a little patriotism. The movie *Wag the Dog*, about an American presidential aide who, with the help of a Hollywood producer, concocts a small overseas war to draw attention away from his boss's sexual indiscretions, had been in American movie theatres prior to the Al-Shifa bombing, a coincidence that Clinton's critics gleefully used against him. Some commentators in the media even began to question whether this Osama bin Laden the government blamed for every terrorist attack was just a scapegoat.[15] It is possible to wonder whether the Clinton administration's grotesque error prompted a complacency in America about the threat bin Laden imposed – a complacency that allowed terrorists to learn to fly commercial jetliners on U.S. soil, then hijack four planes in one day and aim them at symbolic targets.

There have also been questions raised about whether the Clinton administration's hatred of Sudan and its desire to isolate it through its policies (it first labelled Sudan as a terrorist-sponsoring state in 1993) led to an intelligence breakdown that further abetted bin Laden. Several reports have uncovered the fact that in the years following bin Laden's expulsion from

Sudan, the Sudanese government, trying to improve relations with Washington, repeatedly offered the U.S. government extensive files on bin Laden and his operatives. The information had been gathered by Sudanese officials while bin Laden operated his network in that country from 1991-96; the files included photographs and valuable personal information about two hundred Al-Qaeda operatives. In February 1997, the Sudanese government even offered to let the United States send "intelligence, law-enforcement and counterterrorism personnel" into the country. The U.S. dismissed this, as well as the offer of intelligence files on Al-Qaeda, as a "meaningless 'charm offensive.'"[16]

Tim Carney, the last U.S. ambassador to Sudan, told *Vanity Fair* magazine that had Washington looked at the files it was being offered by Sudan, it might have been able to prevent the 1998 embassy bombings that led to the Al-Shifa attack. In the magazine's January 2002 issue, Carney said, "The fact is, they were opening the doors, and we weren't taking them up on it. The U.S. failed to reciprocate Sudan's willingness to engage us on some serious questions of terrorism. We can speculate that this failure had serious implications – at least for what happened at the U.S. embassies in 1998. In any case, the U.S. lost a mine of material on bin Laden and his organization. It was worse than a crime. It was a fuck-up."

Bad government, innocent people. Americans were killed on September 11 not because they were deserving targets but because they were seen by a madman the same way Bill Clinton saw the people of Sudan – as strategic targets in an "enemy" state. At Al-Shifa, the U.S. was heartless, ruthless, and indiscriminate in its use of extreme violence. It was an American government atrocity that arguably killed more people and devastated a country to a greater degree than the September 11 attacks did. Noam Chomsky made this point and, like Susan

Sontag, he was pilloried by media commentators. In his book *9-11*, he has this to say about his critics: "It is difficult to avoid the conclusion that at some deep level, however they may deny it to themselves, they regard [America's] crimes against the weak to be as normal as the air we breathe."[17]

THREE

THE ATROCITIES OF HIROSHIMA AND NAGASAKI

In being the first to use [the atomic bomb], we had adopted an ethical standard common to the barbarians of the Dark Ages.

–Admiral William D. Leahy, President Harry Truman's
Chief of Staff

The Al-Shifa attack was only a small demonstration of the capacity of the United States government to act ruthlessly and use extreme violence for political ends, and of its citizens' capacity to turn a blind eye. The greatest example of this remains the destruction of the Japanese cities of Hiroshima and Nagasaki by atomic bomb at the end of the Second World War. One hundred and seventy thousand Japanese civilians – men, women, and children – were killed instantly by the two American devices dropped on their cities, and as many more died a slow death from radiation poisoning in the days and years that followed. In American mythology, the bombings are pinnacles of scientific and military achievement that brought the war to an end and saved thousands of American lives, as well as the lives of countless more Japanese soldiers and civilians. "Being merciless, they were merciful,"[1] the *Chicago Tribune* wrote in an editorial praising American military leaders after the first bomb was dropped on Hiroshima. The president who authorized the attack, Harry Truman, called it "the greatest thing in history"[2] when an aide informed him the Hiroshima bombing run had been successful. A *New York Times* reporter, William L. Laurence, who had been secretly hired by the U.S. War Department to write its press releases, filed this putatively touching report on the scene inside the B-29 Superfortress bomber carrying the second bomb toward Nagasaki:

> The first signs of dawn came shortly after 5:00 o'clock. Sergeant Curry, who had been listening steadily on his earphones for radio reports while maintaining a strict radio silence himself, greeted it by rising to his feet and gazing out the window. "It's good to see the day," he told me. "I get a feeling of claustrophobia hemmed in in this cabin at night."
>
> He is a typical American youth, even younger looking than his 20 years. It takes no mind reader to read his thoughts.
>
> "It's a long way from Hoopeston, Illinois," I find myself remarking.
>
> "Yep," he replies, as he busies himself decoding a message from outer space.
>
> "Think this atomic bomb will end the war?" he asks hopefully.
>
> "There is a very good chance that this one may do the trick," I assure him, "but if not then the next one or two surely will. Its power is such that no nation can stand up against it very long."[3]

Later in the same press release, Laurence, who describes the bomb sitting in the belly of the plane as "a thing of beauty," asks a question: "Does one feel pity or compassion for the poor devils about to die? Not when one thinks of Pearl Harbor and of the death march on Bataan." Laurence also writes that Nagasaki was a military target – a city "making weapons of war for use against us."

Even if the dialogue is as stilted as that in an earnestly bad B movie, the press release is nonetheless a masterful bit of public relations. It encompasses everything the American people tell themselves about the world's only case of atomic bombs used against human targets: that it ended a war and saved lives, and that it was fitting justice for a cruel enemy that had wiped out hundreds of American military personnel in the sneak attack at Pearl Harbor and had committed terrible war crimes. The detonations of "Little Boy" over Hiroshima on August 6, 1945, and "Fat Man" over Nagasaki on August 9, 1945 (Japan time), were military acts carried out against a despotic nation that had only itself to blame for the misery inflicted on its people. There was even a religious fervour to America's achievement, at least in Truman's mind: "We thank God [the bomb] has come to us instead of to our enemies; and we pray that He may guide us to use it in His way and for His purposes,"[4] he said, giving the bomb's use the air of a fatwa. As such, America has seen little need even to discuss the righteousness of the act, just as there was little desire or perceived need to question the United States' retaliatory military action following the September 11 terror attacks.

But the atomic annihilation of two Japanese cities was never cut-and-dried. During the days leading up to the attack on Hiroshima, important voices were arguing that dropping the bomb was not a military necessity – that Japan was prepared to surrender and had even said so. In the first year or two after the end of the war, serious conservative voices raised questions about the action.[5] And as the years have passed and more facts have come to light, there is now concrete evidence that the two bombings were not inspired by military necessity but, rather, by political expediency: by the need to send a message to the leadership of an expansionist Soviet Union and the rest of the world, and by a desire to show Congress that the costly project to develop nuclear bombs had not been a waste. As well, it is now clear that the alleged military nature of the targets was a fabrication of the War Department. The United States government knew the bombings would kill mostly civilians and wanted it that way. There are a growing number of books, including two American ones released on the fiftieth anniversary of the bombings in 1995, that raise difficult questions about the justifications behind the decision to use the bomb. The release of formerly classified documents, many of which are available on the Internet, and interviews with and autobiographies by aging – and often rueful – participants in the decision also help make the case that the bombings, which propelled the world into the nuclear age and slaughtered innocent civilians in direct violation of international treaties, were as illegitimate and morally indefensible as the mistaken missile attack on the Al-Shifa pharmaceutical plant.

The U.S.' urgent race to develop the atomic bomb during the Second World War was understandable. There were fears the Germans were already well on their way to harnessing the atom; Albert Einstein was persuaded to write to the American government that such was the case early in the war. This prompted the U.S., in 1941, to create the Manhattan Project, at an ultimate cost of $2.6 billion (expensive even by today's standards). The project involved top nuclear physicists, most notably Dr. J. Robert Oppenheimer, and hundreds of personnel working in a top-secret facility at Los Alamos in New Mexico under the command of General Leslie Groves, the man behind the construction of the Pentagon in Washington,

D.C. By early 1945, as the Germans neared surrender and the Japanese were on the ropes in the Pacific, the Los Alamos team thought they had a workable atomic device. When Franklin D. Roosevelt, the president, died late in April 1945, and his vice president, Harry Truman, was sworn in as his successor, the bomb project was one of the first things the new president was briefed on by his aides. On July 16, an atomic bomb containing six kilograms (thirteen pounds) of plutonium was exploded at the Trinity test site in New Mexico. By July 25, Truman, writing in his diary, confirmed that the test had been a success. "The weapon is to be used against Japan between now and August 10th," he wrote.

> I have told the Secretary of War, Mr. [Henry] Stimson, to use it so that military objectives and soldiers and sailors are the target and not women and children. Even if the Japs are savages, ruthless, merciless and fanatic, we as the leader of the world for the common welfare cannot drop that terrible bomb on the old capital or the new. [Stimson] and I are in accord. The target will be a purely military one and we will issue a warning statement asking the Japs to surrender and save lives. I'm sure they will not do that, but we will have given them the chance. It is certainly a good thing for the world that Hitler's crowd or Stalin did not discover this atomic bomb. It seems to be the most terrible thing ever discovered, but it can be made the most useful.[6]

The atom bomb explosion was indeed a terrible thing to behold, as the test explosion at Trinity had made clear. Laurence, writing on behalf of the War Department, glorified the blast with flowery lines like, "One felt as though one were present at the moment of creation when God said: 'Let there be light.'" He also described the huge mushroom cloud as taking the form "for a fleeting instant of a gigantic Statue of Liberty, its arm raised to the sky, symbolizing the birth of a new freedom for man."[7] Some of the scientists who saw the explosion were overjoyed at the sight, as it was conclusive evidence their work had borne fruit, but others were horrified. The blast was several times more powerful than the scientists had anticipated, sending a cloud column as high as 21 kilometres that remained in place for several hours. Subsequent investigation determined that any human within a 3-kilometre radius of the blast's centre would have been killed instantly or injured fatally, and that the flash would have severely damaged, if not destroyed, any unprotected eyes within 10 kilometres. A farmhouse 5 kilometres away suffered extensive damage, its doors blown off. The scientists were also surprised at the extent of the area exposed to dangerous levels of radiation; high intensities were measured as far as 32 kilometres away, prompting officials to start evacuating farms in the area and seek legal advice, in at least one case, concerning their liability.[8] Cattle in the area fell sick, and the researchers found the corpse of a donkey killed by the radiation 32 kilometres from ground zero.[9] Four days later, low-level radiation could still be measured in the air 320 kilometres from the test site. The project team recommended doubling the size of the uninhabited safe zone around any subsequent tests.

The test blast was the equivalent of 10,000 tons of TNT. The two bombs dropped on Japan were capable, depending on the height at which they exploded and other conditions, of creating two times that much destructive force. The Trinity test informed the U.S. as to how deadly a single bomb would be if it were exploded between 500 and 2,500 feet over a target city, both in terms of the blast and the extent of the radiation poisoning that would kill survivors slowly and painfully within days of exposure. The radiation was a difficult subject for the U.S., which knew the rest of the world would not look kindly on the poisoning of Japanese civilians; officials made the conscious decision to detonate the Hiroshima and Nagasaki bombs at higher altitudes than would produce the most blast damage in order to limit radiation exposure. The attacks were thus designed to produce most deaths through explosion and burning – "a manner associated with conventional bombing. ... Radiation symbolized the special horror of the new weapon and introduced an element of moral ambiguity. It seemed comparable to the effects of poison gas, which warring nations had stockpiled but generally refused to use."[10]

Radiation victims develop purple hemorrhages on their skin and fevers; they later develop gangrene and their hair falls out. This painful death, akin to mustard-gas poisoning in the slow torture it inflicts, was not something the Americans wanted the public to focus on after the bombs were dropped. The U.S. had signed treaties in The Hague in 1899 and 1907 banning the use of "poisoned weapons" in war. The U.S. had also agreed to a League of Nations resolution in 1938 outlawing the intentional bombing of civilians. Regardless, the government knew full well what it was unleashing on Japan, and that the bombs' use would be a violation of its treaties. Kenneth D. Nichols, an aide to the general who oversaw the Manhattan Project, "would admit in his memoirs in 1987 that 'we knew that there would be many deaths and injuries caused by the radiation as well as by heat and blast.'"[11]

In determining the targets of the atomic bombs, and in spite of Truman's diary entry to the effect that only military targets would be hit, the U.S. military resolved to use its secret weapon to destroy whatever morale remained in the Japanese people. The American Air Force had already achieved much of that goal with its firebombing of Tokyo in March 1945, which killed 100,000 civilians. The atomic bombs were to be used in a similar fashion. Hiroshima, with a population of 350,000, was listed as a target because its size and layout would mean "that a large part of the city would be extensively damaged," according to the minutes of the May 10-11, 1945, meeting of the Manhattan Project's Targeting Committee. Kyoto was considered because it was "an intellectual center for Japan and the people there are more apt to appreciate the significance of such a weapon," the minutes also reveal.

In a telling bit of history, Henry Stimson, the secretary of war, urged the Air Force, when bombing Tokyo and other cities leading up to the August atomic attacks, to be as precise as possible in their targeting and avoid civilian casualties. "I did not want to have the United States get the reputation of outdoing Hitler in atrocities," Stimson wrote in his diary. "And second, I was a little fearful that before we could get ready, the Air Force might have Japan so thoroughly bombed out that the new weapon would not have a fair background to show its strength."[12] In other words, save some civilians for the atomic bomb.

Having made the difficult decision to use its new weapon to kill and poison civilians, the president and his military chiefs were faced with the task of justifying the military need for such an atrocity. Within the ranks of the scientists working on the project, there were signs of uneasiness. A number of them circulated petitions urging the government to demonstrate the bomb's might to the international community in general, and Japan in particular, before dropping it on a city. Many of them were prescient in their argument that the bomb's use on human targets would lead to a nuclear arms race, a term they used. Japan, said the dissident scientists, should have an opportunity to see what they were faced with; they suggested in a report dated July 11, 1945, that "a demonstration of the new weapon may best be made before the eyes of representatives of all United Nations, on the desert or a barren island. The best possible atmosphere for the achievement of an international agreement could be achieved if America would be able to say to the world, 'You see what weapon we had but did not use. We are ready to renounce its use in the future and to join other nations in working out adequate supervision of this nuclear weapon.'"[13] The same scientists pointed out that the urgent need to harness atomic power before the Germans did had passed, as Germany had surrendered on May 8 of that year. The Americans were clearly the winners of the race to build the bomb; demonstrating its lethality on a live target would only prompt other nations (they did not specifically mention the Soviet Union) to put all their efforts into developing their own version of the weapon.

Oppenheimer himself said he did not think it was feasible to put on an international demonstration of the bomb's might, and given a choice between that and using it on a military target, he recommended the latter. He wanted the war to end and was under the impression the bomb was the only way to achieve that end; he was of this opinion before seeing the Trinity test, however, and he was never told of two other options: allowing the conditional, as opposed to unconditional, surrender of the Japanese; and waiting for a planned Russian invasion of Japan to begin.[14] He changed his mind and thought that a demonstration might do the trick after seeing the magnitude of the Trinity explosion.[15]

Truman was vaguely interested in the idea of a demonstration, too, but other factors were at play. For one, the American public, and many in the administration, had become obsessed with the idea of the "unconditional surrender" of Japan, a mantra created by Roosevelt in 1943.

Through passionate wartime repetition it had become a rallying cry and at the same time an unbending policy. Indeed, when Truman delivered his first speech to Congress upon assuming the presidency, his clear declaration that "our demand has been, and it remains – unconditional surrender" brought the chamber to its feet in resounding applause.[16]

Japan refused unconditional surrender because that meant deposing its revered emperor. This was not an option available to Japanese soldiers, whose kamikaze allegiance to their leader had been shown time and again; or to Japan's people, who saw their emperor as a god. Japan's inevitable refusal to agree to U.S. terms became the death warrant signed out on Hiroshima and Nagasaki.

The United States, meanwhile, was aware that the Japanese wanted the war to end quickly and that, by July 1945, the Japanese military and government leadership saw their defeat as inevitable. Germany had surrendered, isolating Japan; U.S. bombers could make unhindered runs on its cities thanks to the Allied forces' control of the Pacific; the Soviet Union was about to end its neutrality pact with Japan and invade; rice rations had been cut to next to nothing and the Japanese people were eating acorns; scientists, faced with an oil shortage, were trying to develop airplane fuel out of pine root; and the Japanese government had collapsed, with decision-making falling into the hands of an aging admiral "known for his moderation."[17] The combined U.S.-British Intelligence Committee reported on July 8 that "a considerable portion of the Japanese population now consider absolute military defeat to be probable. The increasing effects of sea blockade and the cumulative devastation wrought by strategic bombing, which has already rendered millions homeless and has destroyed from 25% to 50% of the builtup area of Japan's most important cities, should make this realization increasingly general."[18] As well, the Allies had broken Japanese encryption codes and had intercepted a cable in which the Emperor himself stated he wanted the war to end "quickly."[19]

There can be little doubt that a prolonged sea blockade, the precision bombing of Japanese military targets, and Russia's entry into the battle, all of which contained relatively little risk to Allied servicemen, would have brought about the surrender desired by the Americans. Among those who felt so was Admiral William D. Leahy, Truman's chief of staff, who later said, "The Japanese were already defeated and ready to surrender because of the effective sea blockade and the successful bombing with conventional weapons . . . In being the first to use [the atomic bomb], we had adopted an ethical standard common to the barbarians of the Dark Ages."[20] Dwight Eisenhower, the general who later became U.S. president, said, "Japan was at that very moment seeking some way to surrender with a minimum loss of 'face' . . . It wasn't necessary to hit them with that thing."[21] Winston Churchill, the British prime minister at the time, had his doubts, too: "It would be a mistake to suppose that the fate of Japan was settled by the atomic bomb. Her defeat was certain before the first bomb fell."[22] And a U.S. Strategic Bombing Survey from 1946 went even further: "Certainly prior to 31 December 1945 . . . Japan would have surrendered even if the atomic bombs had not been dropped, even if Russia had not entered the war and even if no invasion had been planned or contemplated."[23]

Furthermore, when the end did come, the U.S. abandoned its insistence that the surrender be unconditional. After the Japanese publicly broadcast an offer of surrender on August 10 and the Americans accepted that offer on August 14, the U.S. agreed to allow the Emperor to stay in power, having deemed that such a move would make for a more orderly post-war occupation by Allied forces. In other words, after having refused the one condition Japan insisted on and dropping two atomic bombs on its civilians to force it to abandon that condition, the United States government then agreed to it.

If Truman had ruled out settling for anything less than an unconditional surrender in spite of evidence the war was over for Japan, it was because there yet were other things on his mind. One was the growing power of the Soviet Union, which by 1945 had taken over Poland, Romania, and Hungary. As early as 1944, the Americans had seen the weapon as a "master card"[24] in its dealings with Stalin, and Truman believed a public display of the bomb's capabilities would "make Russia more manageable in Europe," according to Leo Szilard, one of the Manhattan Project scientists who urged the U.S. not to drop the bomb.[25] The other factor was Truman's fear that the American public would take him to task for the huge cost of the Manhattan Project if he could produce no tangible results from its research.

> As [Truman] began to realize that the war had been won, and came to see the Russians as dangerous and the American people as restive, he underwent a shift in focus. As a number of observers have noted, the shift was from military to political imagery. He had said of the Russians when anticipating the success of the weapon, "I'll certainly have a hammer on those boys," and . . . associated the weapon's use with exerting "control" over the Russians. He also shared . . . a profound anxiety about the effects on the American public of a congressional investigation of an unproductive Manhattan Project, all the more so as one who had made his name as a demon congressional investigator of

defense industries. (When interviewed years later . . . and asked about his *first* thought upon hearing about the atomic program [after becoming president in 1945], his reply was: "I hoped that it would be successful, particularly since it cost $2,600,000,000 . . . that was $200,000,000 a pound for the first bomb, an expensive bit of explosive.")[26]

Because of his conviction that America needed to signal its new might to the world, Truman, as early as June 1945, ignored advice to the effect that changing the conditions of surrender and allowing the emperor to remain as the head of a constitutional monarchy would end the war – a decision that prolonged the war and needlessly sent more American servicemen to their deaths in battle.

The order to bomb one of four cities – Hiroshima, Kokura, Niigata, and Nagasaki – was given July 25. The Air Force was to carry out the first attack as soon after August 3 as weather permitted, and continue dropping the weapons on more cities at the pace at which additional bombs could be readied.[27] The U.S. was prepared to destroy four cities to start with, and the order made provisions for further targets. On August 6, Hiroshima was hit. Because of wartime censorship, all the world was told was that the United States had dropped a new weapon on a "military base," as Truman said himself in a radio announcement on August 9 at 10:00 p.m. Washington time, by which time the second bomb had already destroyed Nagasaki. Said Truman in his radio address:

The world will note that the first atomic bomb was dropped on Hiroshima, a military base. That was because we wished in this first attack to avoid, insofar as possible, the killing of civilians. But that attack is only a warning of things to come. If Japan does not surrender, bombs will have to be dropped on her war industries and, unfortunately, thousands of civilian lives will be lost. I urge Japanese civilians to leave industrial cities immediately, and save themselves from destruction.[28]

Hiroshima was no military base; it was a sprawling Japanese city in which forty thousand Japanese troops were stationed. The bomb obliterated the city in seconds, starting from the centre and racing outward. Those near ground zero were eliminated without a trace; farther away they were killed by the blast or burned stiff in seconds. Film footage taken by a Japanese photographer in the days after the blast (the film was seized by the Americans and only returned to the Japanese in the 1960s) showed people dying from radiation poisoning and contained the unforgettable image of the shadow of a painter on a ladder, his arm outstretched, that had been burned by the explosion's flash into a concrete wall.[29] It is estimated that one hundred thousand men, women, and children were killed instantly, while another fifty thousand died from the radiation. Schools, office buildings, churches, stores, homes, and factories were destroyed. Aerial photos taken by the U.S. Air Force over ground zero before and after the blast are stunning: the before photo shows a living, breathing city – a maze of streets and homes punctuated by parks and larger, factory-like buildings; a conglomeration of humanity. The after photo shows a uniform grey surface, with only the faint outlines of major streets giving any indication of prior human existence. One photo is of Earth, the other is of the surface of the moon.

American servicemen, upon hearing the news that the atomic bomb had been used against Japan and that surrender was inevitable, whooped for joy and celebrated openly, much the way Palestinian children were filmed doing after news of the September 11 attacks reached them. There was no thought given to the victims, who anyway were members of a race despised in the United States. A Gallup poll taken in December 1944 revealed that 13 per cent of Americans favoured the elimination of the Japanese people through genocide.[30] The War Department, which had complete control over all information relating to the Manhattan Project and the dropping of the bomb, used this hatred to its benefit. Every press release in the early days after the Hiroshima bombing mentioned the infamous attack on Pearl Harbor; there was no mention of ending the war early to save lives. American journalists, not equipped to handle an event of such magnitude, swallowed whole whatever the War Department told them.

> General Groves left nothing to chance. Before Hiroshima, he had prepared an order prohibiting U.S. commanders in the field from commenting on the atomic attacks without clearance from the War Department. "We didn't want MacArthur and others saying the war could have been won without the bombs," Groves later explained. Indeed, MacArthur and many other of the commanders believed the bomb was not needed to win the war.
>
> [General] Groves would later reflect with satisfaction that "most newspapers published our releases in their entirety. This is one of the few times since government releases have become so common that this has been done."[31]

There were dissenting opinions, though, from "the miscellany of crackpots, columnists, commentators, political aspirants, would-be authors and world savers," as Groves called anyone who did not publish his press releases verbatim, or who questioned the decision to bomb Hiroshima.[32] David Lawrence, a conservative columnist, wrote in *U.S. News*, "Military necessity will be our consistent cry in answer to criticism, but it will never erase from our minds the simple truth that we, of all civilized nations, though hesitating to use poison gas, did not hesitate to employ the most destructive weapon of all times indiscriminately against men, women and children. What a precedent for the future we have furnished to other nations even less concerned than we with scruples or ideals! . . . Surely we cannot be proud of what we have done. If we state our inner thoughts honestly, we are ashamed of it."[33]

For the most part, though, the war-weary American public understandably focused on the fact the fighting was over and their sons and daughters in uniform – those who had not been killed – could return home. They were content to let the War Department tell them the bombing had been the military *coup de grâce* that had brought an evil enemy to its knees; if they had moral concerns about the bomb's use on Hiroshima, they drowned them out with the noises of victory and loss, with jazz music and weeping. When Nagasaki was bombed, it barely made the front pages of American newspapers.

If Hiroshima was a target of dubious military value, Nagasaki was even more so. As per the original order to use atomic weapons against four Japanese cities, the second attack was undertaken without any presidential oversight and came as the Japanese were working to prepare their surrender. Historians argue that, having seen Hiroshima obliterated by a single bomb on August 6 and deciding at that moment to sue for peace, the Japanese command would have needed at least until August 10 to prepare. It was not something that could be done unilaterally and in a single day; it required that political and military leaders be summoned, that messages be sent to commanders across the war front to cease hostilities, and so on. The bombing of Hiroshima clearly had the desired effect of making up the Japanese leadership's mind about surrendering unconditionally; so why was it deemed necessary to drop a second bomb on another city? The American military leadership, who had briefly toyed with the idea of demonstrating the bomb's power on an uninhabited target and then demanding surrender, leapt from that humane consideration to an action in which they killed seventy thousand luckless Nagasaki civilians going about their normal human activities. Instead of waiting to see whether obliterating Hiroshima had done the trick, they simply continued obliterating Japanese civilians with the most horrible and cruel weapon ever devised by man.

Nagasaki, a hilly town in the southern tip of Japan (Hiroshima is also in the south), had been hit steadily since the end of July by an ever-increasing number of American non-nuclear bombs. It was even bombed conventionally the day after the nuclear attack. Many who heard the air-raid sirens on August 9 ignored them, as the sound had become routine. The bomb exploded over the centre of city, away from the shipyards the U.S. later falsely claimed were harbouring Japanese Navy ships. The bomb reduced schools, offices, prisons, homes, churches, and hospitals into dust. At the centre of the attack, everything was turned to fine powder, survivors reported. There were no corpses. Further from ground zero, bodies were scattered everywhere, including those of babies and children.

Yosuke Yamahata was sent by the Japanese Army to photograph Nagasaki the day after the bombing. His pictures show a city utterly flattened, pancaked evenly except for the occasional shard of chimney or metallic framing. He took pictures of a mother dying of radiation poisoning breast-feeding her baby, who was also dying; pictures of rows of corpses; of parents trying vainly to salve the burns on their children's small bodies. Yamahata died of cancer in 1966 at the age of forty-eight.[34]

Nagasaki was a cruel and unnecessary act. America knew from its test at Trinity just how cruel it was. The chief justice of the Nuremberg trials called Nagasaki a "war crime,"[35] although the United States was never charged with any such thing. Had the U.S. waited one day before dropping a second atomic bomb, the Japanese could have surrendered without having to see another of its cities, and a further seventy thousand of its civilians, utterly destroyed.

Similarly, the United States government could have offered Japan surrender terms that allowed it to keep its emperor, ending the war earlier and without the use of the atomic bomb. The U.S. could have waited for sea blockades and conventional bombings of military targets to bring about the inevitable result. It had the most deadly weapon of all time in its hands and could have shown mercy. Instead, against the advice of many in its own inner circle, the government made a political statement designed to secure its advantage over the Soviet Union and placate an American public that had a taste for blood and little patience for expensive military projects that produced no results. By 1950, an estimated 350,000 people had died as a direct result of the atomic bombs dropped on Hiroshima and Nagasaki. Half were killed immediately, the rest slowly by cancer and other radiation-related diseases.

From a political perspective, by using the bomb against innocents, America lost the moral high ground it might have held during the Cold War. It became impossible for the United States "to take the position that we wanted to get rid of atomic bombs because it would be immoral to use them against civilian populations," physicist Leo Szilard has said. "We lost the moral argument with which, right after the war, we might have perhaps gotten rid of the bomb."[36]

Worse still, the bombing launched the arms race. Today, America is paying the price. The former Soviet Union's nuclear arsenal is badly managed, and its underpaid scientists have been found willing to go to work for shady regimes that show the right amount of generosity. One report by a Republican congressman says the U.S.S.R. produced 132 ten-kiloton suitcase-sized nuclear bombs, and that today Russia can account for only 48 of them.[37] That means there are 84 unaccounted-for suitcase bombs out there, possibly in the hands of America's enemies, and they are a direct result of the arms race the U.S. started. There is even speculation that the bombs are already on U.S. soil. Bin Laden, in one of his video-taped messages released to the press after the September 11 attacks, made a pointed reference to Hiroshima and Nagasaki.

More than anything else, Hiroshima and Nagasaki are the seminal atrocities that have led to similar ill-conceived and politically motivated American military actions, such as the attack on the Al-Shifa pharmaceutical plant in Sudan. If Americans can forget something as monstrous as two atomic-bomb massacres, they are surely not going to dwell on a few wayward cruise missiles in Africa.

In Hiroshima and Nagasaki today, there are parks dedicated to peace and to the survivors. In the United States, an attempt in 1995 by the Smithsonian Institution in Washington, D.C., to mount an exhibition on the use of the atomic bomb at the National Air and Space Museum was shut down by veterans' groups and congressmen. The exhibit's sin was to show both sides of the story, an unpopular stance in America when it concerns that country's military history.

FOUR

AMERICA'S IMPERIAL ARMY

Perhaps the Romans did not find it strange to have their troops in Gaul, nor the British in South Africa.
– CHALMERS JOHNSON, *BLOWBACK: THE COST AND CONSE-QUENCES OF AMERICAN EMPIRE*

While the United States government, victorious in the Second World War, went on to compete in the nuclear arms race with the Soviet Union, the scientists who built the bomb gave themselves a different mission: to fight for nuclear disarmament. Perhaps better equipped to understand the human side of the monstrosity they had spawned than politicians and bureaucrats were, former members of the Manhattan Project created the Federation of Atomic Scientists in 1945 "to address the implications and dangers of the nuclear age." The group has since been renamed the Federation of American Scientists; fifty-three American Nobel Prize winners sit on its Board of Sponsors. The FAS devotes much of its energies to arms control and its ultimate goal of disarmament, but it also monitors American military operations and arms shipments. And from that endeavour comes a fascinating and telling Web site.

The FAS Web site (www.fas.org) includes the Military

Analysis Network, wherein the scientists have compiled every U.S. military operation in history, both overseas and stateside. The list dates back to 1689, when a war in Europe between England and France led to local skirmishes between colonial English forces and French and Indian forces. What's interesting is the way the list reveals the United States' steady increase in military activity over the last two centuries, and its dramatic increase in the last twenty-five years. In the two hundred years between the Revolutionary War and 1975, including the many operations involved in the Vietnam War (10 of them, with names like Operation Endsweep, Operations Linebacker I and II, and Operation Freedom Train), the number of U.S. military operations totals under 70. From 1975 to September 11, 2001 – twenty-six years – there were more than 160 completed and ongoing U.S. military operations. From an average of one operation every three years, the United States jumped to an average, in the last quarter-century, of more than one every two months.

A small number of the operations occurred on U.S. soil, such as 1992's Garden Plot, in which 4,500 infantry and Marines were deployed on the streets of Los Angeles to help local authorities quell the so-called Rodney King race riots. (It was not an unqualified success. In one incident, a police officer who was fired upon from inside a house yelled at soldiers, "Cover me!" In police parlance, "Cover me" means ready your weapons in case they are needed; in soldier-speak it means lay down a relentless covering fire. The soldiers obligingly unloaded 200 rounds into the house, in which children were present. No one was injured.[1])

A few of the operations were limited humanitarian gestures, such as 1999's Fundamental Response, in which the U.S. Department of Defense flew water-purification kits and other equipment into flood-ravaged Venezuela. The DoD also provided engineering equipment and personnel to clear and rebuild damaged roads. In this operation alone, the American military machine came to the aid of an estimated four hundred thousand people made homeless by violent flash floods.

About twenty of the operations were anti-drug missions carried out in conjunction with other U.S. government agencies in South America, Central America, Mexico, and the United States.

But the greatest number of operations were carried out overseas and involved U.S. military personnel and equipment acting directly or indirectly in support of various dubious regimes and rebels around the globe, usually on the grounds that the action was needed to stop the spread of communism, and sometimes to deal with the actions of rogue nations such as Iraq and Libya. The operations were given names only an unabashed admirer of military propaganda could love:

• Red Bean in 1978, in which Air Force planes airlifted personnel and supplies into Zaire to help Mobutu Sese Seko, the country's pitiless dictator, repel an invasion by rebel forces. Mobutu, infamous for his human rights abuses and for redirecting hundreds of millions of U.S. dollars worth of economic and military aid into Swiss bank accounts, and using other aid money to buy castles in Europe, convinced the Americans to intervene by making the unproven claim that communists – Cubans and Soviets – were backing the rebels.

• Elf One, a ten-year operation (1979-89) in which American planes provided radar support and other coverage for the Saudi Arabian Air Force during that country's ongoing dispute with Yemen, and later during the Iran/Iraq war, when Saudi Arabia stepped up its air defences as a precaution. In all, U.S. planes flew more than six thousand sorties to protect the airspace of neutral countries during the Iran/Iraq war.

• Arid Farmer (1983), in which the U.S. supplied Chad with

anti-aircraft missiles and launchers in its battle with rebels – rebels who were in turn backed by Libya. The Air Force provided Airborne Warning and Control Squadron (AWACS) aircraft to patrol the Sudan/Libya border as well, but the AWACS were never deployed. Through 1988, the Americans continued to provide small arms, munitions, trucks, Jeeps, and other equipment to the Chad army, and helped France ferry in missile batteries.

• Urgent Fury (1983), the American-led invasion of Grenada whose stated goal was to protect U.S. medical students and other U.S. nationals on the Caribbean island state and restore a representative government after a coup by a rebel faction within Grenada's Marxist-Leninist government. A total of five thousand U.S. Marines and Navy SEALS accomplished the tasks given them, in spite of resistance from "1,200 Grenadians, 780 Cubans, 49 Soviets, 24 North Koreans, 16 East Germans, 14 Bulgarians, and three or four Libyans."[2] The invasion was hampered by poor intelligence, and American journalists were furious that they were prevented by the military from witnessing the invasion. The operation also suffered from poor military communications: in the invasion's most hilarious moment, a field commander had to call long-distance by commercial telephone to Fort Bragg in North Carolina to request air support for his pinned-down troops. The gunships arrived just in time.

• Intense Look (1984), in which U.S. minesweepers were deployed to the Red Sea to remove mines placed there by Libya.

• Golden Python (1990), also known as Steel Box, in which the U.S. military transported one hundred thousand toxic chemical artillery shells from West Germany to the Johnston Atoll. This involved moving the deadly armaments by ship around the equally dangerous Cape Horn.

• Operation Shining Presence, which began in 1998 and involves the deployment of U.S. forces and Patriot missile batteries in Israel.

• Operations Provide Comfort, Provide Comfort II, and Northern Watch, the United States' enforcement of the no-fly zone north of the thirty-sixth parallel in Iraq. The joint operation, which is not authorized by the United Nations, originally involved 1,100 U.S. personnel and 1,400 personnel from coalition partners Britain and France (France has since dropped out). It began in 1991 and was still continuing in 2002, in spite of protests from China and Russia that it is a violation of Iraqi sovereignty and has no international legitimacy. The operation's purported goal is to protect Kurds trapped in northern Iraq from Saddam Hussein's forces. In one sense, it is the least the U.S. can do, as the CIA encouraged the Kurds to rise up against the Iraqi government in the 1970s, then abandoned them at the outbreak of the Iran/Iraq war (1980-88). The U.S. wanted to appear neutral in the war and so did little when the Iraqi leader gassed tens of thousands of Kurds trapped in the northern part of the country in 1988. American officials refused to meet with Kurdish leaders in the aftermath of the attacks for fear of angering Hussein.[3] The genocidal gassings only became a *cause célèbre* for the administration of President George Bush Sr. in 1990, when Iraq invaded Kuwait and triggered the Gulf War. Although little reported until President George W. Bush, in the aftermath of September 11, announced his intention to remove Saddam Hussein from office, Operation Northern Watch has involved near-daily sorties against Iraq air defences that are generally provoked by Iraqi aggression, usually in the form of anti-aircraft missiles. After the United Nations Security Council adopted a resolution in November 2002 ordering Hussein to disarm and allow the return of weapons inspectors or face "serious consequences," the U.S. immediately called these decade-old dogfights a material breach of the resolution.

• Operation Desert Falcon, wherein American forces provide Patriot missiles, and the personnel to operate and protect them, to Saudi Arabia.

There are other lists of American military operations that cover the past 225 years; they do not all contain the same information but they all reveal the same rise in activity since 1975. What emerges is the underappreciated (in the U.S. anyway) fact that the U.S. maintains a relentless military presence throughout the world, one that increased dramatically after the Vietnam War. According to Chalmers Johnson, the author of the prescient book *Blowback: The Cost and Consequences of American Empire*, first published in 2000, "Hundreds of thousands of American troops, supplied with the world's most advanced weaponry, sometimes including nuclear arms, are stationed on over sixty-one base complexes in nineteen countries worldwide, using the Department of Defense's narrowest definition of a 'major installation'; if one included every kind of installation that houses representatives of the American military, the number would rise to over eight hundred [bases]."[4]

There are few, if any, nations, and certainly no regions of the world, that do not live with the presence of American military personnel and infrastructure. The U.S. military machine maintains an especially big presence in the two dozen nations under the direction of CENTCOM, the United States Central Command Headquarters in Tampa, Florida. CENTCOM oversees all U.S. military action in Bahrain, Iraq, Kuwait, Oman, Qatar, Saudi Arabia, United Arab Emirates, Yemen, Djibouti, Eritrea, Ethiopia, Kenya, Seychelles, Somalia, Sudan, Egypt, Jordan, Afghanistan, Pakistan, Iran, and the former Soviet republics of Kazakhstan, Kyrgyzstan, Tajikistan,

Turkmenistan, and Uzbekistan. In other words, it is in charge of the part of the Muslim world considered to be the source of radical Islamic fundamentalism. It is also the branch of the services responsible for protecting 70 per cent of the world's oil supply. (Curiously, it does not have responsibility for Israel.) According to CENTCOM's Web site (www.centcom.mil), there are between 17,000 and 25,000 American military personnel in service in these countries during peace time, and more in times of conflict, such as during the Gulf War, when more than half a million U.S. personnel were sent to force Iraq's withdrawal from Kuwait. In all, there were about 260,000 U.S. personnel in service in foreign areas in 1999 (excluding combat personnel), about half as many as there were during the Cold War. Most were in Germany and in Europe as a whole, while there were large numbers in South Korea and Japan.[5]

In *Blowback*, Johnson focuses on the cost of what he calls America's military imperialism. He writes of a 1998 incident in which an American fighter jet in Italy, clearly flying too fast and too low over a populated area, cut the cable on a chairlift at a ski resort and sent twenty people to their deaths. The American pilots involved in the accident were flown back to the United States, where a military tribunal absolved them of all responsibility. Bill Clinton, president at the time, apologized to Italy and promised to pay compensation, but Congress subsequently killed the bill that would have provided aid to the families' victims.[6] As Johnson notes, this cavalier attitude is routine for the American military and government; and it is an attitude that only a imperialistic nation could adopt.

> There are, of course, no Italian air bases on American soil. Such a thought would be ridiculous. Nor, for that matter, are there German, Indonesian, Russian, Greek, or Japanese troops stationed on Italian soil. Italy is,

moreover, a close ally of the United States, and no conceivable enemy endangers its shores.

All this is too obvious to state – and so is almost never said. It is simply not a matter for discussion, much less of debate in the land of the last imperial power. Perhaps similar thinking is second nature to any imperium. Perhaps the Romans did not find it strange to have their troops in Gaul, nor the British in South Africa. But what is unspoken is no less real, nor does it lack consequence just because it is not part of any ongoing domestic discussion.[7]

Johnson points out that the 1988 bombing of Pan Am flight 103 over Lockerbie was retaliation for a 1986 U.S. missile attack on Libya; that the United States' embargo and blockade of Iraq in the aftermath of the Gulf War has led to the deaths of half a million innocent Iraqis without causing much pain to their murderous leader, Saddam Hussein, but ensuring that Iraqis bear a grudge toward Americans and their government; and that Osama bin Laden was trained and financed by the United States when they needed him to fight the Russians in Afghanistan, making him more dangerous when he turned on the U.S. after the Gulf War because he was opposed to America's relentless military presence in Saudi Arabia.

Johnson also points to America's treatment of Kurds, mentioned above as being the beneficiaries of U.S. military protection as part of Operation Northern Watch. While American fighter pilots patrol the skies over northern Iraq to prevent Saddam Hussein from gassing the Kurds a second time, the U.S. trains and finances Turkish military operatives who are relentlessly wiping out the five million Kurds trapped in the southern part of that country, "destroying some three thousand Kurdish villages and hamlets" since 1990.[8] America needs Turkey as an ally because of its location on the border of the former Soviet Union, or at least it did during the Cold War. From 1991-95, the U.S. supplied four-fifths of the Turkish military's weapons imports. In 1999, the CIA tracked down the Kurdish rebel leader, Abdullah Öcalan, so local authorities could arrest him. A 1995 State Department report documented cases of U.S.-supplied weapons being used in the commission of human-rights abuses in Turkey, according to the Federation of American Scientists.[9] So while, on the one hand, the United States piously protects the Kurds from the evil Saddam Hussein, on the other, it finances and contributes to the destruction of a greater number of Kurds at the hands of the Turks. It is cold-blooded, hypocritical imperialism of the kind Gandhi fought against in India, and it is not the only example of American perfidy.

An equally sad case involves Diego Garcia, a ribbon of land bent like a horseshoe in the middle of the Indian Ocean. It is from this island base, six kilometres across at its widest point and twenty-two kilometres in total length, that the United States patrols the region and, more importantly, the Middle East. Military analysts consider it to be one of America's three most important bases in the world. It is home to America's B-52 Stratofortress bombers, which can fly missions that cover distances of more than twenty-two thousand kilometres. It also has Stealth and B-2 bombers, whose range and capacity mean the U.S. Air Force can bomb a target anywhere in world from Diego Garcia without refuelling. Thousands of bombing runs were flown from the island's airstrip, the longest in the Indian Ocean, during the Persian Gulf War and for the post–September 11 attacks on Afghanistan. As well, the island's deep and protected harbour is home base to U.S. Navy vessels of all kinds. Some four thousand American military personnel and civilian employees working for the contractors who maintain the facilities live on the island. The military does not make a lot of noise about this key base, preferring to keep it something of a mystery in the American and international mind; among other rules, personnel stationed there are not allowed to bring spouses and are told not to wear identifying military badges and uniforms when on leave in neighbouring countries.

The United States is on Diego Garcia because it signed a fifty-year lease with the owner about thirty years ago; the price, it was revealed later, was a discount on the sale of U.S.-made Polaris missiles.[10] The owner is Great Britain, one of the U.S.'s most reliable and loyal allies, who handed Diego Garcia to the Americans on the totally false basis that it, along with the other half-dozen islands that make up what is known as the Chagos Islands, was uninhabited. The American government of the day had made it known to the British that it did not want a "population problem" on Diego Garcia; nor did it want to have to compete for waterways with local boats or worry about the neighbouring islands being launch pads for espionage operations.

So Britain complied. Between 1966 and 1973, it expelled with the use of threats and double-crossing some two thousand Ilois natives, the inhabitants of the island, exiling them to a life of poverty and second-class status in Mauritius and the Seychelles. The resettlement of the Ilois natives came as Britain was granting independence to its territories in the Indian Ocean, including Mauritius; at the last minute and at America's request, it forced a deal on Mauritius allowing Britain to hold on to the Chagos Islands in exchange for £650,000 to cover the cost of absorbing the islands' populations. The British government then set about buying out and closing down the copra plantations on the islands and shipping out the inhabitants, who were made to sign a "deed of acceptance" in which they promised "never to return" to their homes and revoked any future claim against the British government. Some were tricked into accepting what they were told was a round trip to Mauritius, only to arrive and be left stranded at dockside with no way home. The islanders received almost nothing in the way of compensation, and the Mauritius government sat on the money it had been given to pay for resettlement. The British parliament was told the islands were uninhabited, a bald-faced lie. As one senior Foreign Office official wrote about the depopulating of the islands in 1966, "We must be very tough about this. The object of this exercise is to get some rocks which will remain ours. . . . There will be no indigenous population except sea gulls."[11]

By 1975, half the resettled Ilois were unemployed and almost all were living in appalling conditions in settlement camps that had become permanent slums. There are records of at least nine former Chagos Islanders committing suicide, and of many of the daughters of the resettled families turning to prostitution to support themselves.[12] In 1975, when the forced resettlement began to come to light, the *Washington Post* called it an "act of mass kidnapping."[13]

British journalists consider it to be one of the most sordid moments in their country's long history of cold-blooded imperialism; in November 2000, a judge agreed, calling the resettlement an "abject legal failure" and ordering Britain to allow the Ilois to return to their homeland. A contrite British government announced it would not appeal and began searching for ways to repatriate the islanders, or to at least let them visit the islands and, as one former inhabitant said, "put flowers on my grandparents' graves."[14]

The U.S. government did not take part in the court case, which was launched by the exiled natives, but it did file a statement opposing their return on the grounds it would be a threat to national security, even though the nearest island to Diego Garcia is 210 kilometres away and the base is patrolled by the most sophisticated military in the world and would doubtlessly be able to detect and repel an invasion of fishing boats. There was little it could do, though – until September 11. Then American security became the whole world's preoccupation. A planned overnight visit to the islands by the expelled families and their descendants in November 2001 was cancelled by the British government because of the United States' vehement opposition to it. As of spring 2002, the Ilois natives had still not been allowed to see their birthplace.

Chalmers Johnson, an expert on Japan and Asia, writes about a similar example of American military imperialism on Okinawa, the southernmost of the major Japanese islands. Okinawa has been a U.S. military colony since the end of the Second World War. In 1995, Johnson writes, there were forty-two American bases on the island, taking up 20 per cent of the best farmland. Most of the land was seized forcibly from Okinawans in the years after the war, a period of jurisdictional wrangling during which the locals were considered neither American nor Japanese, and thus had no rights. Since then, their island home has been turned back to the Japanese government but is still abused by the U.S. military in a frightening fashion. U.S. servicemen and women in Okinawa were implicated in a crime a day from 1972 to 1995, according to a study by a Japanese newspaper. A disproportionate number (twice the average at any other U.S. military base) were sexual assaults, such as the sensational rape and beating of a twelve-year-old Okinawan girl at the hands of three soldiers in 1995, "just for fun."[15] American military personnel have also been involved in numerous car accidents that killed locals (service vehicles did not have to have licence plates until 1995); and flights by U.S. planes and practice exercises by artillery units contribute to unbearable noise levels that drown out normal activity and harm the environment. In many cases, the American perpetrators of crimes are beyond the reach of local courts because military rules prevent their arrest. Even if they are charged, the suspects are shipped back to the United States before a trial can proceed. As well, the local Okinawan government is obliged to care for an estimated ten thousand orphans of mixed U.S./Okinawan parentage. As if all that were not enough, under the terms of a 1978 agreement, Japan has to pay 78 per cent of America's costs for keeping close to fifty thousand soldiers on its soil (there are eight U.S. bases on Japan proper, plus Okinawa), an amount, says Johnson, "2.2 times greater than Japan's expenditures for university subsidies and 2.1 times the amount it spends for day care."[16] The amount doesn't include the average $1 billion the Japanese have spent on American-made weapons and military equipment in every one of the last ten years.[17]

The Japanese and, needless to say, the Okinawan people deeply resent this heavy-handed American presence in their lives, especially since the Cold War has ended and there is no longer a need for the United States to operate satellites from where it can protect the rest of the world against communism. As well, the Vietnam War and its outcome in favour of North Vietnam has proven that there never really was a risk of the "domino" threat of communism jumping from country to country. American claims that its military presence provides "stability" in the region were debunked, Johnson also says, when the Pacific Rim economy collapsed in 1997, causing widespread regional instability in spite of the troops standing ready in Okinawa. The only reason the Americans are still there, argues the author, is because it is a great place to be posted to if you are in the U.S. Armed Forces (service personnel get generous cost-of-living allowances and access to gorgeous beaches), and "to perpetuate or increase American hegemonic power in this crucial region."[18]

A deeper examination of the Federation of American Scientists' list of U.S. military operations tells an even more compelling story: between the fall of the Berlin Wall in 1989 and September 11, 2001, there have been one hundred such operations – a rate of almost one a month, six times the rate during the period from 1975 to 1989. Since the end of the Cold War, a period that logic dictates should have seen military operations scaled back around the world, the United States has increased its military activities by an exponential amount. In this context, the imperialism described in *Blowback* takes on a new complexion: that of the world's only superpower refortifying itself militarily in order to ensure its domination of all regions of the planet. The United States military, sometimes with the help of the United Nations and NATO but often alone, has become a post–Cold War global police force, using its might to arrange disputes to its master's advantage and prevent other countries from developing the capacity to harm that master's interests. Since September 11, the U.S. has reinforced its dominance by opening new military bases, including at least three permanent ones in Afghanistan and one in Tajikistan. It has also stepped up operations at bases in Qatar, Pakistan, Saudi Arabia, Bahrain, and Kuwait, exacerbating a sore point at the very source of the anger that bin Laden taps into.

America, as Johnson points out, refers to incidents like the chairlift accident in Italy and the problems in Okinawa as "costs" related to protecting the free world from communism. It is an argument most Americans will eagerly accept, and now, seventeen years after the end of the Cold War, they have a new freedom-threatening monster against which all American misdeeds will be measured in terms of a "cost." But how to explain the massive increase in overseas military deployment from 1989 to 2001, when there were no communists or bin Ladens to haunt us? Johnson writes:

> With the disappearance of any military threat faintly comparable to that posted by the former Soviet Union, such "costs" have become easily avoidable. American military forces could have been withdrawn from Italy, as well as from other foreign bases, long ago. That they were not and that Washington is instead doing everything in its considerable powers to perpetuate Cold War structures, even without the Cold War's justification, places such overseas deployments in a new light. They have become striking evidence, for those who care to look, of an imperial project that the Cold War obscured. The byproducts of this product are likely to build up reservoirs of resentment against all Americans – tourists, students and businessmen, as well as members of the armed forces – that can have lethal results.[19]

Chalmers Johnson wrote those words in a book published the year before September 11, 2001. It was a compelling argument, met at the time with praise from both conservative and liberal reviewers. It is the kind of thing Susan Sontag asked Americans to consider in her piece in the *New Yorker* in the days after September 11, and for which she was treated like a leper.

That vehemently uncritical climate was created by American politicians, including the president, who in retrospect clearly saw the terror attacks as a chance to resurrect Americans' unquestioning acceptance of military buildup and its consequent increase in military incursions – an acceptance that had waned in the years since the end of the Cold War. No one should forget that, during the Clinton years, a major U.S. military priority had been to keep American personnel out of the line of fire, even when operating in hostile situations such as Sudan, Afghanistan, Kosovo, and Somalia. America had lost the taste for burying its young, especially in losing causes such as the Vietnam War. It was a stance that did not play well overseas, as Tony Judt, a historian at New York University, noted in an essay in the *New York Review of Books* in the weeks following September 11:

> [Bin Laden] makes much . . . of the "feebleness and cowardice of the American soldier." Americans are "unmanly" – and so, therefore, are those (notably the ruling Saudi family) who align with them or accept their protection. This allusion to U.S. reluctance to accept casualties and Washington's insistence on fighting wars from 15,000 feet up attracts a wide and sympathetic constituency, and not only among Arabs; for it tidily combines the themes of arrogance, hypocrisy, and pusillanimity while reminding his audience of the terrorists' own willingness to die for their cause. I don't think Washington, or many American citizens, have taken the full measure of the propaganda price that America has paid for its manner of waging risk-free war.[20]

Almost immediately after the September 11 attacks, President George W. Bush began telling Americans they would once again have to accept the possibility of casualties and that the war on terrorism would be long and painful.[21] In his State of the Union speech on January 29, 2002, he warned that "tens of thousands of trained terrorists are still at large" and that American armed forces were rounding up suspects and generic terrorists in the Philippines, Bosnia, and Somalia. He also raised the spectre of an "axis of evil" – Iraq, Iran, and North Korea – three countries bent on developing weapons of mass destruction, of "arming to threaten the peace of the world." He promised to "develop and deploy effective missile defenses to protect America and our allies from sudden attack," thereby reviving the defence industry's much-loved Star Wars system. He announced he was increasing the world's biggest military budget by "the largest increase in defense spending in two decades," an amount of $48 billion. And he assured Americans, "We will win this war."

On February 16, 2002, in a speech in Tokyo, Bush reaffirmed the United States' military commitment to Asia. "America, like Japan, is a Pacific nation, drawn by trade and values and history to be part of Asia's future," he said. "We stand more committed than ever to a forward presence in this region." At the same time, American negotiators were in talks with the Philippines to re-establish a U.S. military presence there for the first time since the early 1990s, when the government, angered by the U.S.'s support of the earlier repressive Marcos regime, evicted the military from two bases. The United States has consequently begun sending military aid and equipment to the Philippines again, in spite of documented abuses of Muslims and communists – including assassinations and executions – at the hands of the police force and military there.

In the months after September 11, and for the first time since the Cold War, the American government once again positioned itself as the thin line between the free world and its ruination at the hands of "evildoers" (formerly the communists, latterly the terrorists). It took great pains to use the terror attacks to justify a greater military presences in foreign lands, even though just such a presence was at the heart of bin Laden's complaint against the United States. Furthermore, its citizens had been primed to die, or at least see their neighbours die, in the carrying out of this new global duty. To be fair, in the months after September 11, when anthrax scares were occurring regularly, airlines were facing bankruptcy, the economy was faltering, and nine hundred thousand people had lost their jobs, these were legitimately invigorating words for Americans. As Christopher Patten, the European Union commissioner for foreign policy, told the *New York Times* on February 23, 2002, it was difficult for anyone but an American to "fully comprehend the impact of a grand innocence and a sense of magnificent self-confidence and invulnerability being shattered in that appalling way."

But just as the Cold War, in Chalmers Johnson's words, "obscured America's larger imperialist agenda," so has September 11. Since the attacks, the United States has developed a new goal – remaining the world's sole superpower – that will be disguised by a more noble preoccupation (the war on terrorism). It was not difficult immediately following the attacks for the U.S. to persuade other nations to serve as allies, or to at least remain on the sidelines, while it reinforced its worldwide military presence. Furthermore, thanks to September 11, the American public, still smarting from the misadventures in Vietnam that killed 58,000 of its citizens, was suddenly again willing to swallow American casualties overseas. An article by Nicholas Lemann in the *New Yorker* of April 1, 2002, cited numerous Bush administration insiders and officials who saw September 11 as a "transformative moment" that "drastically reduced the American public's usual resistance to American military involvement overseas."[22] Lemann also quoted two senior members of George W. Bush's government – Condoleezza Rice, the national security advisor, and Richard Haass, the director of policy planning for the State Department, who made it clear the United States wanted to use the terror attacks on its soil to reinforce its superpower authority to police the world.

Rice: "Theoretically, the realists would predict that when you have a great power like the United States it would not be long before you had other great powers rising to challenge it or trying to balance against it. And I think what you're seeing is that there's at least a predilection this time to move to productive and cooperative relations with the United States, rather than to try to balance the United States."[23]

Haass: "What you're seeing from this Administration is the emergence of a new principle or body of ideas . . . about what you might call the limits of sovereignty. Sovereignty entails obligations. One is not to massacre your own people. Another is not to support terrorism in any way. If a government fails to meet those obligations, then it forfeits some of the normal advantages of sovereignty, including the right to be left alone inside your own territory. Other governments, including the United States, might gain the right to intervene. In the case of terrorism, this can even lead to a right of preventive, or peremptory, self-defense."[24]

That was the Bush administration's attitude about overt operations, such as the bombing of Afghanistan. Then there are covert operations: since 1947, when the CIA was created, American agents have actively interfered with the internal politics of foreign countries in order to produce a desired outcome, and trained foreign soldiers in the dark arts of torture, kidnapping, and other human-rights abuses. James Baker, the secretary of state under George Bush Sr., testified at his Senate confirmation hearings in 1989 that covert actions "would not be inappropriate," including "provision of covert support for a political party or candidate to influence the outcome of another's election."[25]

It adds up to a frightening picture: the world's most powerful military and economic force determined to prevent any challengers to its superiority from arising elsewhere in the world, armed with a doctrine that allows it to invade the sovereign territory of any country deemed by it to have failed to meet obligations – obligations set by the U.S. When the Cold War ended, the United States lost its "preemptive right to be where it chooses"[26]; bin Laden gave it back. This rediscovered hubris resulted in an American attitude toward its rejuvenated allies that soon alienated those allies. Within a month of Bush's State of the Union address, European leaders expressed frustration with "a renewed American impulse to disregard them and go it alone."[27] They had heard the president speak of forming a coalition against terrorism, and then watched as he called Iran, Iraq, and North Korea an "axis of evil," when the three were not an axis at all. Perhaps they also noticed that Bush's State of the Union speech did not contain the words "diplomacy," "talk," or "negotiate," and only mentioned the word "listen" once in reference to Congress listening to "the people." Mostly, though, they saw that what had been treated by the American media and government as a historic and transformative moment in U.S. history had not really changed a thing. As Tony Judt wrote in the *New York Review of Books*:

Before September 11 the U.S. was widely seen as arrogant and unhelpful in international affairs, and on the verge of retreat into smug unilateralism, washing its hands of foreign crises and shared concerns. In the aftermath of the attacks on New York and Washington the country was awash in genuine international sympathy. The Bush administration set out to mobilize these good feelings behind its war against terrorists, and it mostly succeeded. But the "coalition" was an inch deep, in large measure a figment of American imagination, energy, and money. Worse, most of its members were not being asked to do anything much beyond lining up behind American military action. In short, the world was expected to place its faith in what amounted to American unilateralism, albeit in a very different key.[28]

Canada began to doubt the sincerity of America's appreciation for its coalition partners when an American plane dropped a five-hundred-pound bomb on Canadian soldiers carrying out live-ammunition training activities in Afghanistan in mid-April 2002. Four soldiers were killed and eight were wounded. President Bush at first expressed no public condolences to Canada, only doing so a day later when the matter became something of a public-relations problem for him. The slow reaction made it that much more difficult for the Canadian government to justify its participation in the invasion of Afghanistan to its citizens.

In Europe, Christopher Patten, the EU foreign policy commissioner, was suspicious of the "axis of evil" contrivance. He pointed out, among other inconsistencies, that Iran, Iraq, and North Korea were not the world's only weapons proliferators; China and Russia both have weapons of mass destruction in their arsenal, yet America prefers "constructive engagement" with those countries.

Why not make a stronger effort with the Russians to get weapons inspectors back into Iraq? [Patten] asked. Why not acknowledge foreign aid and nation-building as important tools in the fight against terrorism? Most important, the United States has permanent friends and allies that need to be heard, he said.[29]

America's coalition allies, so quick to support it in its hour of need, began to wonder why it insisted on a purely military response, an ever-broadening one at that. Why didn't America, so emphatic that the entire world stand with it against terrorism, use European diplomatic experience to bring pressure to bear on unsupportive governments? Why didn't it consult them? Chalmers Johnson, writing before September 11, has an explanation for America's heedless aggression, and for why Bush failed to mention diplomacy as at least one aspect of the fight against terrorism in his State of the Union speech.

Increasingly, the United States has only one, commonly inappropriate means of achieving its external objectives – military force. It no longer has a full repertoire of skills, including a seasoned, culturally and linguistically expert diplomatic corps; truly viable international institutions that the American public supports both politically and financially and that can give legitimacy to American efforts abroad; economic policies that effectively leverage the tremendous power of the American market into desired foreign responses; or even the ability to express American values without being charged, accurately, with hopeless hypocrisy.[30]

Threatened, the United States immediately resorts to its military might, rather than to diplomacy, because that is all it knows. (Some will remember that, in the wake of September 11, the government lamented that it did not have more agents able to speak Middle Eastern and Asian languages and fit unnoticed into the region.) It insists on an international response but it has weakened the value of the United Nations by going for years without paying its membership dues, to the point where a television magnate, Ted Turner, angered by his government's delinquency, chipped in $1 billion in America's name in 1997.[31] When it comes to its vast markets, America uses them more often as a lever for internal political gain than as a diplomatic tool. It imposed import quotas on Russian and European Union steel and tariffs on Canadian softwood after September 11 to help its politicians win re-election in their states in the November 2002 midterms, dousing those allies' economies in uncertainty at the same time as it insisted they support America's war on terrorism.

As for expressing its values, America's historic willingness to support violent and repressive regimes and interfere surreptitiously with the sovereign affairs of foreign countries seems a more honest reflection of those values than any claims of being a defender of freedom. And there are other hypocrisies equally as damaging. The United States boasts of being a nation of peace but it is the single largest builder and exporter of weapons and munitions, a country that regularly supplies both sides in a conflict – Iran and Iraq, for instance, and China and Taiwan. In 1995, it produced 49 per cent of global arms exports, delivering them to 140 countries, 90 per cent of which were not democracies and had questionable human-rights records, according to Johnson.[32] "Military oriented products account for about a quarter of the total U.S. gross domestic product,"[33] Johnson wrote.

In 2002, the Bush administration "brushed aside" legal restrictions preventing the sale of arms to oppressive regimes so that it could buy their loyalty in the war on terrorism, the Federation of American Scientists reported.[34] Countries such as Azerbaijan, Tajikistan, and Georgia, which were not allowed to receive American arms before September 11, permitted the U.S. to use their airspace or set up military bases inside their borders in exchange for a place in line at Guns 'R' Us. According to a report on the FAS Web site:

Among the countless repercussions from September 11 is a new rationale for doling out security assistance: the war on terrorism. Not since anticommunism was used to excuse the arming and training of repressive regimes during the Cold War has there been such a broad, fail-safe rationale to provide military aid and arms to disreputable foreign militaries. Already the largest weapons supplier in the world, the U.S. government is now providing arms and military training to an even wider group of states.[35]

The FAS said oil interests, not terrorism, were the real motive behind the United States' desire to increase its presence in Georgia: "The U.S. government wants a new oil pipeline from the Caspian Sea to go through Georgia and Turkey, and propping up the Shevardnadze regime with military aid and training is an effort to boost security around the planned pipeline."[36] Oil was also behind an increase in aid to Colombia, where the U.S. needs to protect a pipeline from the Marxist rebels waging constant war in that country, and in Azerbaijan "to protect U.S. access to oil in the Caspian Sea from possible Iranian threats."[37]

These new policies show the Bush administration's intention to pursue wide-ranging goals during a time of relatively weak foreign policy oversight. Using U.S. soldiers and tax dollars to protect access to oil is not likely to have the same popular support as fighting terrorism. Many Americans would also balk at helping foreign militaries fight insurgencies, given the Pentagon's poor record with such interventions in the past. But by blurring foreign policy goals before a largely unquestioning American public still shaken by 9/11, the administration may win easy victories.[38]

Using the cover of serving the greater good, such as fighting communism or terrorism, is America's greatest source of hypocrisy. To see where it can lead the world, one only has to look back at Vietnam. And for a more immediate reminder, there is Nicaragua.

FIVE

AN AMERICAN-MADE DEATH SQUAD:

NICARAGUA, HONDURAS, AND BATTALION 316

If any government sponsors the outlaws and killers of innocents, they have become outlaws and murderers themselves.
– GEORGE W. BUSH, OCTOBER 7, 2001

The single worst aspect of communism in the former Soviet Union was the murder and imprisonment of millions of innocent U.S.S.R. citizens by their government. Sent to die in gulags or starved to death in state-manufactured famines, Soviets were killed in numbers almost too large to believe, let alone fathom. What to make of twenty million deaths in order to prop up Stalin's regime? The world does not lament the Communist regime that crumbled, along with the Berlin Wall, in 1989 and the early 1990s.

But, then, what to make of the American government? To fight communism, it needlessly atom-bombed two Japanese cities in a show of its nuclear power designed to send a message to the expansionist Soviet regime of the day. To fight communism, its planes illegally dropped more conventional bombs on rural Cambodia than it did on Japan in the Second World War, killing at least 750,000 innocent civilians.[1] To fight communism, it has propped up psychopathic, brutal dictators in South Korea, Malaysia, and Iran, among other countries, and covertly toppled elected leaders in Nicaragua, Guatemala, and, again, Iran.

Most recently in its fight against communism, it has carried out or has been complicit in the deaths of thousands of innocent civilians at the hands of right-wing dictators and death squads in Latin American countries. Mostly men, but often women and sometimes children, were gunned down, killed by mines, imprisoned, tortured, starved, and impoverished by regimes funded by American tax dollars and trained by the CIA in the 1950s, '60s, '70s, and, in the cases covered in detail in this and the next chapter, the 1980s. Unlike the U.S.S.R., the American government doesn't need to kill its own people to preserve its power (although it has been prepared to sacrifice them when they get caught in its machinations overseas); instead, it massacres people in other lands. What occurred in the 1980s in Nicaragua and Honduras was a travesty of everything the country told the world it stood for and believed in. Americans were horrorstruck when thousands of their innocent fellow citizens were murdered on September 11. In the wake of what they have seen and felt, can they remain unmoved by the pain their country has delivered upon weaker nations? Can they be certain they represent the right side in a battle of good versus evil?

Nicaragua is the kind of country for which the term "banana republic" was invented. Located in Central America between Honduras to the north and Costa Rica to the south, much of its agriculture was controlled by American fruit companies at the beginning of the twentieth century. Consequently, American troops looking after American interests were an almost constant presence in Nicaragua in the 1900s; the U.S. maintained troops and engaged rebels in the country from 1913 to 1933. In 1936, a U.S.-friendly strongman,

Anastasio Somoza García, took control of the government following a bloody coup. He, and then his sons, remained in power until 1979, when the FSLN (the Sandinista National Liberation Front – the Sandinistas) took over in yet another bloody uprising. Officers in the Somozas' brutal National Guard were airlifted out of the country in a U.S. government plane disguised with Red Cross markings.[2] The Sandinistas immediately created a populist regime with socialist overtones. Among other things, they nationalized American-owned businesses and private property. They also abolished most of the remnants of the corrupt Somoza regime, which included municipal governments, the courts, and congress.[3] When Ronald Reagan, the Republican president, took office in 1981, he immediately put in motion policies to undermine what he called the "Communist" Sandinistan government: he suspended aid to the country, and he instructed the CIA to help organize the country's right-wing rebel faction, the Contras, which the United States also funded. A civil war ensued, throwing Nicaragua's economy into chaos and killing thousands. In 1990, in an election declared free and fair by international observers, Nicaraguan voters threw out the Sandinista government and elected the opposition leader, a woman, Violeta Barrios de Chamorro. Subsequent elections in 1996 and 2001 were also deemed free and fair. The companies that were nationalized were returned to private hands, and the current president, Enrique Bolaños, signed up for America's war on terrorism after September 11.

Most of the above history of Nicaragua has been provided to you courtesy of the United States Department of State Web site (www.state.gov). It is the kind of U.S. foreign-policy story Americans like to believe in: a strategic use of funds and intelligence services to keep the communists from gaining a foothold in Central America. But it is not a story that bears scrutiny.

One rather important point about Nicaragua's recent history that the State Department fails to mention is that there was another free and fair election there – in 1984. In it, the people of that country elected the Sandinistas to power, an outcome the United States at first tried to prevent and then strove to undermine. The American government, such a fierce defender of the right to vote, the shining beacon of freedom for the individual, systematically destroyed the democratic will of the people in Nicaragua. Everyone seems to know this but the American people themselves.

While the Reagan administration portrayed the Sandinistas as Marxist-Leninist dictators with links to international terrorists, more neutral and academic studies of their voyage to power and the way they handled themselves upon arrival describe a model of democratic and humanitarian altruism tainted only by a mild revolutionary fervour. The consecutive Somoza dictatorships, whose only power source was the ruling family's connections to the United States government and American businesses, were brutal and corrupt, enriching themselves and their friends at the expense of the population and enforcing their rule with the brutal National Guard. The Sandinistas, who had waged a guerrilla campaign against the hated Somozas for decades, had massive popular support and control of the army when they took over in 1979. They could have been equally ruthless had they so chosen. Instead, they made mercy and democracy their guiding principles.

Within a month of seizing power, the FSLN had created a seven-member Supreme Court with three judges from the Sandinista party, three from opposition parties, and one unaffiliated judge. The new government also created the Fundamental Statute of Rights and Guarantees of the Nicaraguan People.[4]

This remarkable document, comparable to the preamble of the U.S. Declaration of Independence and the Bill of Rights, incorporated, often verbatim, key provisions of the U.N. Covenants on Civil and Political Rights and on Economic, Social and Cultural Rights, recognizing these as binding in the legal order. But it went beyond that by placing enormous emphasis on the "right to life" (Article 5), described as "inviolable and inherent to the human person." The death penalty, established in Article 38 of Somoza's constitution of 1974, was abolished for all crimes, even in times of national emergency.[5]

Where other incoming regimes routinely go about chopping off the heads of defeated leaders and lining their loyalists up against a bullet-pocked stone wall, the Sandinistas rejected such atrocities because they knew it would make them no better than the Somozas. They outlawed "cruel, inhuman, or degrading treatment" and set a maximum prison sentence of thirty years.[6]

The Sandinistas interpreted their "right to life" mandate as being a requirement to provide for the well-being of Nicaragua's citizens. They launched a literacy campaign in 1980, and also set out nationalizing banks, resources, and foreign-owned companies, as well as instituting land reforms. These takeovers – a reaction to the Somoza years that is still felt in Nicaragua today in the form of thousands of unsettled property claims – were implemented to benefit citizens who had been impoverished by years of corruption at the hands of the Somoza clan and its friends. It was these reforms that prompted the country's elite to flee, mostly to the United States, and caught the Reagan administration's eye.[7]

The other remarkable thing the Sandinistas did was to announce, upon seizing power, that they would hold elections as soon as possible, and no later than 1985 – and then see that promise through. So many new regimes that come to power in developing countries in coup d'états make a similar vow and then fail to deliver, but not the Sandinistas. Overturning a Somoza election law that reserved one-third of the seats in Congress for the ruling conservative party, they guaranteed the right to form political parties and made it ludicrously easy to register them with the government: all that was required was the "submission of a name, emblem, political platform, and names of a few dozen party officials."[8] The FSLN created a ninety-member National Constituent Assembly elected by proportional representation, and an executive office – president and vice-president – elected by popular vote. Thus, in the Assembly, every party that ran candidates was given its share of the ninety seats proportional to the percentage of the popular vote it received. This virtually guaranteed a minimum of one seat for every opposition party. As well, "all participating political parties were guaranteed the right to equal shares of public campaign financing, to equal time on radio and television, and to have poll watchers present during registration, voting and counting of ballots."[9]

This burst of democracy was inconvenient for the Reagan administration, which was doing its best to tar the Sandinistas as the worst kind of communists. Fortunately for the Americans, the Sandinistas' openness also gave the administration a way to tarnish the elections: the relaxed rules made it simple for the U.S. administration to run its own candidate as leader of one of the opposition parties – a candidate instructed to pull out of the election at the last moment on the grounds the vote was unfair and fixed in the Sandinistas' favour. The U.S. did just that, pushing the well-connected and fluently

English-speaking Arturo Cruz into the leadership of a marginal party called the Nicaraguan Democratic Coordinator. According to a senior CIA official quoted in the *New York Times*, "the administration never contemplated letting Cruz stay in the race, because then the Sandinistas could justifiably claim that the elections were legitimate."[10] In 1988, Cruz admitted to the *Times* that he was paid $6,000 a month by the CIA while he campaigned in the 1984 election. Another CIA mole in the elections was Enrique Bolaños, one of the leaders of COSEP, a pro-business group, and the man elected president of Nicaragua in 2001. He and others in COSEP – for the most part former Somoza cronies whose property had been seized by the Sandinistas – met with CIA officials in 1984 to help develop plans to sabotage the vote's credibility.[11] One of those strategies included an invented story planted in the U.S. media about a shipment of Russian MiG fighter planes to Nicaragua just prior to the election, a complete invention that was later revealed to have come from the mind of Oliver North, the National Security Council officer who took the fall in the Iran/Contra scandal.[12]

The election was held on November 4, 1984. Not surprisingly, the FSLN – the party that had liberated the country and then shown mercy to its vanquished enemies – won easily; its leader, Daniel Ortega, became president. Three-quarters of eligible voters cast a ballot; the two communist opposition parties received less than 4 per cent of the tally. Official delegations from the Irish and British parliaments, among others, declared the election to be clean.[13] In a little more than five years, a revolutionary government had created an electoral system that guaranteed the right of citizens to control their own destiny. It was as proper and remarkable an election as has ever been organized in modern times. Three years later, in 1987, after eighteen months of public consultation, the new government went on to adopt a constitution that reinforced the rights of Nicaraguan citizens. The United States, as the world's leading democracy and advocate of human rights, should have celebrated these events; instead, as the State Department Web site demonstrates, it does not even acknowledge they took place.

That omission is understandable: throughout most of the 1980s, both before and after the election, the United States spent millions of dollars, much of it illegally, to support and encourage human-rights abuses in Nicaragua and neighbouring Honduras, all in the name of preventing the people of a small Central American nation from choosing a destiny that was inconvenient to the White House. For the U.S. to acknowledge that the election took place and was clean would be to admit that it had interfered with a legitimate government and sabotaged the will of another people for its own ends. Nicaragua in the 1980s is sadly remembered today not for its democratic achievements but for Oliver North and the Iran/Contra scandal, in which the Reagan administration was forced to admit it had sold $50 million in arms to Iran, an illegal transaction aimed at freeing American hostages believed to held by Iranian-backed Hezbollah terrorists in Lebanon,[14] and forwarded the money to the Contras, the rebels opposing the Sandinistas, in yet another illegal transaction. As embarrassing as it was, and in spite of the convictions of four conspirators and the guilty pleas of seven others, the administration got off lightly. As Chalmers Johnson notes, in that era the American public generally accepted these kinds of dirty tricks to be the "cost" of keeping America safe from communism, or at least from people labelled as such by the White House. (Not that the independent counsel who investigated the scandal was able to see all the evidence against the Reagan administration: Oliver North destroyed valuable records while John Poindexter, the national security advisor, erased key e-mails that might have led to more convictions. "Congress was defrauded," the independent counsel noted in his concluding observations.)

There was also evidence during the Nicaraguan civil war that the U.S. State Department gave funds designated for humanitarian aid to drug traffickers in exchange for their help in running guns and supplies to the Contras,[15] another attempt to get around the 1984 legislation prohibiting the U.S. from funding the military activities of the Nicaraguan rebels. The CIA admitted in 1998 that it knowingly worked with some two dozen Contra rebels even though they were trafficking in drugs; it also admitted that the decision to stick with the drug-runners was made by senior officials at CIA headquarters in Langley, Virginia.[16] Some writers have speculated that the sudden increase in cocaine and crack cocaine use in the United States in the 1980s is linked to the CIA's look-the-other-way attitude on drug dealers.[17] In spite of this, these misdeeds, too, never seemed to get under the skin of the American people, and that will probably never change.

But in the wake of September 11, would Americans be so forgiving if they realized their government ran a campaign of terror and murder in Nicaragua and its neighbour, Honduras, of a kind that Osama bin Laden could only dream of having the power and resources to orchestrate? A campaign that targeted innocent civilians, and which employed an Argentine psychopath who named his son after Erwin Rommel, the Nazi general?

None of this would have come to light without the *Baltimore Sun*, an American newspaper that in 1995 ran a series of articles revealing how the CIA recruited General Gustavo Álvarez Martínez to run the Honduran national police and armed forces in the early 1980s, and how General

Álvarez, in July 1983, organized a special Honduran Army death squad known as Battalion 316. Battalion 316's members were trained in part by the CIA, according to documents uncovered by the newspaper. The squad's official mission was surveillance and interrogation; its unofficial one was terror through torture and the "disappearance" of uncooperative Hondurans, and it was key to the United States' success in its war against Central American "communism."

Honduras, one of the United States' most reliable friends in the region, was the staging ground for arming and training the Contras in their U.S.-backed war against the Sandinistas; by the early 1980s the country was so overrun with American military personnel and equipment that it was dubbed the USS *Honduras*. To keep the flow of arms moving through the Honduran jungle into Nicaragua, the CIA needed to ensure that anyone in Honduras who spoke up against America's presence there would be silenced. They knew where to turn for help: General Álvarez was an expert in counterinsurgency, having learned his trade in Argentina in the 1970s, when at least ten thousand people were killed or disappeared at the hands of men like him. He was perfect for the job, and became head of the Honduran Armed Forces. He was a White House favourite, visiting President Reagan in the Oval Office in 1982; in 1983, Reagan awarded him the Legion of Merit for "encouraging the success of democratic processes in Honduras."[18]

At the time of General Álvarez's visit to Washington, D.C., officials there were aware of the abuses he was carrying out in their country's name. In 1981, after being recruited by the CIA and installed in Honduras, the general told Jack Binns, the U.S. ambassador to Honduras from September 1980 to October 1981, that he admired the way the Argentine military dealt with subversives and "said that he planned to use the same methods in Honduras."[19] Binns immediately cabled Washington and warned his superiors about General Álvarez's pathology; he cabled again four months later after the abduction and permanent disappearance of a thirty-three-year-old university professor who had raised questions about the United States' presence in his homeland. In both cases Binns was ignored. By the end of that year he had been replaced, after only a year on the job, by John Negroponte, a career diplomat and old friend of the Bush family who was sympathetic to the Reagan administration's pursuits in Central America. Negroponte's posting was essential to the American government's success in the region. The last thing the Reagan administration wanted in Central America was an ambassador concerned about human rights. Most of the governments in the region that were friendly to the U.S., particularly El Salvador and Guatemala, were enthusiastic murderers and detainers of "subversives." The policy of the Carter administration prior to Reagan's arrival had been to stress human rights – a policy that would have only served to alienate regimes useful to the United States' efforts to prevent the Soviet Union (which we now know was in a state of collapse in the mid-1980s) from establishing an imagined beachhead in Central America. Negroponte was the right choice for the job. Confronted upon his arrival with conclusive proof prepared by embassy staff that the Honduran military was kidnapping, torturing, and killing people "to control a perceived subversive threat,"[20] he knew what he had to do.

Rick Chidester, then a political officer in the U.S. Embassy in Tegucigalpa, told the *Sun* that he compiled substantial evidence of abuses by the Honduran military in 1982, but was ordered to delete most of it from the annual human rights report prepared for the State

Department to deliver to Congress. Those reports consistently misled Congress and the public.

"There are no political prisoners in Honduras," the State Department asserted falsely in its 1983 human rights report.[21]

As the *Baltimore Sun* noted, "The truth could have triggered congressional action under the Foreign Assistance Act, which generally prohibits military aid to any government that 'engages in a consistent pattern of gross violations of recognized human rights.'"[22] It was therefore Negroponte's job to ensure that Congress and the American public remained unaware that the administration was propping up and training a mini-Taliban to further its jihad on Nicaragua's government and people. The newspaper documented instance upon instance of reports prepared during Negroponte's posting in which the embassy lied about what was going on in Honduras. While the embassy claimed in 1982 that students, peasants, workers, and unions were able to organize demonstrations unhindered, it was fully aware of three cases of union and student leaders disappearing forever at the hands of Battalion 316 and ELACH, the Honduran Anti-Communist Liberation Army, a shadowy group that worked for Battalion 316 and which is thought to be responsible for many disappearances. The embassy insisted that Hondurans arrested by police were arraigned within twenty-four hours, even though it knew prisoners were often moved to secret locations where their families could not find them.[23] Negroponte's staff feigned ignorance even though, in 1982 alone, more than three hundred stories were published in Honduran newspapers about student and union leaders going missing and bodies being discovered in unmarked graves. The Americans in Honduras were apparently unaware of near-daily protests in the streets of Tegucigalpa, the capital city, by the families and friends of missing people. And in at least one documented case in 1982, Negroponte himself got involved in the release of a couple being held by Honduras's paramilitary infrastructure – Oscar Reyes Bacca, a journalist who was an open supporter of the Sandinistas in Nicaragua, and his wife, Gloria. Their arrests sparked such loud protests and so many newspaper articles that the noise threatened to reach the U.S. and spark the interest of Congress. Cresencio S. Arcos Jr., the embassy spokesperson at the time, told the *Sun* he warned Negroponte that if Reyes and his wife were hurt, "it would be a disaster for our policy."[24] He said Negroponte subsequently approached General Álvarez, the founder of Battalion 316 and by then commander of the Honduran Army, to express his concern. The couple was released a week later, tried in court, and convicted to six months in prison.

> Two weeks before their sentences ended, they were allowed to leave for the United States on the condition that they kept quiet about the torture they endured. The condition was laid down personally by Álvarez, said the Reyeses, who now live in Vienna, Va. The U.S. Embassy also kept quiet publicly about the Reyes case.[25]

In 1989, when Negroponte underwent confirmation hearings before the Senate Foreign Relations Committee before being appointed ambassador to Mexico, he was asked about Battalion 316 and other abuses of human rights in Honduras. "I have never seen any convincing substantiation that they were involved in death-squad-type activities," he responded.[26] He at first refused to comment to the *Baltimore Sun* on its investigation but relented several months later, saying in a 1995 interview that he stood by the claim he made to the

Senate confirmation hearings. He insisted that he pushed the government to improve its human-rights record but that, overall, the country was on the path to democracy. "I do not have any regrets about the way we carried out U.S. policies [in Central America]," he told the *Sun*.[27]

Negroponte has subsequently gone on to become a key member of George W. Bush's team assuring America's dominance in the post–September 11 world. Three days after the attacks, Negroponte was confirmed by the U.S. Senate as the permanent United States representative to the United Nations. As such, he became an architect of the international coalition to fight terrorism – a coalition led by the aggrieved and freedom-loving American government. The *New York Times*, on August 18, 2001, wrote in an editorial that Negroponte's record in Honduras needed to be thoroughly investigated before his nomination to the U.N. position, because the "job is symbolically important, especially in the areas of human rights and adherence to law."

If Negroponte and his embassy staff were unable to find convincing evidence of abuses by Battalion 316 or ELACH, the same was not the case for the Honduran government. In 1993, it released a report entitled *The Facts Speak for Themselves*, in which the government accepted responsibility for the abuses of the 1980s and listed 184 people as still missing and presumed dead. The Hondurans subsequently made attempts to bring members of its military to justice, arresting and charging eleven former and current military officers in 1995.[28]

The Americans have never been so upfront or forthcoming, even though declassified government documents made plain the extent to which Battalion 316 was created, funded, and trained by the American government. The documents, mostly based on testimony to a Senate committee by a CIA official named Richard Stolz, show that the CIA flew members of the death squad to a secret location in the U.S. where they were trained and equipped; that they were given further training at CIA bases in Honduras; and that one CIA official routinely visited the secret prison where many abductees were held and tortured to assist the death squads by analyzing the answers they had beaten out of prisoners.[29] The CIA to this day says there is no evidence to substantiate that allegation.

The *Sun* also obtained a CIA manual dated 1983 that outlined interrogation and torture methods similar to the ones used by Battalion 316. These techniques included "stripping suspects naked and keeping them blindfolded" in interrogation rooms that were "windowless, dark and soundproof, with no toilet."[30] Interrogators were counselled to make prisoners stand in rigid positions for long periods and deprive them of sleep. It also advised arresting people in surprise raids carried out early in the morning, to achieve "the maximum amount of mental discomfort" – a typical tactic of Battalion 316 members.

The *Sun* also unearthed the KUBARK manual, a CIA torture how-to from the Vietnam War era that advised agents setting up an interrogation site to check the electrical current, "so that transformers and other modifying devices will be on hand if needed" – a reference to the electric-shock torture that was another Battalion 316 favourite.[31]

> The KUBARK manual is mentioned in a 1989 memorandum prepared by the staff of the Senate intelligence committee on the CIA's role in Honduras, and some members of the intelligence community during that period believe it was used in training the Hondurans. One said that some of the lessons from the manual were recorded almost verbatim in notes by CIA agents who sat in on the classes.[32]

Not that Battalion 316 needed much guidance in the ways of torture. General Álvarez brought a distinctive South American style to the proceedings when he arrived from Argentina. Torture victims who lived to tell their stories, as well as some of the torturers themselves tracked down in Toronto, Canada, by the *Baltimore Sun*, described methods such as holding a prisoner's head underwater to the point of drowning, attaching a basket to a man's scrotum and slowly filling the basket with stones, raping women, and wrapping *la capucha* – a rubber mask – around a prisoner's face and slowly suffocating him or her.[33]

The CIA promised to investigate the *Baltimore Sun*'s findings but never did. Nor has it turned over the many documents requested by the Honduran government in its attempts to investigate its own part in the doings of Battalion 316. And in 1998, Republicans in the Senate killed a bill that would have required the administration to declassify the same documents.[34]

A 211-page report by the CIA's inspector general dated August 27, 1997, released in a heavily censored form (entire pages are blacked out), confirms the CIA failed to live up to a commitment made by then-director William Casey to report to Congress on the doings of Battalion 316 and ELACH. According to the *New York Times*, "CIA officers in Honduras knew that the military operated a right-wing assassination squad [but] the officers' poor reporting on human rights problems left senior CIA officials unaware of their seriousness or scope."[35]

The CIA also sometimes gave misleading information to Congress, the 1997 report indicated, downplaying Honduran involvement in abuses at least in part so as not to jeopardize the country's crucial support for rebels fighting against the Sandinista government in Nicaragua.[36]

The report also made it apparent that, even though Battalion 316 was formally disbanded in 1987, many of its members were subsequently transferred to other intelligence and counterintelligence units in the Honduran army.

As for General Álvarez, he suddenly fell out of favour with the Honduran army in 1984 and was summarily deported to Costa Rica. Later the same year he moved with his family to Miami, where he joined an evangelical church and found God. He ill-advisedly returned to Honduras in 1988 and began preaching the Gospel on street corners. On January 25, 1989, he was gunned down by five men wearing hard hats and armed with submachine guns. His last words were, "Why are they doing this to me?"[37]

POSTSCRIPT

John Negroponte, who became the U.S. ambassador to the United Nations in September 2001, is not the only person directly involved in Ronald Reagan's Central American dirty tricks who has gone on to prominence in the administration of George W. Bush. As noted in the *Economist*, Elliott Abrams, who pleaded guilty to lying to Congress about America's role in Nicaragua but was later pardoned by George Bush Sr., "has reemerged as head of the [National Security Council]'s office for democracy and human rights. . . . But the most controversial figure is the man mainly responsible for policy in the region: Mr. [Otto] Reich, a Cuban-American who ran the State Department's office of public diplomacy in the 1980s, which, according to Congress, helped Oliver North raise money for the Contras."[38]

These connections were raised after a failed coup in Venezuela in April 2002, in which the populist president, Hugo Chávez, was ousted momentarily by the opposition, and then returned to power after demonstrations by hundreds of thousands of Venezuelans who supported him. The coup was triggered by Chávez's attempt to take control of the state oil company and increase production against the wishes of OPEC, the U.S.-supported cartel that controls the price of oil by setting production quotas. Within days of the coup, there were rumours that the Bush administration was involved in its planning, partly because the plotters were in Washington prior to the coup and met with administration officials. It did not help that the administration seemed by its silence to welcome Chávez's ouster when it occurred; the White House protested the violent overthrow of another government only after Latin American leaders condemned the lack of response.

The Bush administration swore it had no prior knowledge of the coup and was not part of its planning or financing. The truth will only be known twenty or thirty years after the coup, when the relevant CIA or other documents are declassified. Still, America's history in Central and South America is such that when a coup does occur, even in 2002, many in the region rather understandably include the U.S. in their roundup of the usual suspects.

SIX

FROM GUATEMALA TO NICARAGUA, BY WAY OF CHILE

We're right and they're wrong. It's as simple as that.
    – RUDOLPH GIULIANI, OCTOBER 1, 2001

When the CIA and the United States government got around to training torturers in Honduras and sabotaging the democratic will of the Nicaraguan people in the name of fighting communism, both were well practised in the commission of such atrocities in Latin American countries. The first to go was Guatemala, where the democratically elected president, Jacobo Arbenz Guzmán, granted legal status to the communist labour party in 1952 and let communists hold key positions in his government. He also instituted modest land reforms that angered American corporations growing bananas there.[1] It was the original American-made dictator in Nicaragua, Anastasio Somoza García, who proposed to Harry S. Truman, the president, that they work together to overthrow Arbenz and install the type of right-wing dictatorship that had proven to be so useful to American interests in his country.[2] Truman told the CIA to go for it.

The first attempt, a five-week effort to run guns and money to the Guatemalan exiles, was uncovered by the Arbenz government and consequently abandoned. It was then that the CIA came up with perhaps one of its most regrettable plots of all time: a plan to assassinate fifty-eight Guatemalan supporters of the Arbenz government suspected of being communists. According to heavily censored declassified CIA documents, in 1953, under President Eisenhower, the Agency drew up a "disposal list" of the targets and trained assassins to kill them. The plans were discussed at the highest levels of the State Department and were included as a key part of Operation Success, the name of the operation to topple the Guatemalan government. Eisenhower's National Security Council gave the CIA the go-ahead to carry out Operation Success.

No record of the formal approval or disapproval of the plans by President Eisenhower . . . has been made public. None likely exists. The newly released files include a 22-page how-to manual on murder that says, "No assassination instructions should ever be written or recorded."[3]

The assassinations were never carried out because they were ultimately unnecessary. Instead, the CIA paid off officers in the Guatemalan Army not to resist the coup and targeted recalcitrant officers, as well as some those on the "disposal list," with a "nerve war" in 1953 and 1954. The nerve war involved "sending them death threats, telephoning them, 'preferably between 2 and 5 a.m.,' with bloodcurdling warnings, and denouncing them to their supporters with accusations ranging 'from treason to tax evasion.'"[4] As the U.S. State Department background notes on Guatemala today read, "The army refused to defend the Arbenz government when a U.S.-backed group led by Col. Carlos Castillo Armas invaded the country from Honduras in 1954 and quickly took over the government." The State Department makes no mention of the fact the military was on the CIA payroll and continued to be for the following decades while it committed atrocity after atrocity against its own people.

The obvious consequence – or at least it is obvious now – of the right-wing Guatemalan government's autocratic injustices was a series of coups that ultimately drove the rebels into the arms of the only superpower available to them – the U.S.S.R., via Cuba. In the 1960s, several left-wing guerrilla groups "conducted economic sabotage and targeted government installations and members of government security forces in armed attacks."[5] They assassinated the U.S. Ambassador to Guatemala, John Gordon Mein, in 1968. In 1982 the various factions merged to form the Guatemalan National Revolutionary Unity. By that time the country was under the control of Efraín Ríos Montt, a fanatically violent dictator who promised to wipe out indigenous tribes if they supported the rebels. This he did. Thanks to American training in counterinsurgency methods, as well as American financing, the Guatemalan Army "destroyed some four hundred Mayan villages in a campaign of genocide in which approximately two hundred thousand peasants were killed."[6] Two reports into the atrocities by separate bodies – the United Nations–sponsored Commission for Historical Clarification, and the Archbishop's Office for Human Rights in Guatemala – made it impossible for the United States to turn a blind eye any longer. Both reports said the right-wing puppet government was responsible for the deaths of the mostly unarmed peasants; in 1999, Bill Clinton, the president, travelled to Guatemala to apologize to the people there.

That apology needs to be put in the light of American foreign policy of the time. By the 1990s, the U.S. had realized that propping up right-wing dictators to protect its interests

often led to the "blowback" identified by Chalmers Johnson –
a virulent hatred of the United States and the creation of anti-
American governments that feed off that hatred. The most
clear-cut case of this is Iran, where the U.S. for years supported its despised martinet, the shah, only to see Iran fall into
the hands of the Islamic fundamentalist regime of Ayatollah
Khomeini in 1979. Khomeini, an Islamic radical as fanatical
as Mullah Omar, the spiritual leader of the Taliban, was
among the first to label the U.S. "the great Satan," and he
made the U.S. miserable for years, beginning with the seizure
of the American embassy in Tehran (a critical moment that is
unmentioned by the Department of State in its background
notes on Iran). If, in 1999, the American government was
getting around to apologizing for its past sins, it was doing so
because it had become apparent that those transgressions
created more enemies than friends in the long run. (For more
on Iran, see Chapter 7.)

From Guatemala we move to Chile, where the CIA was
instrumental in the overthrow of Salvador Allende, a left-
leaning senator elected president in 1970. Allende undertook
land reforms and nationalized banks and industries, including
a proposal to nationalize the U.S. interests in major Chilean
copper mines. His policies prompted American businessmen
to press President Richard Nixon directly to prevent Allende's
confirmation as president on October 24, 1971. Nixon,
according to Christopher Hitchens in his book *The Trial of
Henry Kissinger*, felt sufficiently indebted to the president of
Pepsi-Cola, in particular, to agree to try organize the overthrow of a democratically elected leader of a foreign country.

[Nixon] was personally beholden to Donald Kendall,
the President of Pepsi Cola, who had given him his first
corporate account when, as a young lawyer, he had

joined John Mitchell's law firm. A series of Washington meetings, held within days of Allende's electoral victory, essentially settled the fate of Chilean democracy.[7]

According to a declassified CIA report about the U.S. administration's activities in Chile, the CIA was meddling in elections there as early as 1962, when it began financing preferred candidates with an eye to keeping the leftist Allende from being elected in the 1964 presidential elections. Among others, ITT, which owned valuable copper mines in Chile, was urging the CIA, as well as the American government, to prevent the rise of a left-wing, nationalist leader.

As early as the 1964 Chilean Presidential election, American businessmen with interests in Chile had offered to provide the CIA with funds to prevent Allende from being elected. All of these early offers were rejected. In early 1970, a Station officer was contacted by a United States businessman employed by International Telephone and Telegraph (ITT) urging the U.S. government to provide financial support to one of Allende's opponents, Jorge Alessandri. The Station provided the businessman the name of an individual who could securely funnel ITT funds to Alessandri.[8]

Leading up to the 1964 elections, the CIA regularly undertook "propaganda and political action" programs and gave "covert assistance" to its preferred candidates. As well, "thousands of Chilean military officers came to the United States for training, which included presentations on the impact of global communism on their country."[9] Allende lost the 1964 vote to the CIA-supported Eduardo Frei of the

Christian Democratic Party, a "milestone in the CIA's Chilean election effort," according to the report.

Allende made it clear he would run again in 1970. In 1967 the CIA "set up a propaganda mechanism for making placements in radio and news media,"[10] mostly warning Chileans of the dangers of an Allende-led Marxist regime. As well, "in the run-up to the 1970 Presidential elections," the CIA carried out "spoiling operations to prevent an Allende victory," an effort that ultimately failed in spite of the cooperation of Chilean politicians in other parties.

After Chileans elected not to vote for the CIA's candidates, the Agency was subsequently directed to "instigate a coup to prevent Allende from taking office."[11] One paragraph of the CIA report describes a meeting between then CIA Director Richard Helms and Attorney General John Mitchell and President Nixon and his National Security Advisor, Henry Kissinger, on September 15, 1970:

> Nixon and . . . Kissinger directed the CIA to prevent Allende from taking power. They were "not concerned about the risks involved," according to Helms' notes. In addition to political action, Nixon and Kissinger, according to Helms' notes, ordered steps to "make the economy scream."[12]

Nixon told the CIA to carry out the plot without telling the departments of State and Defense, or the U.S. ambassador to Chile, and gave them $10 million to get the job done.[13] The CIA immediately began contacting "key Chilean military and Carabinero (national police) officers to convince them to carry out a coup." They and their Chilean co-conspirators soon concluded that "any coup would require the kidnapping of Commander [sic] Rene Schneider, who felt deeply that the

Constitution required that the Army allow Allende to take power."[14] General René Schneider, who put his country's constitution before America's interests, was killed in an attempted kidnapping carried out by one of three "groups of plotters" working for the CIA, one of which had been armed by the agency with "tear gas, submachine-guns and ammunition." The botched kidnapping/assassination shocked the other plotters and the coup was shelved. The CIA subsequently paid a member of the group that killed Schneider $35,000 to "keep the prior contact secret, maintain the good will of the group, and for humanitarian reasons."[15]

Allende managed to hang on to power until 1973, when a coup led by General Augusto Pinochet Ugarte finally succeeded. The one-day coup took place on September 11, 1973. The CIA insists it did not instigate it but the report acknowledged that "because the CIA did not discourage the takeover and had sought to instigate a coup in 1970 [it] probably appeared to condone it." Allende was killed in his palace, or committed suicide, depending on who is telling the story. Pinochet declared himself "Supreme Leader" of Chile in December 1974.

Pinochet, of course, went on to become one of the most repressive and murderous dictators in South American modern history. He took control of a country with an intellectual, left-leaning middle class that posed a threat to his rule, and so undertook years of arrests and disappearances that have been well-documented by journalists and novelists. Within days of his coup, the mutilated bodies of prisoners who had been held at the National Stadium in Santiago began to turn up in rivers, canals, and ditches. In one case, the CIA said that Pinochet's right-hand man, General Sergio Arellano Stark, gave instructions that led to the summary execution of twenty-one political prisoners.[16]

Over the course of four years, as many as three thousand people were killed by Pinochet's henchmen while the CIA looked the other way or even put the killers on its payroll, as in the case of General Juan Manuel Contreras Sepúlveda, who was chief of Pinochet's most feared secret police unit. The CIA maintained contacts with Contreras even though he was "the principle obstacle to a reasonable human rights policy within the Junta."[17] In May and June of 1975, "elements within the CIA recommended establishing a paid relationship with Contreras," an idea that was overruled but not before he had received a one-time payment from the Agency.[18] As well, the report concludes, "There is no doubt that some CIA contacts were actively engaged in committing and covering up serious human rights abuses."[19]

It was Contreras who helped mastermind a plot to track down and kill Allende sympathizers that led to the car-bombing deaths in Washington, D.C., of Orlando Letelier, who had been Chile's foreign minister under Allende, and his American assistant, on September 21, 1976. That same year, Kissinger himself told Pinochet the U.S. was sympathetic to his brutal regime, "although Kissinger advised some progress on human rights in order to improve Chile's image in the U.S. Congress."[20]

It was not until the 1990s that revelations about Chile prompted the CIA to be less friendly with Latin American murderers, torturers, and dictators; the Agency now claims to have "new standards . . . that would likely have altered the amount of contact we had with perpetrators of human rights violators in Chile,"[21] it concludes in its report on Chile. Guatemala and Chile were thus lessons that reshaped American thinking in the 1990s. Prior to that, under Reagan, a president who, according to Kissinger, was "elected on the promise of militant anti-communism,"[22] the experiences of

Guatemala and Chile were instructive demonstrations of how to get things done. America's abusive policies in Nicaragua were carried out by experts who were fully aware of the pain and destruction they would bring the Nicaraguan people. By the time the CIA and the administration turned their attentions to the Sandinista regime in 1981, both were well-endowed with the know-how and the indifference to human suffering required to turn events their way.

They had secured Honduras as a staging ground, its dissidents silenced by Battalion 316. In Nicaragua, the economy was near collapse, thanks to Reagan's suspension of $100 million in aid in 1981 on the unproven grounds that the Sandinistas were running guns to El Salvador. (This suspension was followed by a 90-per-cent reduction in sugar export quotas to the U.S. and a total trade embargo in 1985.) The stage was set for the U.S. to wage its campaign against the Nicaraguan people.

The campaign had a simple goal: "to see the Contras debilitate the Sandinistas by forcing them to divert scarce resources toward the war and away from social programs."[3] The Sandinistas had already established themselves as an interim government dedicated to the welfare of the Nicaraguan people. They had vowed to create social services to serve the impoverished population, including health care and education. The government also planned to rebuild the nation's infrastructure, and had vowed to hold free elections by 1985. The CIA thus came up with the idea not so much of targeting the Sandinista Army as carrying out hit-and-run operations on clinics, schools, agricultural co-operatives, road-building equipment, telephone and power lines, and other essentials of life.

The results of this strategy were documented by members of a group that observed the war first-hand, the First Veterans

Peace Action Team, in a letter to the U.S. Ambassador to Nicaragua, Harry Bergold, in March 1987.[24] The attacks on innocent civilians, combined with the trade embargo that prevented doctors from getting the supplies they needed to treat the wounded, led to thousands of innocent deaths, the group stated. They also discovered that the Contras were planting tank mines on roads that were known to carry not tanks but heavy civilian traffic. As a result of the civil war, Nicaragua is today one of the most heavily mined countries in the world.

Edgar Chamorro, a former Contra leader turned peace activist, testifying in a trespassing case in Boston, Massachusetts, resulting from an anti-CIA demonstration at the University of Massachusetts in 1986, told the world how the agency trained the Contras:

> The CIA hired hardened Argentinean soldiers to teach the Contras how to commit atrocities against the civilian population, Chamorro said. "The philosophy was that you have to fight in ways that people will be really scared, or otherwise they will not respect you." Chamorro said the Agency asked him to translate a stack of blue mimeographed sheets that bore the title *Psychological Operations in Guerrilla Warfare*. The manual, a copy of which was admitted as evidence, advises Contra leaders to assassinate respected citizens of small towns, such as judges and doctors, and to make it appear as if the Sandinista government were responsible. Chamorro said the document also asked the Contras to "create martyrs of our own followers, someone who is well-liked that gets killed in a way that looks like the government did it." The CIA also delivered to the Contras mines powerful enough to maim but not kill civilians, Chamorro testified, in hopes of overburdening

the Sandinista health-care system. "The CIA was telling us, in this kind of war, there is no difference between civilian and military," Chamorro said.[25]

Back in America, Reagan and his administration were portraying the Sandinistas as an invading Red Army sent by Moscow. It must be remembered, as Henry Kissinger wrote in one of his memoirs, that Reagan had been elected in 1980 to "reaffirm traditional verities of American exceptionalism."[26] Americans were tired of watching the U.S.S.R. make gains in Afghanistan, Angola, and Cambodia, and had suffered through the humiliating Iranian hostage crisis that had made their country seem so ineffectual. Reagan promised the American people he would push back against communism and enforce the ideals of democracy around the world. Soon after his inauguration in 1981, "he labeled the Soviet Union an outlaw empire prepared 'to commit any crime, to lie, to cheat,' in order to achieve its goals," Kissinger recalled.[27] In 1983, Reagan dubbed the U.S.S.R. the "empire of evil" (the precursor to George W. Bush's "axis of evil"), and he authorized massive new defence spending to keep them in check. Thus, when a revolutionary government in Central America seized power from a right-wing puppet regime and American interests were at stake, Reagan was perfectly positioned to portray the new government's politics as proof the Soviet Union wanted nothing less than to start building Ladas in Detroit. Hugh Brogan, in *The Penguin History of the U.S.A.*, notes:

> The [Reagan administration was] as unreasonably obsessed with the Sandinistas of Nicaragua as the Kennedy brothers had been with Fidel Castro. Reagan at times talked as if he expected a red tide to come lapping up at any moment at the borders of Texas.[28]

In a speech he made to a fundraising dinner for the Nicaraguan Refugee Fund in 1985, Reagan told the audience the Sandinistas had "embraced" communism and "moved into the Soviet orbit." He called the government – democratically elected and guided by an American-style bill of rights – a "communist dictatorship" that has "done what communist dictatorships do: created a repressive state security and secret police organization assisted by Soviet, East German, and Cuban advisers; harassed, and in many cases expunged, the political opposition, and rendered democratic freedoms of speech, press and assembly punishable by officially sanctioned harassment and imprisonment or death."[29]

Reagan described prison camps to which thousands of peasants were sent forcibly; he spoke of a "scorched-earth policy" that caused thousands of refugees to flee the country, and he claimed the Sandinistas had massacred the country's native Miskito Indians because they resisted their indoctrination into Marxist dogma.[30] Reagan also claimed the communist Nicaraguan regime was threatening the rest of Central America. He named as being under threat Costa Rica, whose president had in fact praised the Sandinistas for their humane policies, as well as what he told the audience were the "democratic movements" in El Salvador and Guatemala, both of which at that time were still in the control of American-supported right-wing dictatorships, in spite of recent cosmetic elections. He also mentioned Honduras, where the government was rounding up and killing anti-American dissidents with the help of the CIA.

The speech was almost entirely a string of lies; there were grains of truth in the treatment of Miskito natives, many of whom had been recruited by the Contra rebels, and there is no denying that Daniel Ortega, the Sandinista president, had visited Moscow and Cuba and that "advisors" from the

U.S.S.R. and Cuba were in Nicaragua. But where else was Ortega to turn? Eight months after Reagan's inauguration, the new president had sent a senior envoy to Nicaragua to tell the Sandinistas to protect American interests in the country or "be prepared for the worst."[31]

Moreover, Reagan's speech came after the 1984 election that had been declared open and fair by international observers – the election in which less than 4 per cent of the population had voted for communist candidates. Nicaragua was by that time a legitimate democracy; the Sandinista government's only sin was to refuse to embrace the superpower that had propped up the brutal regime before it and had inflicted so much misery on its people.

It must also be remembered of Reagan that he was, in Hugh Brogan's words, a "lazy man"[32] – a president happy to delegate, without question, all responsibilities after establishing the bigger picture, which in this case was stopping an imagined spread of communism in Central America. As Henry Kissinger wrote in *Diplomacy*, "Reagan knew next to no history, and the little he did know he tailored to support his firmly held preconceptions. He treated biblical references to Armageddon as operational predictions."[33] Nor was Reagan much interested in the niceties of moral consistency, at least not when it came to fighting communism.

> He was also far too casual about questions of legality and constitutionality, which encouraged similar attitudes in his subordinates. . . . In his usual idle way Reagan let things get out of hand; he forgot that he had sworn to uphold and execute the laws. The Iran–Contra caper was as potentially damaging to the Constitution as Watergate itself; but Congress could not bear the thought of dragging itself and the country

through the misery of another impeachment, this time of an immensely popular president. It was content to lay bare the truth through a series of reports and investigations, and to let Reagan exhibit himself as a shuffler, if not a liar, when he responded to investigators' questions with such answers as "I just have no way of recalling anything specific as to what you are asking."[34]

It is further worth noting that Reagan's speech came at the same time as the Soviet Union was opening up to reform and pulling back on its military ambitions and not, as he claimed, trying to establish an entire new orbit of satellites in Central America. A month prior to the speech, Mikhail Gorbachev had become the Soviet secretary-general – the fourth man to hold the position in three years. Four months before Reagan's speech, Gorbachev, as chairman of the Supreme Soviet Foreign Affairs Commission, had first mentioned that glasnost (openness) was "a compulsory condition of socialist democracy and a norm for public life."[35] Within two years, Gorbachev had pulled Soviet troops out of Afghanistan and opened serious disarmament talks with the United States. Two years later the Berlin Wall came down, and two years after that the U.S.S.R. collapsed. The Soviet menace Reagan described in his 1985 speech was not reality; rather, it was propaganda to shore up his administration's controversial incursion into Nicaragua.

Which is why Reagan did not mention one important matter in his speech, and this fact still generally goes unacknowledged in the United States: CIA operatives in Central America known as UCLAs, or Unilaterally Controlled Latino Assets, laid mines in several Nicaraguan harbours in late 1983 and 1984. Reagan, at the time, claimed the mines were "homemade" jobs planted by the Contras, but administration officials and Senate Committee reports demonstrate they were planted by American agents. The mining damaged more than a dozen ships (many of them commercial and foreign vessels), caused insurance rates to rise, closed the harbour for two months, and prompted a number of shipping lines to stay away from Nicaraguan ports, further hurting the economy. After the mine incidents, Nicaragua took its case to the International Court of Justice in the Hague, a tribunal more commonly called the World Court. The United States originally contested the World Court's jurisdiction to hear Nicaragua's case; when the court ruled that it did have jurisdiction, the U.S. pulled out of the proceedings. The court did its best to find evidence in favour of the absent United States, even admitting as evidence a document the U.S. circulated at the U.N. justifying its incursion.

In 1986, the court found the United States government to be responsible for the mines in the harbour and for other direct actions against Nicaragua. These included the sabotage of an underwater oil pipeline and part of the oil terminal at Puerto Sandino on September 13, 1983; an attack by air and sea on the port of Cortino on October 10, 1983, that destroyed five oil tanks and forced the evacuation of large numbers of the local population; another explosion on the underwater oil pipeline at Puerto Sandino on October 14, 1983; and a two-day attack involving speedboats and helicopters using rockets against Potosí Naval Base on January 4 and 5, 1984. In all these cases, the court ruled, the United States planned, directed, and executed the attacks, even if they did not involve American military personnel. In other words, the U.S. had directly attacked Nicaragua in violation of U.N. and other international treaties.[36]

The court also found that the funding the United States sent to the Contras had helped to increase the number of rebel forces from five hundred to ten thousand in a short time. It determined that the training manual entitled *Psychological Operations in Guerrilla Warfare*, mentioned by ex-Contra leader Edgar Chamorro in the Massachusetts trial, was a real CIA document. Its judgment quoted the sections advising Contras to target judges and "notables" in order to terrorize the populace, as well as the advice to create martyrs by killing popular community leaders and making it look like the Sandinistas were responsible. The court noted that the CIA subsequently denounced the document, saying assassination was repugnant to its principles, not to mention in direct violation of an executive order signed by Reagan in 1981 banning assassination as a tool of the government and its intelligence agencies. The CIA blamed its creation on agents who were apparently unaware of the executive order.

The World Court found that the United States' justification for cutting off aid to Nicaragua in 1981 – the allegation that the Sandinistas were running arms to the guerrillas in El Salvador – remained largely unproven. The court said guns did find their way from Nicaragua to El Salvador but not in any significant number, and there was no proof the Sandinistas were behind the operation. It also rejected the United States' claim that its military actions in Nicaragua were taken in self-defence. "Where collective self-defense is invoked," the court ruled, "it is to be expected that the State for whose benefit this right is used will have declared itself to be the victim of an armed attack." El Salvador never declared itself to be under attack by Nicaragua until August 1984 – several months after Nicaragua had filed its suit with the World Court.

The court also found the U.S. trade embargo to be a breach of its treaty obligations. Most damning of all, it ruled that the CIA training, financing, arming, and provision of logistical support to the Contras constituted an unjustified and "clear breach of the principle of non-intervention" in the affairs of a sovereign nation. The fact the U.S. believed the Nicaraguan government was taking "significant steps towards establishing a totalitarian communist dictatorship" was not justification for this violation of a nation's basic rights: "to hold otherwise would make nonsense of the fundamental principle of State sovereignty, on which the whole of international law rests, and the freedom of choice of the political, social, economic and cultural system of a State," the court noted. The U.S. was ordered to pay Nicaragua an unspecified amount of reparations: Nicaragua had asked for $370,200,000.

This, then, is the nation that, in new world order following the September 11 attacks, has given itself the near-holy mission to interfere with the sovereign affairs of any country it deems to have failed to meet its obligations to fight terrorism. As Nicaragua showed, America is capable of using the cover of a higher calling, such as the Cold War, to pursue unjustified covert operations that deliberately kill thousands of innocent civilians. It will back murderous regimes as long as they toe an American line. It will sell arms to an enemy nation harbouring terrorists to raise money illegally for its operations, and its intelligence agents will trade with known drug dealers, even at a time the United States has declared a "war on drugs." When judged by anyone other than itself, the U.S. is seen not as the noble protector of the free world but as something of a rogue nation, mining international waters, breaching the sovereignty of foreign countries for political purposes, organizing hit squads to terrorize innocent, non-military populations, and lying to its own people about its activities. It is a nation that, regardless of its "historic ideals," as Kissinger calls U.S. democratic pretensions,[37] does not stand on higher moral ground than the rest of the world, and the rest of the world is wise not to let those historic and still precious ideals blind it to America's capacity for what could only be called evil. Given what the U.S. has done in the name of fighting communism, what is it willing to perpetrate in the name of fighting terrorism?

POSTSCRIPT

The Nicaraguan government notified the International Court of Justice it was discontinuing its suit in 1991, after the Sandinistas lost power in free elections in 1990 to a government sympathetic to the United States. The U.S. administration had spent an estimated $45 million on the winning party's campaign. When Daniel Ortega lost the election by a slim margin, he immediately conceded defeat, paving the way for a smooth transition to the new government. He ran again in 1996 and 2001, each time losing to an American-backed candidate. In the November 2001 election, he appeared to be heading for a comeback when polls showed him ahead of his nearest opponent by more than six percentage points; the United States immediately dispatched its ambassador to warn that an Ortega win would hurt the country's relations with the Bush White House. Subsequent pressure from Congress in the form of demands on President Bush to re-evaluate his policies toward Nicaragua if the Sandinistas won was heavily reported in the Central American country. A third-party candidate was then pressured to drop out of the race for president, preventing a split in the right-wing vote.[38] Enrique Bolaños, who had worked with the CIA in its attempts to discredit the 1984 election, was elected president, and Ortega was sent back to the sidelines. By then, even some in his own party were wearying of his obstinate hold on the leadership of the Sandinistas, a fatigue that had been exacerbated in 1998 when Ortega was accused by his then-thirty-year-old stepdaughter of sexually abusing her from 1979 to 1990. Ortega denied the allegation, and a Nicaraguan judge ruled he would not have to face a rape charge because his position in the legislature gave him immunity. The woman's mother denied the charge and called her daughter a liar.[39]

Augusto Pinochet has not had a glorious epilogue to his time as the chief spokesman for U.S. values in Chile. Pinochet finally left office in 1990 after being ousted in a 1988 referendum, and Chile has been relatively stable since his departure. Pinochet probably hoped to live out his days in seclusion. Instead, during a trip to Great Britain in 1998, he was arrested and held on an extradition warrant from Spain, which wanted to question him about the torture and disappearance of Spanish nationals in Chile during his rule. The arrest was followed by an international debate about the ethics of bringing former dictators to justice. The Left saw it as a victory, while right-wing commentators pointed out that the Left had never insisted on the legal pursuit of murderous dictators in communist regimes, such as the former Soviet Union, East Germany, and Cuba. After seventeen months in detention, the aging Pinochet was freed when a British judge ruled he was suffering "mild to moderate dementia" and was thus unfit to stand trial. He returned to Chile, where he lives in the countryside and is cared for by a male nurse. It seems the world is so crawling with former death-squad hitmen, deposed dictators, and superannuated torturers that singling one out for punishment is considered unfair, as opposed to a good start.

A final question: America breached Nicaragua's sovereignty in every possible way and was criticized by the international community for doing so. When Richard Haass, the director of policy planning for the State Department, told the *New Yorker* in its April 1, 2002, issue that any country that fails to meet obligations set by the United States in its war on terrorism "forfeits some of the normal advantages of sovereignty,"[40] was he thinking of Nicaragua? Is America's new self-given right to decide who is sovereign and who isn't a retroactive justification of its Central American enormities?

SEVEN

THE "AXIS OF EVIL"

North Korea is a useful whipping boy for any number of interests in Washington.

– CHALMERS JOHNSON

Perhaps the greatest evidence that the United States government would like to bring that old Cold War feeling back to American politics came when President George W. Bush referred to Iran, Iraq, and North Korea as an "axis of evil" in his now historic State of the Union address on January 29, 2002. Ronald Reagan, at the height of his anti-communist crusade, had referred to the former Soviet Union as an "empire of evil" (or "evil empire" – it depends who quotes him). Reagan's simplistic view of the Soviets, based on his equally oversimplified understanding of history, actually served him well, in that it prevented him from losing his focus. Not even his conscience was able to interfere with his ambitions. In American right-wing circles, Reagan's single-mindedness is credited with delivering the *coup de grâce* to the Soviet regime. If oversimplification as a policy worked for the Gipper, it could work for Bush, a president considered by many overseas and in his own country to be something of a bumbling nonentity who had fallen into the job.

And work it did. In the aftermath of September 11, Bush's image was transformed by his Reaganesque response to the attacks. He immediately made it clear there could be no neutral ground. The coming days were to be "a monumental struggle of good versus evil." Bush put nations on notice that they were either with the United States in its fight against terrorism, or with the terrorists. The public responded, and Bush's popularity ratings rose to the same levels Reagan had enjoyed while in office. America's allies, profoundly sympathetic to the country's suffering, agreed to let the United States do their moral thinking for them, at least for a while. In late January 2002, with the military operation in Afghanistan going better than expected, Bush sought to reinforce his country's new authority in his State of the Union speech. Harkening back to Reagan's words, he sought to establish a tone worthy of a president bent on ridding the world of an ubiquitous malevolent presence:

> North Korea is a regime arming with missiles and weapons of mass destruction, while starving its citizens. Iran aggressively pursues these weapons and exports terror, while an unelected few repress the Iranian people's hopes for freedom. Iraq continues to flaunt its hostility toward America and to support terror. The Iraqi regime has plotted to develop anthrax, and nerve gas, and nuclear weapons for over a decade. This is a regime that has already used poison gas to murder thousands of its own citizens – leaving the bodies of mothers huddled over their dead children. This is a regime that agreed to international inspections – then kicked out the inspectors. This is a regime that has something to

hide from the civilized world. States like these, and their terrorist allies, constitute an axis of evil, arming to threaten the peace of the world. By seeking weapons of mass destruction, these regimes pose a grave and growing danger. They could provide these arms to terrorists, giving them the means to match their hatred. They could attack our allies or attempt to blackmail the United States. In any of these cases, the price of indifference would be catastrophic.[1]

But rather than reinforcing America's moral authority in the wake of September 11, the speech produced the opposite effect. You could almost hear the air being let out of the allied coalition. Within weeks, France, Germany, and Britain had reacted poorly to what they saw as a simplistic use of hawkish adjectives that limited the coalition's options to a single strategy – the use of force. They also felt America was using the coalition as window dressing for a militaristic agenda, requiring of its European members only that they quell any opposition to the United States' goals from their citizens. It did not feel like an alliance between equal partners. The response of Joschka Fischer, the German foreign minister, was typical:

> A world of six billion people will not be led into a peaceful future by the mightiest power alone. I do not support anti-Americanism at all, but even with all the differences in size and weight, alliances between free democracies should not be reduced to following. Alliance partners are not satellites.[2]

East Asian countries were also put on edge by Bush's remarks. He had to reassure the leaders of China, Japan, and South Korea that he had no intention of invading North Korea when he visited the region a month after his speech.[3] The problem was that the United States government had its own, simple-minded definitions of words like "coalition" and "axis." For the U.S., its allies' membership in the anti-terrorism coalition was a moral obligation. For those allies, the coalition was both a show of solidarity for a grieving friend and a geopolitically sound reaction to the threat of a new common foe. Morality had little to do with it. As for the word "axis" – a loaded word in Europe given that it triggers memories of the Berlin-Tokyo-Rome Axis of the Second World War – it seems Bush used it more as a pun than a historical reference.

An axis is an alignment of countries that want to promote common goals, according to the usual understanding of the word. The president had taken two countries – Iran and North Korea – that were trying to improve relations with the United States and lumped them together with Iraq, a country that was clearly at war with America. Iran, Iraq, and North Korea were not aligned diplomatically or by treaty. All they shared was a justifiable animosity toward the United States and its roguish character. The threats Bush referred to in his speech were old ones that were not connected to the events of September 11. Bush was simply using the opportunity to create a new rhetorical threat to America, the way Reagan had done – somewhat more convincingly – when he called the U.S.S.R. an "empire of evil."

The obvious irony in Bush's use of the term "axis of evil" was that it bolstered the existing anti-American elements in all three countries. Hardliners in Iran, under pressure from a younger generation to soften the country's foreign policies and liberalize its internal laws, suddenly found themselves back in favour. In North Korea, delicate reunification talks between it and South Korea immediately broke down, and efforts to reach out to the U.S. fell apart. And in Iraq, a country that needs little convincing to rally against America, the leader, Saddam Hussein, saw his stock rise, and not just within his own borders but in the Arab and Muslim world as a whole.

To be fair, reunification talks between North and South Korea resumed in the following months, and Bush's intractable warmongering was partly responsible for moving them forward. But otherwise, the "axis" remark was a diplomatic failure. Bush rarely referred to it afterwards, at least not in international circles (although the American media made daily use of the term). For one thing, whatever agenda had inspired it was overtaken by a sudden and massive increase in hostilities between Israel and the Palestine territories in spring 2002. While the Bush administration threw its weight behind the Israelis, the rest of the world demanded that Israel withdraw its troops from Palestinian villages and cities. America stood isolated, the sole proponent of a tough military response by an Israeli military, equipped with the latest in U.S. weaponry, to the terrorism of Palestinian suicide bombers. All that remained of the coalition against terrorism was the ongoing battle in Afghanistan, and even that was losing steam as the months passed and no one knew whether Osama bin Laden was alive or dead, in Afghanistan or Pakistan.

The zing was gone from the coalition, partly because it was clear from Bush's "axis of evil" formulation that America was going to use the war on terrorism to settle old scores and advance its interests, regardless of the wishes of its allies. Iran and North Korea were not threats to U.S. national security before September 11, and they certainly were not working together. Iraq is a different matter: it is America's most intractable enemy. By lumping the three together, Bush exaggerated the threat of Iran and North Korea, prompting an international reaction that resulted in the downplaying of the threat posed by Iraq.

Of greater issue here is that, if the three "axis" countries were united in anything at all, it was the degree to which U.S. foreign policy had affected their governments and circumstances. America's rogue history, in particular its psychopathic ability to switch allegiances and turn a blind eye to suffering, were key in all three countries' makeup on September 11, 2001. At the very least, Americans need to recognize that it is thanks to their country's direct intervention that there are two states on the Korean peninsula today, rather than the historic, and more natural, one. Koreans are a homogeneous people with a distinct language; their great historical misfortune is to be situated near Russia, China, and Japan, all of which have repeatedly invaded the country. Japan was the last to do so, annexing Korea in 1910 and subjugating it to a brutal and repressive rule most notorious for forcing young Korean women to become "comfort women" serving the sexual demands of Japanese officers. The United States, on its Department of State Web site, takes credit for "liberating" Korea when Japan surrendered in 1945, a moment in their history that should have been a blessing to Koreans. It was anything but.

Within days of Japan's surrender, the United States and Russia, the country's supposed liberators, were divvying up the spoils between themselves. The separation of North and South Korea was the result. How did it happen? The State Department offers the strange explanation that "the unexpectedly early surrender of Japan led to the immediate division of Korea into two occupation zones, with the U.S. administering the southern half of the peninsula and the U.S.S.R. taking over the area to the north of the 38th parallel."[4]

Japan did not surrender "unexpectedly early"; it surrendered precisely when it was expected to, atomically speaking. A more convincing and accurate description of how a homogeneous nation was carved in two for political reasons is found in *The Oxford Companion to United States History*:

As the Pacific war moved toward conclusion, American officials worried that the impending entry of the Soviet Union into the fight against Japan would result in Soviet occupation and domination of the entire peninsula. Some Soviet troops entered Korea after the Soviet Union declared war on Japan on August 8, 1945, but they did not advance rapidly. A week later, Washington proposed that the Soviets occupy the country as far south as the 38th parallel and that the United States occupy the rest. Soviet Premier Joseph Stalin agreed.[5]

And that was that. What had for thousands of years been a single state was offhandedly and overnight turned by its occupiers into a natural stage for aggression between two ideologically contrary factions. Families were cut in two by the arbitrary dissection, much as the Berlin Wall would do to Germans in 1961. (Cross-border visits by family members are still permitted only at the pleasure of the North Korean government.) In 1948, the United States organized elections in the South that led to the creation of the Republic of Korea. In the North, the Soviets created the Democratic People's Republic of Korea. The line, as it were, was even more deeply drawn.

The two Koreas, an American invention, would go on to become a defining element of the Cold War. The leader of the North, Kim Il Sung, pressed the Soviets to finance an invasion of the South that would reunify the peninsula. On June 25, 1950, after China had agreed to go along with the plan and supplied the necessary troops, the attack was launched. The Korean War lasted until 1953, and during it Korea lost two million civilians and one million soldiers. The Chinese suffered hundreds of thousands of casualties, while more than 50,000 American servicemen and women were killed; the total number of Americans killed and wounded was 142,000.[6] The peninsula was devastated physically and economically.

In the United States, the Korean War was seen as the required evidence that communism was the single greatest threat to national security. Before the war, the U.S. military budget was $13 billion annually. Within two years it had jumped to $50 billion, and, as the *Oxford Companion to United States History* says, "the modern defense budget was born."[7]

In Korea, the legacy of the war was the creation of the world's most heavily defended border and a half-century of hostilities. Both Koreas suffered through economic depression for the first twenty years after the war, until the South shot ahead in the 1970s thanks to its friendly relations with the West. Its gross domestic product in 2001 was a robust $434.5 billion; the North's was $21.8 billion.[8] As well, the post-war period in both countries was marked by repressive and antidemocratic governments. The North is still that way; South Korea liberalized to a great degree in 1987.

For its part, the United States has washed its hands of the political chaos it created in 1945. The Department of State says on its Web site, "The question of peace and security on the Korean peninsula is, first and foremost, a matter for the Korean people to decide." Still, the U.S. maintains a military force of 37,000 in South Korea, making it a key base for U.S. activities in the region.

Which leaves the beleaguered North. No longer propped up by the Soviets and under constant pressure from the United States, it has not fared well. Its people are desperately poor, partly because of rigid economic sanctions imposed by the U.S., and partly because it spends a quarter of what little revenue it has on its military – the military that American-Soviet intervention made necessary in the first place, and whose current need is exacerbated by the U.S.'s consistent efforts to paint the tiny nation as a "rogue" and, now, as one-third of an axis of evil.

The question is, assuming North Korea *is* a rogue nation, who is to blame? In *Blowback*, Chalmers Johnson argues that North Korea cultivates its image as an international nuclear outlaw (mostly in the form of missiles it sells to, or swaps for oil with, other roguish nations, such as Pakistan, Iran, Syria, or Libya) because the bartering helps feed its people and also forces the United States at least to engage it in dialogue. If North Korea did not practise nuclear brinkmanship, Johnson argues, as a post-Soviet communist holdover it would have become as isolated as Cuba.[9]

The dialogue brought about by North Korea's arms race resulted in the 1994 Agreed Framework, a deal with the United States, Japan, and South Korea under which North Korea would stop developing its nuclear arsenal in exchange for a lifting of trade sanctions, including ones related to banking and the export of magnesite, which is used in the making of U.S. steel and of which, with China, North Korea is the world's primary source. The United States, Japan, and South Korean also agreed to organize and finance the replacement of North Korea's nuclear power plants with light-water plants whose spent fuel cannot be used in nuclear weapons. In the interim, the U.S. was to provide the oil needed to replace the power produced by the older reactors. North Korea agreed to dispose of its dangerous spent fuel rods (this was completed to the American government's satisfaction in 2000, according to the State Department Web site), and both sides agreed to work toward the normalization of relations.

The Americans did not uphold their end of the deal. As Johnson states, "Instead of delivering fuel oil, as promised, or opening diplomatic and economic relations, as the North Koreans expected, the U.S. government has vacillated, often blaming Congress for its failure to fund the new relationship. Its impulse seemed to be to provide North Korea with just enough food to keep it from starving while hoping that its collapse would be 'soft,' relatively nonviolent, and controllable."[10]

In August 1998, the United States told the world in the gravest tones that North Korea had launched a test missile over Japan, an announcement that threatened to send the Agreed Framework crashing to the ground. The test missile turned out to be the launch of a satellite "in connection with the country's fiftieth anniversary." As Johnson recounts, "Like the famous 1970 Chinese satellite that broadcast the Maoist anthem 'The East Is Red' into outer space, Pyongyang Radio announced that its satellite was transmitting the 'Song of General Il-sung' and 'Song of General Kim Jong-il,' which it labeled 'immortal revolutionary hymns.' The satellite seems to have malfunctioned, and no one ever recorded these melodies."[11]

In October 2000, following renewed efforts by the United States and its regional allies to settle the North Korea question, Chairman Kim Jong-il sent a special envoy to the United States for talks. The envoy, North Korean Vice Marshal Jo Myong Rok, the first vice-chairman of the National Defence Commission, and his United States counterparts signed a joint communiqué "in which the two sides stated that neither government would have hostile intent toward the other and confirmed the commitment of both governments to make every effort in the future to build a new relationship free from past enmity," according to the Department of State Web site page relating to North Korea, which was updated that month.

In late 2002, as the United States was pushing the United Nations Security Council to adopt a resolution calling on Iraq to disarm or face "serious consequences" (the resolution was finally adopted in November 2002), American government officials suddenly announced that North Korea had admitted it was refining plutonium for use in atomic weapons. The Bush administration called it a breach of the Agreed Framework, a deal the U.S. government had never respected in the first place. Rather than demand that North Korea disarm in the same no-uncertain terms as Iraq, however, the Bush team said it would seek a diplomatic solution and began immediately calling for a complete embargo of oil shipments to the country. The U.S. also stepped up its presence in South Korea, a move that was met with much hostility in that country. South Koreans are not happy about the 37,000 American soldiers stationed inside their borders; that unhappiness spilled over in June 2002, after two soldiers killed two teen-aged Korean girls in a road accident. The girls, on their way to a birthday party, were crushed by an armoured vehicle during a routine exercise on the outskirts of Seoul. When the U.S. military refused to let the two soldiers stand trial in a South Korean court and said they would instead face court-martial at an American base north of Seoul, protestors staged demonstrations outside the base and at other U.S. army camps. BBC News reported that some of the protests turned violent, and U.S. personnel were attacked.[12] The soldiers were later acquitted.

Of course, there would be no need for American soldiers in South Korea if the United States had not created North Korea in the first place in 1945. As it is, it is a weak nation, behind the times (it was to get its first limited cellphone and Internet services in 2002). So why the fear and enmity? For Chalmers Johnson, it is a simple matter:

Even though it remains a small, failed Communist regime whose people are starving and have no petroleum, North Korea is a useful whipping boy for any number of interests in Washington. If the military needs a post–Cold War opponent to justify its existence, North Korea is less risky than China. Politicians seek partisan advantage by claiming that others are "soft" on defending the country from "rogue regimes." And the arms lobby had a direct interest in selling its products to each and every nation in East Asia, regardless of its political orientation.[13]

For the record, the United States arms manufacturers delivered a total of $42,171,789,000 in military equipment to the region from 1990 to 2001, according to the Federation of American Scientists.[14] Of that total, $7.2 billion went to South Korea and $10.6 billion went to Japan. The biggest recipient, in dollar figures, was Taiwan, with $14.6 billion; others in the region included Australia at $3.6 billion, Thailand at $2.3 billion, and Singapore at $1.8 billion. China, Taiwan's enemy and a supplier of missiles to Iran and Pakistan, received $44.3 million worth of American military hardware during the same period. North Korea received none and remains an untapped market for American arms manufacturers.

EIGHT

IRAN: HOW TO CREATE A ROGUE NATION

It was a day that should never have ended for it carried with it such a sense of excitement, of satisfaction, and of jubilation that it is doubtful whether any other can come up to it.
– Dr. Donald N. Wilber, writing about the mood at the CIA after the Agency successfully carried out the overthrow of the Iranian prime minister in 1953

Iran was the country that first made an entire generation of Americans aware of the fact there are Islamic nations out there who do not like the United States at all. Ayatollah Ruhollah Khomeini, the religious fundamentalist who took over the country in a revolution in 1979, made "the great Satan" a catchy synonym for America. It was under his rule that a student mob seized the American embassy in Tehran on November 4, 1979, and held fifty-two embassy staffers hostage for 444 days, the so-called Iran Hostage Crisis. Khomeini was the unsmiling and unbending leader of an orthodox sect of Muslims, the Shiites, that made up 95 per cent of Iran's population at the time. The Shiites are activists who believe in conducting religious wars to establish Islamic fundamentalist governments wherever they are lacking. The

Iranian government has, since 1979, supported Shiite radicals in other countries and was suspected in 2002 of shipping arms to the Palestinians for their terrorist activities against Israel. Shiites are also well-known for having little tolerance for blasphemy. It was Khomeini who issued the infamous fatwa, or religious decree, calling on Iranian Shiites to assassinate novelist Salman Rushdie on sight for his allegedly sacrilegious writings. Khomeini, who died in 1989, and subsequent ayatollahs, also imposed varying degrees of abuse on Iranians, among other things sentencing homosexuals, religious and political opponents, and Kurdish nationalists to death, sometimes by stoning.

Thus, it was not difficult for Bush to convince Americans that Iran, ruled in 2002 by a relatively moderate elected president under the control of an orthodox council of religious leaders, had all the qualifications for membership in the "axis of evil." His main beef with Iran turned out to be that the U.S. believed the country was harbouring Taliban and Al-Qaeda members fleeing the American onslaught in Afghanistan, Iran's northern neighbour. Iranian officials could not rule out the possibility that some had fled over its six-hundred-mile border with Afghanistan but complained that the U.S. had not provided information about whom to be on the lookout for. At the same time, the Iranian leadership was dealing with a surge in anti-American sentiment and rallies, and renewed support for its more hardline elements, none of which was helpful to the United States' cause in the region.

Of course, what would have been most useful to the U.S. was a friendly government in Iran to start with; instead, it was faced with a militant Islamic government leading a people guided by anti-Americanism and mistrust of all things Western. Commentators in the U.S. writing after September 11 attributed Iran's dislike of America to the country's fundamentalist regime. Many explained it away as a clash of civilizations; an ideological and political battle between an oppressive, unevolved theocracy and a freedom-loving, secular superpower. Iran's anti-Americanism is more straightforward than that. Iranians have a lasting distaste for the United States because the CIA, under the cover of stopping the spread of communism, malevolently toyed with their country in the early 1950s. The Agency, under the direct guidance of the U.S. president of the day, toppled a popular and populist Iranian prime minister and cemented the power of a U.S.-friendly regime that went on to become one of the most brutal on the planet.

In typically disingenuous fashion, the State Department Web-site entry for Iran sums up the country's twentieth-century history as something that occurred in a U.S.-free vacuum:

> Modern Iranian history began with a nationalist uprising against the shah (who remained in power) in 1905, the granting of a limited constitution in 1906, and the discovery of oil in 1908. In 1921, Reza Khan, an Iranian officer of the Persian Cossack Brigade, seized control of the government. In 1925, he made himself shah, ruling as Reza Shah Pahlavi for almost 16 years and installing the new Pahlavi dynasty.
>
> Under his reign, Iran began to modernize and to secularize politics, and the central government reasserted its authority over the tribes and provinces. In September 1941, following the Allies' (U.K.-Soviet Union) occupation of western Iran, Reza Shah was forced to abdicate. His son, Mohammed Reza Pahlavi, became shah and ruled until 1979.[1]

The shah did indeed reign as the country's monarch from 1941 on, but he might not have remained on his throne as long as he did were it not for what *Time* magazine called a "CIA-inspired" coup in 1953.[2] Referring to the events in question as "CIA-inspired" is rather like saying the film *Saving Private Ryan* was "Steven Spielberg–inspired." An internal CIA history of the coup first made public by the *New York Times* in 2000,[3] and now available on the Internet in its near-entirety,[4] makes it plain the Agency controlled the coup with the same creative vigour a Hollywood director brings to his signature movies. The CIA wrote the twisting and nail-biting plot, chose the many colourful characters – including the playboy shah with his slick hair and dark glasses, and the dedicated lead agent with the memorable name of Kermit Roosevelt – carried off the critical ad-lib scenes, and controlled the emotions of the audience with expert ease. One stands in awe of the sheer nerve involved (the CIA, which teamed up with British intelligence to carry out the coup, used the partnership to spy on the Brits), not to mention the brazen indifference to Iran's sovereignty and the right of its people to choose their own destiny.

The document, "Overthrow of Premier Mossadeq [*sic*] of Iran, November 1952–August 1953," by Donald N. Wilber, was a CIA "clandestine service history" dated 1954, the year after the coup. Wilber, a field agent, ostensibly wrote it "because it seemed desirable to have a record of a major operation prepared while documents were readily at hand and while the memories of the personnel involved in the activity were still fresh."[5] The unspoken reason for the report was that the coup was the CIA's first successful overthrow of a foreign government (the Agency had only come into being five years before, in 1947). As the document triumphantly noted of the shah's return to power, "it was a day that should never have ended for it carried with it such a sense of excitement, of satisfaction, and of jubilation that it is doubtful whether any other can come up to it."[6]

In those early, pre-Vietnam years, the CIA was not a political liability to the United States government. The White House made little attempt to distance itself from the Agency's activities or to set up the "plausible deniability" so important to subsequent presidents. The very highest levels of the American government of the day were quite happy to be associated with the CIA's doings. There is an innocence to the report. The coup went on to serve as a model for the CIA's successful overthrow of the government of Guatemala in 1954 and the catastrophic Bay of Pigs invasion of Cuba in 1961.[7] It was only after the 1979 revolution in Iran that the American government began to distance itself from its role in the 1953 coup, and it might have been able to maintain its distance had the report never surfaced.

The plot begins in 1952 with Britain, under an aging Prime Minister Winston Churchill, going to the Americans with the idea of overthrowing the Iranian government of Premier Mohammed Mossadegh. The British government controlled the country's oil production after the Second World War through the Anglo-Iranian Oil Company. Mossadegh was a militant nationalist who came to power in 1951 after the assassination of a pro-Western prime minister. Mossadegh despised the West, and especially Britain, for the way it exploited his country's oil resources. His politics also clashed with that of the shah, who was decidedly pro-Western.

Mossadegh was the first modern Middle Eastern leader to challenge the West's presence in the region, and as such is still beloved in Iran. Readers of Iranian.com, a free-spirited Web site dedicated to the politics and life of the country, voted Mossadegh "Man of the Century" – ahead of Ayatollah

Khomeini and the shah – in a 2000 poll.[8] His refusal to bow to the West was so shocking for its era and so well received in the Middle East that *Time* magazine made Mossadegh its "Man of the Year" in 1951.[9] The magazine called him "the Iranian George Washington." *Time* also noted that Mossadegh represented a growing anti-American feeling in the region.

> The word "American" no longer has a good sound in that part of the world. To catch the Jewish vote in the U.S., President Truman in 1946 demanded that the British admit 100,000 Jewish refugees to Palestine, in violation of British promises to the Arabs. Since then, the Arab nations surrounding Israel have regarded that state as a U.S. creation, and the U.S., therefore, as an enemy. The Israeli-Arab war created nearly a million Arab refugees, who have been huddled for three years in wretched camps. These refugees, for whom neither the U.S. nor Israel will take the slightest responsibility, keep alive the hatred of U.S. perfidy.[10]

Mossadegh's first order of business as premier was to nationalize the Anglo-Iranian Oil Company, a move that won the instant support of the Iranian people. In 1951, he forced a law to that effect through the country's parliament, the Majlis. As *Time* noted:

> The Anglo-Iranian Oil Co., most of whose stock is owned by the British government, had been paying Iran much less than the British Government took from the company in taxes. The U.S. State Department warned Britain that Iran might explode unless it got a better deal, but the U.S. did not press the issue firmly

enough to make London listen. Mossadegh's nationalization bill scared the company into concessions that
were made too late. The Premier, whose mind runs in
a deep single track, was committed to nationalization –
and much to the surprise of the British, he went
through with it, right down to the expulsion of the
British technicians without whom the Iranians cannot
run the Abadan refinery.[11]

Rather than negotiate to get its oil back (Churchill would
later say that the AIOC had "fouled things up"),[12] the British
turned to the CIA for help. The Americans were at first reluctant to arrange a coup, perhaps realizing the region's burgeon-
ing independence required a more sensitive form of diplomacy.
They changed their minds in 1953, however, after President
Dwight D. Eisenhower was inaugurated. Eisenhower was concerned with the presence of Soviet agents in the country and
the growing influence of Iran's communist party, the Tudeh.
The joint British intelligence (SIS) and CIA plan, code-named
TPAJAX, quickly gained steam under the leadership of
Kermit Roosevelt, the CIA chief of the Near East and Africa
Division (and a grandson of Theodore Roosevelt).[13] By the
middle of July 1953, TPAJAX had been approved by
Churchill and Eisenhower. The CIA was immediately authorized to spend $1 million on the coup, and no further approvals
were needed to disburse the money.

The British spies, told by London to placate the vastly
better-trained and better-funded Americans, stepped aside
and let the CIA do its job. The plan involved getting the shah,
who under the Iran constitution could name the country's
prime minister, to sign three firmans (royal decrees) – one dismissing Mossadegh, one naming the United States' choice as

the new prime minister, and one calling on the army to remain loyal to the Crown. Pressure to get the timid shah to sign the documents was to be applied by his twin sister, the strong-willed Princess Ashraf Pahlavi, and U.S. General H. Norman Schwarzkopf, the father of "Stormin'" Norman Schwarzkopf, the leader of the United States forces in the Gulf War.

The shah was to be approached first by his sister, who was tracked down on the French Riviera and flown to Tehran. Her arrival further aroused the country's already volatile political climate. The easily upset shah, who hadn't been told she was coming, at first refused to receive his sister. He relented, and she told him of the plot and that he was to be visited by Schwarzkopf, who would carry a similar message to hers. The next contact was the British intelligence services' man in Iran, who had to convince the shah the British government sup-ported the coup. The agent told him the BBC would broad-cast a key phrase on its Iranian services on specific dates as proof of his credentials. This was done, and it worked. Next, Schwarzkopf visited the shah at his palace on what appeared to the rest of the world to be a routine call. Wilber wrote in his report that Schwarzkopf was struck by the man's paranoia.

Fearful of planted microphones, the shah led the General into the grand ballroom, pulled a small table to its exact center, and then both sat on the table.[14]

Schwarzkopf told the shah the CIA wanted him to sign the three royal decrees. The shah, worried that the army was not behind him, refused and said he needed to think about it. This scenario was to become an oft-repeated one in July and August 1953, the shah unable to act while the persistent American and British agents pressured him. Agents told him the Peacock Throne, as the shah rather grandiosely liked to call his royal lineage, would cease to exist if he did not sign the necessary decrees. The CIA called it "relentless pressure . . . exerted in frustrating attempts to overcome an entrenched attitude of vacillation and indecision."[15] The shah was warned his failure to act would "lead only to a Communist Iran or a second Korea."[16] The British and Americans agreed to hammer home the communist threat and play down the true motivation for the coup, Britain's oil interests.

By this time, the CIA had settled on the man it wanted as the country's new prime minister. General Fazlollah Zahedi was a former member of Mossadegh's cabinet and the only one in the government to oppose the prime minister. He was thought to be a courageous man by the CIA, which considered most "Persians," as the Agency referred to Iranians, to be military losers limited by a lack of logic, and who compensated for their multiple defeats with silly chest-thumping. As well, Zahedi "was known to be pro-American and had permitted his son, Ardeshir, to study in the United States for six years."[17] The CIA also mentioned that an American doctor had once saved Zahedi's life. Zahedi was approached and quickly brought on board; if he had hesitated at all, a "loan" of $50,000 was sufficient to ensure his enthusiasm. The same kind of persuasion was used to enlist Iranian army officers who would switch allegiances when the coup began in earnest.

Also by this time, the CIA's propaganda machine was busily building support for Zahedi and opposition to Mossadegh. The Agency's "Art Group" prepared realistic protest posters and flyers that appeared to be the work of legitimate dissent groups and passed them around Tehran and the countryside. CIA-invented stories critical of Mossadegh were placed in American and local media (although that aspect of the plan did not go as well as the Agency would have liked).[18] As well, the United States government began to destabilize Mossadegh's regime through statements planted on the lips of members of Eisenhower's cabinet by the CIA; on July 28, the secretary of state of the day, John Foster Dulles, told a press conference that, "The growing activities of the illegal Communist Party in Iran and the toleration of them by the Iranian Government has caused our government concern. These developments make it more difficult to grant aid to Iran." The statement was "made at [the] CIA's suggestion."[19]

Mossadegh reacted badly. He tried to ensure his control of the government through an obviously faked referendum on August 4 in which he asked the Iranian people whether the Majlis should be dissolved. The results were reported by the government to be more than two million in favour and only several hundred opposed. It was a clear abuse of the country's constitution, and CIA agents exploited it in their propaganda to build further opposition to Mossadegh. The same day, by pure chance, Eisenhower deviated from a scripted speech in the United States "to state by implication that the United States would not sit by idly and see Iran fall behind the Iron Curtain."[20] With the pieces falling into place and pressure mounting, the shah finally agreed to sign the royal decrees on August 12. He did the actual signing the next day, by which time the CIA had decided only two decrees were necessary: one dismissing Mossadegh and one naming Zahedi as the new prime minister. Wilber wrote:

> At this same time the psychological campaign against Mossadeq [*sic*] was reaching its climax. The controllable press was going all out against Mossadeq, while [a newspaper whose name was deleted from the report] under station direction was printing material which the station considered to be helpful. CIA agents gave serious attention to alarming the religious leaders at

Tehran by issuing black propaganda in the name of the Tudeh Party, threatening these leaders with savage punishment if they opposed Mossadeq. Threatening phone calls were also made to them, in the name of the Tudeh, and one of several planned sham bombings of the houses of these leaders was carried out.[21]

On August 14, the CIA station in Iran cabled its headquarters in Washington that the Zahedi government, when established after the coup, would need an immediate injection of $5 million to allow it to meet its payroll and other obligations. The stage was set for TPAJAX to begin in earnest, which it did on August 15. It immediately fell apart.

The CIA concluded later that one of the Iranian army officers thought to be onside betrayed the plotters to Mossadegh. This was not necessarily a fatal problem, except that a large number of the other officers recruited to the cause "proved to be inept or lacking in decision at the critical juncture." Regardless of exactly who let down the team, the bottom line was that Mossadegh's chief of staff, General Taghi Riahi, knew the details of the coup by 5:00 p.m. on August 15, including the fact that pro-shah soldiers would begin making arrests later that night. The soldiers managed to make exactly three arrests, the highest-profile being that of Mossadegh's foreign minister. The pro-shah general assigned to deliver the royal decrees to Mossadegh was arrested at Mossadegh's house. By 2:30 a.m., the remaining pro-shah officers abandoned the cause, and by morning Mossadegh was firmly in control of Tehran.

Or so it seemed. The CIA agents in Tehran proved themselves at that point to be determined and resourceful, and unwilling to abandon the plot. Zahedi also felt there was still hope. They quickly decided to spin the night's events in their favour by spreading rumours that it was in fact Mossadegh who had carried out a coup, and that Zahedi was the rightful prime minister. Kermit Roosevelt disingenuously sent a U.S. general "to see General Riahi . . . to ask whether the U.S. Military Mission was still accredited to Mossadeq [*sic*] or to someone else, as the Embassy had heard that an imperial firman had been issued naming Zahedi as Prime Minister. Riahi denied that the firman had been 'authentically signed . . .'"[22]

The following days were marked by a propaganda war. Radio Tehran was still in the government's control, and Mossadegh used it to announce that the country's parliament had been dissolved. This, combined with some intemperate verbal attacks by Mossadegh and his cabinet on the shah that underestimated the Iranian people's affections for their monarch, as well as growing riots and demonstration carried out by the Tudeh Party, began to backfire on the government. The CIA, meanwhile, was able to plant local newspaper stories about the existence of the shah's royal decrees. Its agents were also able to compose and publish a fake interview with Zahedi, who was holed up at either the U.S. Embassy or in the nearby homes of U.S. personnel. Pro-government newspapers fired back with stories conclusively linking the attempted coup to the CIA, stories that even named Schwarzkopf as the mastermind.

The shah, meanwhile, living up to his reputation as a man with no taste for adventure, had fled to Baghdad, where he was eventually convinced by the British to make statements over local radio in the hope they would reach the people of Tehran. The CIA circulated copies of the firmans to the general public, which began to catch the attention of the Iranian people. Still, the Mossadegh government remained in firm control of Iran, causing the CIA agents there to begin to despair that their first attempt to overthrow a government – the Agency's equivalent of putting a man on the moon – was doomed to fail in spite of their efforts. The shah did not help matters. On the morning of August 18 he flew from Baghdad to Rome, where he issued vague statements that did little to shore up his support. Tehran newspapers supporting Mossadegh reported that the Pahlavi dynasty was over. The CIA started to organize the evacuation of key players.

That evening, the tide changed. The CIA reckoned later that the shah's flight to Rome made Iranians aware of the fact they might lose their king. The communist Tudeh Party also went too far, tearing down statues of the shah's father and postering Tehran with literature that implied they were ready to install a "people's republic" in Iran. The CIA, meanwhile, had continued its "black propaganda" against the Tudeh Party, sending fake party members to ransack and loot stores in the city. The army was called in to clear the streets, and some of the soldiers began shouting slogans in favour of the shah as they arrested Tudeh members.

By nine the next morning, pro-shah demonstrators had assembled in Tehran's bazaar area. "Members of these groups had not only made their personal choice between Mossadeq [*sic*] and the shah, but they were stirred up by the [CIA-invented] Tudeh activity of the preceding day and were ready to move," Wilber wrote. "They needed only leadership."[23]

Two CIA agents who happened by pure luck to be at the Tehran bazaar that morning on another mission saw the crowds and provided the necessary leadership. Apparently well-versed in the clichés of revolutionary behaviour, one of them led part of the crowd toward the parliament "and on the way incited them to set fire to the offices of . . . the semiofficial paper owned by [the] Minister of Foreign Affairs."[24] The second agent led a group to the offices of three Tudeh papers and encouraged the mob to sack them thoroughly, which it did. Word began to spread through the city that something was afoot. An American colonel turned up in a U.S. tank at the square where the Parliament was located and was soon joined by two American trucks. "By 1015 hours there were pro-shah truckloads of military personnel at all the main squares."[25] Two British agents began to rally citizens to head to Radio Tehran, which in a surreal moment during the height of the coup that day stubbornly broadcast cotton prices and music while gun battles and riots raged outside. Demonstrators began to display posters of the shah and to chant pro-shah slogans. At 10:30, General Riahi, Mossadegh's chief of staff, informed the prime minister that he had lost control of the Army. Mossadegh ordered him to stand fast, and the last remaining troops loyal to the government took up position around Mossadegh's house.

By 2:30 in the afternoon, Radio Tehran was in the hands of pro-shah forces and the coup was over, other than the usual mopping up and getting the word to the provinces. Almost all of the Iranian Army's generals had lined up behind the shah. The CIA arranged for a tank to carry Zahedi triumphantly to the radio station, where he broadcast his first message at 5:15 p.m. By 7:00 p.m., Mossadegh's house had been reduced to rubble and his possessions were being sold to passersby.

Clearly, Iran's political life from 1953 on was a creation of the American government, not the Iranian people. Iranians were manipulated into thinking their country was in the midst of a homespun political revolution, when in fact it was in the grips of determined CIA agents equipped with a million dollars, a few Photostat machines, and a conscience that allowed them to terrorize people and bomb their homes and make it look like someone else had done it. The shah, propped up by the U.S. government and the CIA during the remainder of his reign, went on to develop a prodigious appetite for American fighter jets and values; it suited his desire to make

Iran appear like a modern Western country. He instigated reforms that took land away from the country's leading clerics (as they were not American fruit-company owners, the U.S. remained unconcerned about this blatant socialism), and he heedlessly moved a deeply religious people away from its Shiite roots through policies of secularization. He also spent heavily on weapons supplied by the United States and Israel, a move that alienated his Arabic neighbours – from 1968 forward, the U.S. gave Iran $100 million in military credits, according to State Department documents. These policies might not have gone over so badly had the shah not been so insistent: anyone who dissented was arrested, tortured, and killed by SAVAK, a secret police and intelligence force so brutal that Amnesty International declared Iran to be the most repressive country in the world in 1976. Those too powerful to kill were imprisoned or sent into exile. Such was the fate of Ayatollah Khomeini in 1964.

In 1979, Khomeini returned from exile and seized power in the wake of anti-shah riots in which hundreds were killed. The mobs were exasperated with the poverty, corruption, and cruelty of the shah's rule, problems that Iranians blamed on the United States. The door was open for Khomeini to reintroduce the strict orthodoxy of the Shiite religion, with its possibility of martyrdom in the battle against American infidels. The shah once again fled Iran, this time on the pretext that he was tired and needed a rest. When the United States took him in as an honoured guest, it was too much for Iranian university students; it was that gesture that prompted the seizure of the American embassy in Tehran and precipitated the hostage crisis.

So who is to blame for all this? Every new government, whether elected or installed in a revolution, is a reaction to the old government, which makes the United States directly responsible for the existence of a devotedly anti-American, Islamic fundamentalist regime in Iran in 2002. Even in 1952, at least some in America were aware that clumsy, self-serving U.S. interference – a CIA coup, for instance – might exacerbate the region's growing animosity toward the West. In its "Man of the Year" essay on Mohammed Mossadegh, *Time* magazine approvingly quoted a Lebanese politician who said, "The disturbing rise of fanaticism in the Near East in recent years is a reaction to the thoughtlessness and superficiality of the West."[26] Subsequent United States governments, pre–George W. Bush, also recognized America's complicity in the rise of Islamic fanaticism, as the *New York Times* reported when it first published the CIA history of the coup in 2000.

The Islamic government of Ayatollah Ruhollah Khomeini supported terrorist attacks against American interests largely because of the long American history of supporting the shah. Even under more moderate rulers, many Iranians still resent the United States' role in the coup and its support of the shah.

Secretary of State Madeleine K. Albright, in an address in March [2000], acknowledged the coup's pivotal role in the troubled relationship and came closer to apologizing than any American official ever has before.

"The Eisenhower administration believed its actions were justified for strategic reasons," she said. "But the coup was clearly a setback for Iran's political development. And it is easy to see now why many Iranians continue to resent this intervention by America in their internal affairs."[27]

In January 1980, *Time* named Ayatollah Khomeini its Man of the Year for 1979. In its accompanying essay, the magazine encouraged United States leaders to learn from Khomeini's rise. It said America should "avoid getting tied too closely to anti-Communist 'strongmen' who are detested by their own people," and "to look for ways to foster material prosperity in Third World countries without alienating their cultures."[28] These were wise words that fell on deaf ears – *Time*'s very next Man of the Year was Ronald Reagan, the president whose brutal and self-serving policies in Nicaragua and Honduras made it clear the United States had learned nothing from its Iran debacle.

In 2002, George W. Bush followed in Reagan's footsteps. His "axis of evil" edict sabotaged Iran's slow evolution toward moderation. The country's leadership will always have to deal with a political right wing populated by religious hardliners who capitalize on the country's post-shah anti-Americanism. It does not take much for the United States to "recreate the revolutionary fervor in Iran," as one Islamic conservative put it after Bush's comment.[29]

The United States can perhaps find solace in the fact Iran, unlike North Korea, is not a communist regime on the Soviet model. But it must accept that the governments of both countries are American creations, inadvertent or otherwise. The two countries' circumstances and attitudes in 2002 were also U.S.-defined and U.S.-created. They were repressive regimes unfriendly to the United States, unlike the friendly repressive regimes of Saudi Arabia or Indonesia, for instance, and were thus singled out for harsh judgment on that score. And their peoples' mistrust of America was the direct result of U.S. interference in their lives, not a consequence of cultural, religious, or political differences. Perhaps the United States will one day elect a president wise enough to acknowledge and confront these truths while there is still hope of reconciliation – before Iran and North Korea become as irretrievably lost as the third member of the "axis of evil," Iraq.

NINE

THE CORNERED RAT: IRAQ

Air strikes against Iraqi troops retreating from Kuwait were being launched so feverishly from this carrier today that pilots said they took whatever bombs happened to be closest to the flight deck.

– FROM A NEWS REPORT DESCRIBING THE AMERICAN BOMBING OF DEFEATED IRAQI TROOPS AT THE END OF THE PERSIAN GULF WAR

Is there a more evil country in the world than Iraq? Certainly not in the eyes of the United States. Iraq is the axis in the axis of evil; the centre of gravity for America's endless game of spin-the-bottle with its allies and enemies, where it is in love with a country one week and won't be seen by decent company with it the next.

From 1975 to August 2, 1990, the day it invaded Kuwait, Iraq was a right-wing dictatorship like any other, at times courted by the United States and at other moments reviled for the sins the Americans willingly overlooked during better times. From the Gulf War forward, it has been America's international post–Cold War public enemy number one, a country the United States nearly bombed out of existence and has since backed into a diplomatic and economic corner with relentless sanctions. It is also the country most likely, in its pursuit of revenge against a much larger nemesis, to have sponsored the 1993 bombing of the World Trade Center's north tower and the attacks of September 11. There is no love lost between Iraq and the United States, and that will not change until either Saddam Hussein, Iraq's president for life, or the U.S. is dead and buried.

In 2002, Iraq was the closest thing the Arab world had to a secular state. Saddam Hussein's Baath party, which took control of the country in 1968, inclines toward Arab nationalism rather than Muslim orthodoxy. The state's Muslim religious leaders are watched closely, and paid by, the government. The mustachioed Hussein is more often seen in Western military garb of the kind favoured by leftist revolutionaries, and in weirdly cut three-piece suits, than in traditional Arab dress.

As one of the most populous Arab nations in the region (Iran is three times the size but its people are Persian), Iraq has always had a dominant voice in the conversation in the Middle East. In 1988, it officially recognized the Palestinian claim to independent statehood, an act of Arabic solidarity and a blow to Israel and the United States. Iraq has long been a direct backer of Palestinian terrorism in Israel and of the leadership of the disputed territories Israel so unsuccessfully shares with Yasser Arafat.

The United States has had its eye on Saddam Hussein from the day he took control of the Baath party in 1980. A fascinating declassified State Department document called "Saddam Hussein: The Cult of Personality," dated August 1980, goes into detail about the man.[1] The report is essentially an opinion as to whether Hussein could be overthrown by a popular uprising; its conclusion, no doubt a disappointment to the CIA, was that he was too crafty and brutal to be removed that way (though the report did hold hope for "the assassin's bullet or palace coup. End summary").

Hussein, the report noted, held power thanks to a security service that rooted out all dissent in the most cold-blooded fashion. There was and remains no hope of a legitimate in-country opposition to the Baath party, there is no free press, and people whose family members disappear at the hands of the government often only find out what has become of their loved one when they receive a bill from the state for the disposal of his or her mutilated body. Things are even worse if you are a Kurd, a member of a non-Arabic (but nevertheless Muslim) race that makes up about 20 per cent of the Iraqi population and has been struggling for independence for two generations. State Department documents reveal the U.S. has long considered Kurdish independence a "delusion and unrealistic"; it is a struggle America does not support, mostly because there are millions of oppressed Kurds in Turkey, a critical U.S. ally in the region, who would also like to run their own lives. As it is, Hussein has undertaken the genocide of the Kurds in his country, including a gas attack in the northern part of the country in 1988 that may have killed as many as ten thousand people. The gas used was made from chemicals most likely provided by German arms manufacturers – a hideous collaboration, if true, given the fate of Jews in the Holocaust.

Hussein maintains popular support in his country, and has done so from the beginning, by playing up its independence from foreign influence, in particular that of the United States. His most loyal followers are from the lower classes, which he originally won over by improving the welfare system and other basic services when he came to power. He is known for making personal appearances in poorer neighbourhoods, for doling out clemency, and for siding with people accosted by

Baath party members who attempt to use their status to get around the law. He also appeals to their sense of national pride by promising to make Iraq a prominent player in the Mideast.

Had Hussein been at all pro-American, he would have been the perfect U.S. ally in the region. In many ways he is the very model of the brutal, efficient, pompous, self-aggrandizing psychopath the United States routinely puts to work in Latin America and, notably, in Iran right next door, prior to Hussein's arrival on the scene. There was little difference between the shah of Iran and Hussein in terms of their enthusiastic oppression of dissenters; American policy-makers in the 1970s and 1980s must have often stayed up at night imagining how sweet life would be if only Hussein, and the Baath party leadership before his arrival, were as compliant as the weak-kneed shah.

Imagining doesn't make it so. In 1980, the United States was faced with a new leader in Iraq, one who was strongly suspicious of American policies and practices in the Mideast, and not without reason. The U.S. was supporting the Kurds in their war with the Iraqi government, and America's close ties to Iran during the shah's reign were well-known.[2] But the U.S. had too many other worries in the region to bother itself with Hussein: the shah had been overthrown by Ayatollah Khomeini the year before, the hostage crisis was in its early days, and the Soviet Union, entering its final decade of superpowerdom, was at war in nearby Afghanistan while its agents sniffed out possible allies in the Mideast. It was a situation that called for a delicate hand. As early as 1974, the United States had ruled out toppling the Iraqi government, and even talked the shah of Iran out of trying it himself. A change of regime in Iraq "may suit [the] shah, but it is difficult to see how it would serve U.S. or western interest in regional stability," an officer in the United States Interests Section wrote to his Washington bosses in December 1974.[3] The fear was that a successor regime "would be more radical and disruptive, and probably be forced to rely heavily on [the] U.S.S.R."[4] As always, the United States was willing to live with a murderous dictatorship for the sake of convenience. As the officer wrote in his report:

> [The] Ba'ath regime, for all its abhorrent traits, has given Iraq over six years of stability. In addition, it is now concentrating on economic development and energetically attempting to bring about full rapprochement with western Europe and conservative Arab states. Whatever motives lay behind this twin policy of development and rapprochement and whatever [the] radical rhetoric used to conceal it, characteristics of Ba'ath regime if policies successful likely to be quite different [from] current characteristics, which admittedly often resemble those of a cornered rat.[5]

This cornered rat remained a useful American interest through the Iran-Iraq war, which lasted from 1980 to 1988 and killed 1.5 million people. The war began in an atmosphere in which both regimes were actively trying to disrupt the internal politics of the other, usually through the support of dissident terrorists, minor border incursions, and the odd assassination. Both regimes spent much of their energies on staying in power, making these distractions a real nuisance. By September 1980, Iraq had had enough; it carried out lightning strikes against Iranian military training targets, and the war was on. The United States government, by then almost a year into the hostage crisis, saw the outbreak as having certain advantages for it. A State Department memo written in Baghdad in September 1980 came to the erroneous conclusion the war might lead to the end of the Ayatollah.

> A persistent theme shared by both western and East Bloc diplomats here is that the U.S. and the West might somehow benefit from the Iraq-Iran confrontation, which could force the Iranian people to rally around . . . the army as a counterweight to the ineffective religious leaders. It would also force Iran to turn to the U.S. and the West for arms supplies. We have made a point of not agreeing with this assessment, though it has some merit.[6]

The United States adopted a neutral stance on the war; it refused to pick sides and hoped for an outcome "without victor or vanquished."[7] It is now well-known that the U.S. was negotiating with Iran at the time for the release of the embassy hostages and may have provided weapons in exchange for their freedom. The hostages were let go the day Ronald Reagan was inaugurated in January 1981. By then, Iraq was already suspicious that the U.S. government had chosen a side in the war; Hussein kept America on its toes by making the claim in the press as often as possible. The fact of the matter is, throughout the eight-year war, the U.S. maintained ties with both regimes, supplying them with arms, both legal and illegal, while also trying to monitor the flow of unconventional weapons into the region, most of which seemed to be coming from U.S. allies such as West Germany.

This tone of neutrality continued until 1988, when Iran started disrupting commerce in the Persian Gulf and the war ended in a series of civilian tragedies. The Iraqis gassed the Kurds in the north, a massacre that took years to come to light in a concrete way. And, on July 3, 1988, an American warship in the Persian Gulf brought down a commercial Iranian jet-liner, Flight 655, killing all the passengers. The Americans have always maintained that the jet flew directly toward the U.S.S. *Vincennes*, whose captain at the time was engaged in a battle with Iranian gunboats, and refused to identify itself. George Bush Sr., then the vice president to Ronald Reagan and campaigning for the election of November 1988, placed the blame for the incident squarely on the shoulders of Iran. His argument was that if Iran had only abided by a U.N. Security Council resolution to end its war with Iraq, the tragedy would have been avoided. In a speech to the U.N. Security Council in the days after the downing of Flight 655, and against the back-drop of the American media's criticism of the attack, Bush Sr. also defended the presence of American warships in the Persian Gulf, ships dispatched there after Iran began mining the waters of the Gulf to disrupt commercial shipping. "If [Iran attacks] innocent shipping and place[s] mines in international waters, that's the business of all who value freedom,"[8] he said – a bloodcurdling example of American government hypocrisy, given that the CIA had mined Nicaraguan ports only a few years earlier, damaging as many as nine innocent ships travel-ling in international waters.

Iran and Iraq eventually agreed to a ceasefire in 1988. By then, Iraq had the largest army in the Middle East, surpassing even Israel's. It was a military built partly with the help of the United States, in spite of strict regulations during the war about the nature of equipment and munitions that could be shipped to Iran and Iraq. Sperry Corporation, a U.S. com-puter manufacturer, wrote directly to George Shultz, then Secretary of State, in April 1985, asking that he allow Sperry to complete the sale of $9 million worth of computers used in aviation. The sale was being held up by the Department of

Defense, which feared the technology could be used by the Iraqi military for its missile technology. Shultz immediately wrote the Secretary of Defense on Sperry's behalf urging him to allow the sale. There is no record of that sale going through, but there is a 1991 report by the Wisconsin Project on Nuclear Arms Control called "U.S. Exports to Iraq: 1985-1990" that outlines other sales of American products that were clearly used by Iraq to develop its nuclear missile technology.

The U.S. also maintained an open business relationship with Iraq throughout the war and after. In 1986, twenty-eight American corporations exhibited at a U.S.-government-organized pavilion at the Baghdad International Trade Fair.[9] The Americans continued to give Iraq credits to buy U.S. agricultural products right up to the outbreak of the Persian Gulf War in 1991. And in 1989, Saddam Hussein met a delegation of American executives from such giant U.S. corporations as Westinghouse and Bell Helicopter. By then, American exports to Iraq were valued at $1.5 billion, an impressive increase from $600 million in 1986. The 1989 meeting was cordial. Concerns about human rights and the gassing of Kurdish civilians were not raised, and Saddam Hussein made it clear he was willing to forgive the Americans for selling arms to Iran during the war. At the time, Hussein was faced with pending U.S. legislation that would have imposed sanctions on his country relating to weapons inspections, so it was in his interests to make nice with the American businessmen. But on one point he would not bend – a request from the travelling executives to restructure his country's short-term debt so that Iraq would be eligible for more credit and, presumably, be able to purchase more American products. The U.S. businessmen were quite persistent on this point but went home disappointed. A group of American bankers made the same pitch to Hussein and were also rebuffed; the Iraqi leader's position was that he could solve his country's debt problems through increased oil sales.[10]

That same year, a group of U.S. congressmen wrote Lawrence Eagleburger, the deputy secretary of state, urging him to work with Volvo GM and the Iraqi government to secure financing for a truck assembly plant in Iraq. The parts would be made in the U.S. and shipped to Iraq for completion, before being sold in the Middle East. As the letter noted, "For trucks and many other industrial products, the Middle East and Africa offer the only major opportunities for U.S. exports."[11]

Within a year, the United States was preparing to go to war with Iraq because it had invaded Kuwait. Hussein's justification for the invasion was that Kuwait, an American ally, had been overproducing oil, causing a drop in prices that cost Iraq $14 million – money it had been relying on to turn around its economy. President George Bush Sr. demonized Hussein as a modern-day Adolph Hitler, playing up the gassing of the Kurds and the country's complete lack of basic democratic freedoms as proof of the regime's illegitimacy and of the necessity for the Americans, backed by the United Nations, to counterattack. It was a complete turnaround of American policy of a decade earlier, when Iraq – no less an inhumane regime then than it was in 1990 – invaded Iran and the U.S. remained neutral. What had sparked America's reversal?

For one thing, the Soviet Union was not a threat any more. The regime there was tottering after the fall of the Berlin Wall in 1989 and was only months away from its final disintegration. Its leaders were seeking better relations with the U.S. This time, the U.S.S.R. would not be available to Iraq as an ally. It also seems Hussein was not as open to the financial advice of American business interests as those interests would have liked, thereby slowing their expansion into the lucrative

Middle Eastern market. There was also Iraq's support of the Palestinians and the aid it gave to terrorists working for Arab causes. There was the fact that Iraq now had the largest army in the region. And, finally, it was apparent that Saddam Hussein was not going anywhere; his grip on the country was as resistant to CIA interference as ever. Once again, America's moral flexibility on the sovereign rights of other nations came in handy; this time it would act in defence of another country's borders, a consideration it had not extended to Iran in 1980, or, for that matter, most of Europe at the beginning of the Second World War.

The Persian Gulf War was not so much a war as a turkey shoot between the world's only superpower and a country about the size of California. It lasted barely a month – forty-two days, to be exact. The U.S.-led coalition – basically the American armed forces with a few foreign militaries tagging along, all with the blessing of the United Nations Security Council – decided the quickest way to rout the Iraqi invading force from Kuwait was to target military and government installations back in Iraq, as well as civic infrastructures such as water-treatment plants and power-generation stations. Once the country lay in ruins, thirty-eight days into the war, the coalition forces put ground troops in Kuwait and ran the remaining Iraqi soldiers out of the country.

The amount of ordnance the Americans fired into Iraq from warships and missile batteries, and dropped on the country from aircraft, was alarming, to say the least. The total tonnage was 88,500, more than the U.S. had dropped on Japan in the Second World War, atomic bombs not included. Three thousand bombs were dropped on Baghdad alone, out of a total of 250,000.[12] The U.S. portrayed the missile attacks and bombings as precision military exploits that limited so-called collateral damage; the television news was filled with images of laser-guided missiles as they slammed into Iraqi Defence Ministry targets. But only a small fraction of the explosives dropped on Iraq were of the "smart" variety; 90 per cent were of the "stupid" type that destroy everything they come close to. These included cluster bombs, daisy cutters, and FAEs, a massive explosive that obliterates anything within a range of half a hectare (fifty thousand square feet) and is considered a weapon of mass destruction rather than a conventional bomb. The U.S. also used fire bombs and napalm in Iraq.[13] It carpet-bombed Basra, a city of eight hundred thousand that the U.S. rather ludicrously claimed was a military target and devoid of civilians by the time the bombs reached it. And, in what is probably the most offensive U.S. tactic of the war, American planes bombed and strafed Iraqi soldiers under the white flag of surrender as they retreated from Kuwait. The attacks massacred thousands on what became known as the "Highway of Death." A reporter on the American aircraft carrier the U.S.S. *Ranger* filed this description of the activity on the ship as planes took off for the site of the slaughter:

> Air strikes against Iraqi troops retreating from Kuwait were being launched so feverishly from this carrier today that pilots said they took whatever bombs happened to be closest to the flight deck. The crews, working to the strains of the *Lone Ranger* theme, often passed up the projectile of choice . . . because it took too long to load.[14]

Once Iraq had pulled out of Kuwait, the war was over. The United States did not have authority from the United Nations to continue on to Baghdad and oust Hussein. Nor did it really want to go through the work required to set up a temporary government or become involved in the rebuilding of a country it had destroyed. So it pulled out, abandoning a large number of dissidents who had risen up against Hussein at President Bush's urging, only to be rounded up and killed by the still well-ensconced Iraqi leader.

America also left behind a shattered country with a reduced capacity to care for its citizens and under the heel of sanctions that Hussein manipulated to further oppress his people. It was left to the United Nations to monitor and rebuild Iraq, a position it had put itself in by supporting and authorizing the United States' war in the first place.

And then in 2002, Iraq became a charter member of George W. Bush's "axis of evil." Of the three countries in the axis, Iraq was the only one that could fairly be considered a threat to the United States. Saddam Hussein has simply refused to bow to the U.S. He kicked out U.N. weapons inspectors in 1998, and in 2002 was America's most dangerous enemy. Laurie Mylroie, an American author and university professor, published a book in 2000 about the bombing of the World Trade Center that she revised after September 11, 2001.[15] She provided solid evidence that the Iraq government was the mastermind of the bombing and was almost certainly in cahoots with Osama bin Laden in the attack that finally brought down the twin towers. She pointed out that Saddam Hussein was the only foreign leader who praised the September 11 attacks and quoted this statement from him:

> Regardless of the conflicting human feelings about what happened in the United States yesterday, the United States reaps the thorns that its rulers have planted in the world . . . Those who consider the lives of their people as precious and dear must remember that the lives of people in the world are also precious and dear to their families.[16]

Mylroie's evidence of Iraqi involvement in the 1993 bombing is not conclusive – there is no smoking gun – but it is damning. As for whether Iraq was involved in the 2001 Al-Qaeda attack, "We already have the clues to show us that Iraq is probably involved. Bin Laden has known ties to Iraqi intelligence. Bin Laden's aims, moreover, coincide with Iraq's agenda: to overthrow the Saudi government, to end the U.S. presence in the Gulf, and to have the sanctions on Iraq lifted."[17] There is also Hussein's unquestionable desire for revenge against the United States for his defeat in Kuwait and the destruction of his country.

Like every other decent person, Mylroie does not seek to defend or justify the September 11 attacks; she merely makes the point that Saddam Hussein was not created in an America-free vacuum. In 1988, the United States was seeking rapprochement with the Iraqi leader, and in 1980 it had turned a blind eye to his invasion of Iran. In 1991, it bombed his people into near oblivion after he invaded a different neighbour. America isolated a regime it once tolerated, and in 2002, it was faced with the task of finishing what it started.

The "axis of evil," then, is not an axis at all, and not really "evil." In 2002, there were no alliances between the three countries, and only one of them could be considered a direct threat to the United States' homeland. North Korea's inclusion in America's unholy trinity most likely had to do with its location in the Pacific, where the U.S. always needs a reason to maintain its forces. Iran is an American-made Frankenstein the U.S. would rather chase down with an angry mob than understand. Iraq is an enemy the United States has been unable to bring to the negotiating table, and it is the only true military opponent to American hegemony in the Middle East, where 70 per cent of the world's oil is produced, the largest glob of which flows to the United States at cut-rate prices.

Hussein's desire to unite the Arab world is furthermore a direct threat to the United States' new mantra of never again letting another country get in the superpower game. There were fears in the spring of 2002 that Hussein had been armed by America and its allies with chemical weapons, and possibly biological ones, as well as the missile technology to deliver these weapons of mass destruction to countries as far away as Western Europe. As well, the Iraqi leader, faced with an economic crisis and a corresponding increase in dissent, was becoming more ruthless. Amnesty International reported that in the year 2000, Hussein's security forces resorted to beheadings of prisoners of conscience and the amputation of the tongues of people who allegedly slandered the government or its president. In one incident that needs no adjectival embellishment, a former general who had fled into exile received a videotape by mail from Iraq's intelligence service showing the rape of one of his female relatives. He later got a phone call from Iraqi intelligence asking whether he had enjoyed the "gift" and informing him the relative was still in their custody.

In the spring of 2002, it appeared that the United States and Iraq were headed for a showdown, one that would end badly. By the fall of the same year, it was an absolute certainty (see Epilogue).

TEN

FUNDAMERICA

We thank God [the bomb] has come to us instead of to our enemies; and we pray that He may guide us to use it in His way and for His purposes.
    – HARRY TRUMAN ON THE ATOMIC BOMB

Read a translated interview with Osama bin Laden and you are forced to wade through lines of invocation of, and praise to, the man's god. It is not unlike watching an evangelical preacher working his flock into a lathered stampede toward paradise on Sunday-morning television in the United States.

> ABC News: You have been charged with masterminding the bombings of the two U.S. embassies in Kenya and Tanzania. Are these charges true?

> OSAMA BIN LADEN: Praise be to God, the Cherisher and Sustainer of the Worlds. Peace and blessings be upon Prophet Muhammad, his companions and his kin. Let me begin by stating . . .[1]

And so it goes throughout the interview. Bin Laden's answers are regularly preceded by, or punctuated with, "By the Grace of God, praise and glory be to him . . ." The man is announcing himself as a pious Muslim to his followers. To his detractors, he comes across as a religious fundamentalist – someone who justifies his actions with the help of a simplistic interpretation of his god's scriptures; a man who clothes himself in a piety that he believes requires him to kill men, women, and children. When Americans hear bin Laden, alarm bells undoubtedly go off in their heads when he says things like, "We will continue this course because it is part of our religion, and because God, praise and glory be to him, ordered us to carry out jihad so that the word of God may remain exalted to the heights." At that point, they know what they are up against.

So how does the rest of the world feel when an American president, Harry Truman, thanks his god for giving the United States the atomic bomb?

> "We thank God [the bomb] has come to us instead of to our enemies; and we pray that He may guide us to use it in His way and for His purposes."[2]

Under the same circumstances, bin Laden would not have put it any differently. Nor would a suicide bomber in his final moments before sending himself to paradise and a dozen Israelis to Islamic hell. Nor George W. Bush when he demonizes America's enemies, invokes God in the name of retribution, and begins preaching about "evil versus good." It is troubling talk that mimics what many so fear from the reactionary Islamic world. Andrew Reding, a senior fellow of the World Policy Institute, thinks it has a troubling effect on the United States' allies:

When President Bush uses words like "war" or "crusade" to describe the U.S. response to terrorist attacks, alarms ring all over Europe. The words may play well in Peoria, but in Paris, Madrid and Berlin, they have an unpleasant undertone of national and religious fanaticism. . . . When Jerry Falwell and Pat Robertson suggest that the terrorist attacks may have been God's punishment for America's departure from Christian morals, Europeans flinch even more. In fact, by those standards, Europe would have been a much more logical target. Prostitution is legal in Amsterdam and Copenhagen. Gay and lesbian marriage is a reality in the Netherlands. Belgium has just decriminalized possession of marijuana. Beer is sold in Coke dispensers in Brussels. Nakedness is permitted on public beaches throughout Europe.

From the European point of view, the United States, though in many ways a great nation, has all too many points in common with the forces with which it is in conflict. Its government is unduly responsive to the interests of religious fundamentalists. To conform to religious notions of morality, it denies its citizens all sorts of personal freedoms. And its gut response to violence by Islamic extremists is to respond with calls for a "war" and "crusade" against "evil."

How, Europeans wonder, is that so different from calls for a "jihad" against the "Great Satan"?[3]

Reding's is the kind of thinking that causes conservative Americans to sputter with indignation. How dare he compare the American way of life, with its individual freedoms, democratic traditions, and secular centre, with the reactionary theocracies, dictatorships, and terror camps of the Arab world? The two are night and day, black and white, them and us. Average Americans, too, are affronted by suggestions that they are not much different from the average Arab, that they are not intrinsically better people by virtue of living in the freedom-loving United States of America. Isn't the United States the country to which everyone wants to emigrate? The beacon of freedom whose light shone so bright that an Islamic terrorist attempted to snuff it out?

True in parts, but Reding is on to something important. As this and the next chapter will attempt to demonstrate, the United States has long been – like Iran, for instance – in the sway of its religious fundamentalists, and never more so than in the twenty years leading up to September 11, 2001. Like Iran, it pins a forked tail on its enemies and over-worships its heroes and idols to the point of deification; meanwhile, its leaders regularly invoke their lord's name to guide them down a path of politically convenient righteousness.

When it comes to morality, American citizens can be killed for walking into an abortion clinic and arrested for being too kinky in bed. The country's non-violent criminals are sentenced to inhumane sentences of hundreds of years, and are subjected to torture in the form of institutionalized rape at the hands of fellow prisoners. Drug dealers do not get their hands chopped off or suffer a caning in a public square; instead they are squeezed into cages in maximum-security prisons where they are deprived of all human contact. Like Iran and Iraq, and unlike Canada and all the members of the European Union, the United States executes prisoners, even the mentally retarded[4] and those who commit capital crimes as children. It is the democratic world's leading killer of the incarcerated.

And when it comes to democracy, the sacred foundation of the American identity, the United States has let its most precious institution be so corrupted by partisanship and dishonesty that less than half the population bothers to vote any more. It has reached the point where there are many in the country who are not sure that George W. Bush didn't steal the election that made him president in 2000. Could there have been a palace coup in America?

FROM FUNDAMENTALISM TO THE MORAL MAJORITY

The United States, by most measures, is home to the world's largest churchgoing population. Estimates vary but the fact remains that, while church attendance has declined in almost all other Christian countries in the past twenty-five years,[5] it has stayed relatively steady in America and was higher in 2002 than it was ten years earlier.[6] This is not hard to understand. In its earliest days, America was a refuge for people whose religions got them thrown into jail or limited their chance of escaping poverty in European countries. It was and remains, as *Scientific American* points out, "a free market in religion, and a free market promotes competition among denominations for new members."[7] While European churches have stagnated or declined by adhering to traditions and values that no longer appeal to a modern constituency, American churches, including the Protestant and Catholic ones, have successfully adopted populist tones that attract every conceivable variety of devotion. This populism dates back to the 1800s, when branches of the Protestant church became the country's leading religions:

> Soon the old-line denominations were eclipsed by the Methodists and the Baptists, who, with their revival meetings and circuit riders, promised life everlasting for the saved and hellfire for sinners. Moreover, their relatively uneducated ministers had a natural rapport

with the people, coming as they did mostly from the same class. Methodists were the leading group in the mid-1800s, but as they became more affluent and as their ministers became seminary-trained, their fervor declined, and members who yearned for a more evangelistic faith left to found new churches.[8]

The American Catholic church adopted the evangelism of the Methodists and Baptists, and by the 1990s it was the single largest denomination in the land (although there are still twice as many Americans who are members of the various Protestant denominations). The 1996 edition of the *Encyclopedia of American Religion* listed more than 2,150 organized religions in the U.S., from the traditional churches to the slightly wacky designer versions with names like New Enlightened Inspired Living, Nudist Christian Church of the Blessed Virgin Jesus, and Original Hebrew Israelite Nation.[9]

This dilution of religion has long been a sore spot for traditionalists, at various times throughout U.S. history prompting calls for a return to basic tenets. One of the most important such movements occurred in the Protestant church in the early part of the twentieth century. This was the movement that gave birth to the idea of religious fundamentalism. More to the point, that is what the movement was called – fundamentalism. The term is said to have come into existence at a bible conference in 1910 in Niagara Falls as a reaction to what was perceived as a weakening of Protestant morals and values. Two brothers, Milton and Lyman Steward, published *The Fundamentals*, a twelve-volume tirade calling on Protestants to return to a literal interpretation of the Bible, one so strict that it required adherents to believe that Adam and Eve had to fence off their home to keep out the dinosaurs.[10]

It was the fundamentalists who led the charge in the 1925 Scopes trial, in which a teacher was taken to court for teaching evolution in school after the state of Tennessee had outlawed the practice. The teacher lost and was fined $100, but the highly publicized trial was an embarrassment for fundamentalists, who came to be seen as ill-informed and intolerant backwater folk, unable to live by the (largely ignored) First Amendment requirement to separate church and state. The fundamentalist movement subsequently moved out of the mainstream, but did not disappear. As historian William Vance Trollinger noted, "Instead, fundamentalists created a rapidly expanding network of nondenominational organizations, including publishing houses, mission boards, and radio stations. At the center of this fundamentalist network were approximately seventy Bible institutes across the country."[11]

The Bible institutes produced a renaissance in the fundamentalist movement after the Second World War, making stars of evangelical preachers like Billy Graham. The movement was split at this point between the hard-core old-timers and a younger generation willing to at least tolerate the theory of evolution, if not espouse it. But the most dramatic comeback the movement was to enjoy came in the 1970s, when, according to Trollinger, the American psyche was somewhat adrift and searching for renewal.

> Fundamentalism had always been associated with patriotism, militarism, and free-market economics; in post-Vietnam, post-Watergate America, when such sentiments came back into vogue, politically energized fundamentalists, who had long yearned to recreate a "Christian America," played an important and visible role in the resurgence of the Right.[12]

Enter Jerry Falwell, the founder and leader of the Moral Majority, a neo-fundamentalist organization that came into being in 1979, the year before the election of Ronald Reagan. Falwell, an old-time television evangelist, tapped into the dormant fundamentalist sentiment in the United States and turned it into a powerful political lobby.

A "pro-life, pro-family, pro-moral, and pro-America" political organization, the Moral Majority mobilized grassroots Americans to oppose pornography, abortion, the gay and lesbian rights movement, and the welfare state; to support increased defense spending, the death penalty, and the free-enterprise system; and to elect candidates who shared these goals.[13]

The Moral Majority became a key player in the 1980 election and one of the most vociferous supporters of Reagan's candidacy. When Reagan was elected, Falwell's organization earned a new prestige and a high profile. The Moral Majority folded in 1989, however, because of internal disorganization and the fall from grace of other televangelists, such as Jim Bakker, who was caught cheating on his wife, Tammy Faye, in 1987 and then convicted in 1989 of wire and mail fraud related to the fundraising activities of his religious empire. The Moral Majority morphed into the Christian Coalition, another – and much more successful – neo-fundamentalist group whose founder, Pat Robertson, failed in a bid for the Republican Party presidential nomination in 1988.

The Christian Coalition waged many campaigns at the local level, in school board, city council, and mayoral elections. But it also wielded substantial clout nationally by helping boost the arch-conservative victory in the North Carolina senatorial election in 1990 and mobilizing public support for the confirmation of Clarence Thomas to the Supreme Court in 1991. The Christian Coalition's most visible success came in 1994, when it contributed much to the Republican sweep of congressional elections.[14]

Robertson, who agreed with Falwell after September 11 that the attacks were God's punishment on America "for tolerating feminists, gays and lesbians, libertarians and certain federal judges,"[15] was never one to allow moderation and tolerance, let alone Christian forgiveness, into his fundamentalist discourse. He sounded, more often that not, like someone who would be better suited to a position of moral authority in the Iranian government of the Ayatollah Khomeini than to being a leading spokesman for "American values," as a sampling of his quotations demonstrates:

- How can there be peace when drunkards, drug dealers, communists, atheists, New Age, worshippers of Satan, secular humanists, oppressive dictators, greedy moneychangers, revolutionary assassins, adulterers, and homosexuals are on top?[16]
- When lawlessness is abroad in the land, the same thing will happen here that happened in Nazi Germany. Many of those people involved in Adolph Hitler were Satanists, many of them were homosexuals – the two things seem to go together.[17]
- The feminist agenda is not about equal rights for women. It is about a socialist, antifamily political movement that encourages women to leave their husbands, kill their children, practice witchcraft, destroy capitalism and become lesbians.[18]

Robertson and Falwell lost credibility after they blamed September 11 on godless homosexuals, etc., though they are no less well-off for it. The Jerry Falwell Ministries is an evangelistic powerhouse, as is Pat Robertson's Christian Broadcasting Network. Robertson resigned as president of the Christian Coalition in December 2001, but the legacy and influence of American religious fundamentalism was undiminished in the administration of George W. Bush, in spite of the Coalition's Taliban-eqsue preachings about women, homosexuals, and Jews. Its control over the Republican Party and its purges of unacceptable voices, according to one observer, "killed the conservative intellectual movement,"[19] thereby eliminating moderate and nuanced thought from the right wing of American politics. Its influence is still felt today, as pornography, abortion, homosexuality, and evolution remain key rallying points for the right. In Alabama, where the state's 1901 constitution still contains a provision (since overruled by the Supreme Court) outlawing interracial marriage, biology text books must bear a disclaimer stating that evolution is a "controversial theory" in order to appease the Christian Coalition. John Ashcroft, Bush's hawkish, anti-abortion, anti-birth-control, gun-friendly attorney general, was appointed to the position "to reward [the president's] supporters on the religious right."[20]

Bush himself, a southern Methodist who decided to "recommit" his heart to Jesus Christ in the 1980s when he had a problem with alcohol, brought an evangelical tone to the White House before and after his election. During his campaign he said Christ was his favourite political philosopher,[21] and after coming to power he constantly referred to the importance of "faith in God" as a healing power in America, although he remained carefully ecumenical in his references to

"Almighty God."[22] Among his first acts as president was to cut federal funding to international aid groups that support abortion and birth control. His pious tone won him admiration in some circles and caused worry in others, especially believers in the separation of church and state. "He went from a kind of post–September 11 pluralism to presidential evangelism today," Rev. Barry Lynn, the executive director of Americans United for Separation of Church and State, was quoted as saying in the *New York Times* in April 2002.[23] "This man now seems to have an enormous difficulty separating his personal religious commitments from his public policy positions."

The Bush administration's evangelism served it well in its effort to demonize its new enemies after September 11. Some writers noticed that the White House's relentless characterization of bin Laden and his followers as evil was similar to America's campaigns of dehumanization against the communists in the Cold War and the Japanese in the Second World War – when, remember, 13 per cent of Americans favoured the elimination, by genocide, of the Japanese race.[24]

America's discovery of an enemy who is not merely an enemy, but "evil", has impeccable historical credentials. In a long history of responding to real and perceived threats, it seems clear that this large, heterogeneous country defines itself in part through its nemeses. The language Mr. Bush and others have used to describe Al Qaeda terrorists sometimes sounds as though it could have been written by Cotton Mather. Ever since the Puritans arrived in New England, civic and political leaders have often issued the same warning: sinister conspirators are spreading invisibly through the land, a cabal of evil and dangerous men who are bent on subverting this shining city on a hill. As Attorney General John Ashcroft put it recently: "A calculated, malignant, devastating evil has arisen in our world."[25]

By calling its enemies an "evil" of biblical proportions, America stakes its claim to biblical righteousness, a high-handed stance that is galling to the rest of the world and to a minority in America, but which gives the government more room to manoeuvre among its like-minded majority. Americans are less likely to oppose the wishes of a president devoted to defeating something or someone as frightening as the Devil himself. The president's demands for moral clarity in the wake of September 11 were no different than those of the Baptist brothers who wrote *The Fundamentals* at the beginning of the twentieth century. Fundamentalism is alive and well in the world today – in Iran, in the cells of bin Laden's terrorist network, and in the United States of America. Some writers suggest it might serve America's interests to lighten up a little.

Ultimately, of course, terrorism does present a real threat, just as cold-blooded killing presents a moral outrage. But the history of American crusading, even against unmistakable evil, suggests that it can be more effective to start from a position of humility. Righteousness easily becomes self-righteousness, and it can be hard for crusaders to distinguish between the two.[26]

HELL ON EARTH:
THE AMERICAN PRISON AND JUSTICE SYSTEMS

Americans love to tell tales of the medieval justice meted out in fundamentalist Muslim countries: lurid stories of people being stoned to death for being homosexual, women being whipped for alleged adultery, dissidents' tongues amputated for slandering government leaders, vandals caned in public squares, as happened to an American teenager in Singapore in 1994 (and which many in America supported as fitting punishment). Americans, however, are less apt to concern themselves with the brutality and unfairness of their own justice system, even though, year after year, human-rights groups rank the United States as one of the world's worst regimes. The U.S. no longer imprisons people for being gay (although, unlike some European countries, it still discriminates against them when it comes to the right to adopt children or get married) or for having sex out of marriage (although sodomy practised between consenting adults can land a person in jail in some states), but it still imposes ludicrously long sentences on non-violent offenders, most often drug dealers and users, and then warehouses them in prisons that Charles Dickens would have had a hard time imagining. One of the most populated states, California, has a "three strikes" rule, under which a repeat offender whose first two offences are serious felonies can be sentenced to life in prison for committing a third offence as minor as stealing a slice of pizza. America also remains one of the few democracies that still executes criminals, in spite of evidence that far too many people are wrongly convicted and sent to their deaths unfairly, and that capital punishment does not reduce crime. In fundamentalist, evil-hating America, crime and punishment have barely evolved in two hundred years.

The most hideous aspect of the United States prison system is the institutionalized rape and torture of inmates that occurs across the country. Human Rights Watch published an exhaustive report in April 2001 outlining the extent of the debauchery. As many as one in five inmates in municipal, state, and federal prisons is raped and assaulted by other inmates, out of a total prison population of about two million.

Many of the victims are men sentenced for relatively minor offences, such as drunk driving, drug abuse, and, in one notorious case, unpaid library fines. Often they are teenaged boys, some under the age of eighteen, who are required to do their time in adult prisons. Anyone, regardless of his age, who is small, weak, intellectual, or has feminine features is immediately preyed upon in American prisons and suffers the most outrageous horrors, such as repeated anal rape, gang beatings, and treatment as slaves to their tormentors.

In the most extreme cases, Human Rights Watch found that prisoners unable to escape a situation of sexual abuse may find themselves the "slaves" of their rapists. Forced to satisfy another man's sexual appetites whenever he demands, they may also be responsible for washing his clothes, massaging his back, cooking his food, cleaning his cell, and a range of other chores. They are frequently "rented out" for sex, sold, or even auctioned off to other inmates.[27]

Human Rights Watch also found that prison staff and managers were unconcerned with the inhumane activities going on under their watch. Prisoner after prisoner reported being disciplined by wardens and guards for complaining about the rape they had endured, or being advised to find a man who would protect them in exchange for gentler sexual favours.

A central problem is the deficient – and, in many instances, callous and irresponsible – response of correctional staff to complaints of rape. When an inmate informs an officer he has been threatened with rape or, worse, actually assaulted, it is crucial that his complaint be investigated and that he be protected from further abuse. Yet Human Rights Watch found that correctional staff frequently ignore or even react hostilely to inmates' complaints of rape.[28]

In one case documented by Human Rights Watch, a sixteen-year-old boy named Rodney Hulin was convicted of arson in Texas and sentenced to eight years in an adult prison. Once incarcerated, the five-foot-two, 125-pound boy was immediately subjected to beatings and, within a week, had been anally raped. When he reported his abuse to prison authorities, he was ignored. For protection, he broke prison rules and got himself placed in solitary confinement, which is where he hanged himself two months after his arrival in prison. He fell into a coma and died four months later. His parents sued the state of Texas and obtained a substantial award in an out-of-court settlement.

Even when prisoners are not raped, they are still subjected to appalling, dehumanizing conditions, especially in the United States' new breed of "supermaximum" prisons. Children under the age of eighteen are often housed in these new horrors, according to the human rights organization Amnesty International:

> Isolation conditions in Wisconsin's supermaximum security Boscobel prison are harsh and in breach of international standards, Amnesty International said today, asking for under-18 inmates to be urgently removed from it. Prisoners at Boscobel prison are allowed no outdoor exercise and can see their relatives only through a video screen. In the most restrictive custody levels, inmates are confined alone for 24 hours a day in sealed, sparsely equipped, concrete cells with no view of the outside, and are deprived of reading

and occupational materials, educational and other programs, and even watches or clocks to enable them to tell the time.

"These conditions would constitute 'cruel, inhuman or degrading treatment' when imposed in any case for a protracted period, and they should never be inflicted on vulnerable young inmates," Amnesty International said. The organization noted that international standards contained an outright ban on the use of punitive solitary confinement in the case of incarcerated juveniles.[29]

How such grim horrors can be compatible with the values of a civilized country must seem a mystery to non-Americans, but they become less incomprehensible when seen in the light of the United States' fundamentalist approach to good and evil. American voters, urged by groups such as the Christian Coalition to oppose the "coddling" of criminals, constantly demand that their elected judges and prosecutors impose harsher sentences and invent more brutal, supposedly more deterring, conditions for convicted criminals. Prisoners who complain about their treatment behind bars are generally considered either unreliable, and thus not to be believed, or deserving of whatever fate they suffer. In a very real way, American criminals are victims of the same dehumanizing that the U.S. doles out to all enemies of its crusades. Ronald Reagan's "War on Drugs" in the 1980s produced similarly stark results, with tens of thousands of Americans – usually poor, black ones – incarcerated for sentences often exceeding the human lifespan. In New York state, "A person convicted of a single sale of two ounces of cocaine faces the same mandatory prison term as a murderer – fifteen years to life."[30]

Long prison sentences may be proportionate for traffickers who run large and violent drug distribution enterprises. But in New York, the vast majority of drug offenders sentenced to prison are nonviolent minor drug dealers or persons only marginally involved in drug transactions – people who make $20 sales on the streets, one-time couriers carrying drugs for a small fee, addicts who sell to finance their own habits. For these people, even a few years of imprisonment can be disproportionately severe punishment that violates the inherent dignity of persons, the right to be free of cruel and degrading punishment, and the right to liberty. Such sentences contravene the Universal Declaration of Human Rights, the International Covenant on Civil and Political Rights, and the Convention Against Torture and Other Cruel, Inhuman, or Degrading Treatment or Punishment.[31]

As for the death penalty, the United States[32] is in the tiny but elite class of killer nations whose only other members are China, Iran, and Saudi Arabia. Together, these four countries combined to produce 90 per cent of the world's known state executions in 2001. China leads the way with thousands of executions annually; it is by far the most brutal country when it comes to capital punishment. After a crackdown on crime in 2001, China executed 1,781 people between April and July of that year – "more than the total number of people executed in the rest of the world in the previous three years."[33]

Iran finished second in the death-sentence sweepstakes in 2001, with 139 reported executions. Saudi Arabia was third with 79, and the U.S. was fourth with 66.[34] The only other democracies that put their citizens to death for common crimes, as opposed to high crimes like treason, are the English-speaking island nations of the Caribbean, and Japan. As a sentencer-to-death of criminals, America keeps company with such swell places, along with the three mentioned above, as Iraq, Libya, the Palestinian Authority, Syria, and Malaysia. The United States reached a peculiar milestone in the spring of 2002 when Ray Krone became the one-hundredth person sitting on death row in an American prison to be exonerated since 1972, the year the Supreme Court ruled that capital punishment was unconstitutional.[35] Krone was convicted of murdering a cocktail waitress in 1991, a conviction that was based on poor detective work and unreliable forensic evidence.[36] He was cleared by DNA evidence that implicated a man who was serving a sentence for child molestation. In roughly the same period that 100 people were exonerated, 767 were put to death, leading many to conclude that there were some who died innocently. The Supreme Court had abolished the death penalty in 1972 precisely because it was being applied in an arbitrary and capricious manner. One study found that as many as 350 innocent people were wrongly convicted of capital offences in the United States in the twentieth century, and 25 executed, and not always because of error but also because of "conspiracies by the police, prosecutors, defense attorneys, judges, witnesses, and even jurors."[37] Still, individual states have pressed on, electrocuting, hanging, shooting, gassing, and lethally injecting criminals by the dozen. Christopher Simmons, who was convicted of a murder committed in 1993, when he was seventeen, was scheduled to be executed by the state of Missouri on June 5, 2002 (the Missouri Supreme Court stayed the execution at the last moment). The death penalty is a fate he should be spared under UNICEF's Convention on the Rights of the Child,[38] as well as article 6(5) of the U.N. High

Commissioner on Human Rights International Covenant on Civil and Political Rights.[39]

> Both prohibit the imposition of the death penalty against child offenders, defendants who were under 18 at the time of the crime. It is a ban now so widely respected that it has become a principle of customary international law, binding on all countries no matter which treaties they have or have not ratified.[40]

But not the United States, the country whose president, as Amnesty International pointed out, vowed in his State of the Union speech in January 2002 to "always stand firm for the non-negotiable demands of human dignity." In the land of good and evil, there is a heavy fog obscuring the treatment of criminals, convicted or otherwise. This was never more apparent in the days after September 11.

President Bush declared a national emergency on September 14, and the country immediately began rounding up anyone who looked like a terrorist. Within a matter of weeks, the United States had arrested 1,200 people, all foreign nationals and mostly Arab or Middle Eastern in origin, on minor criminal charges and immigration violations. On October 23, 2001, Amnesty International reported some were being held not as suspects but as material witnesses, and many were being held in locations unknown even to their families and lawyers. As well, the conditions they were held under were less than humane.

> Two men held in solitary confinement in the Metropolitan Correctional Center in New York . . . are reportedly denied exercise; given certain foods which

they cannot eat on religious grounds; kept in cold cells, with only one blanket; subjected to full strip searches twice a day despite having non-contact visits; and are shackled hand and foot whenever they are taken from their cells.[41]

The suspects' lawyers complained they could not get even minimal information about their clients, and fears arose that it would become more difficult, not more easy, to provide suspects with basic American justice. That is just what happened when, two months after September 11, Bush issued an order under which detainees would be tried by a semi-mysterious body called a military commission. There were some who confused "military commissions" with courts martial, but they were nothing like the military's long-standing and open process of meting out justice to members of the armed forces. Courts martial featured, among other standard legal niceties, due process, openness, and the right to an appeal. Bush's military commissions so coldly eliminated all these protections against abuse that they were immediately characterized even by conservative critics as being nothing more than a "foolproof shortcut to a guilty verdict."[42]

Bush's November 13, 2001, order creating the military commissions took pains to remind Americans of their new world order. He included language in the order's preamble that made it sound as though the country was an inch from Armageddon, and, to be fair, that is how things felt to Americans at that moment. Envelopes containing anthrax spores had been delivered to government and media offices, killing at least two people and sending the country even deeper into crisis. Americans felt vulnerable, something to which they were utterly unaccustomed. The country needed reassuring, and not even its precious democratic principles were beyond adjustment. Bush had a receptive audience when he said:

> Individuals acting alone and in concert involved in international terrorism possess both the capability and the intention to undertake further terrorist attacks against the United States that, if not detected and prevented, will cause mass deaths, mass injuries, and massive destruction of property, and may place at risk the continuity of the operations of the United States government.[43]

In Bush's November 13 order, non-American citizens in the United States or in other countries who were suspected of being terrorists could be arrested, detained, and tried in secret hearings that denied the suspects access to the evidence against them and took away their right to appeal, even in cases involving a death sentence. The military commissions were based on a formula used in the Second World War to try eight German saboteurs, a formula that was not popular even then,[44] during a period of declared war on an identifiable enemy.

The Bush administration further empowered itself with a series of decrees, such as one allowing it to wiretap conversations between suspects and their lawyers, and it relaxed rules that prevented it from spying on religious groups. The combined effect was to create a parallel system of justice under which suspects could be held indefinitely in unknown locations under uncertain conditions, and be sentenced to death away from the public eye. As had become the practice in the United States at the time, those who questioned these developments were accused of working for the terrorists – of giving "ammunition to America's enemies and pause to America's friends."[45] Those who defended the use of military commissions did so on the grounds that their judicious use would protect both the country and the rights of suspects, and that there was no requirement for them to be held in secret, only the possibility to protect vital information, if deemed necessary. The only problem was that there was no way for the public to judge whether this was the case. Even after John Ashcroft, the attorney general, released the names of 93 people who had been charged in early December 2001, there were still 548 unidentified people being held by the U.S. and another 400 who were missing and presumed held but who could not be accounted for.

Six months later, after the Bush administration made minor adjustments to the original order creating the military commissions (suspects were given the right to appeal, but only to a military panel, not a civilian one), there were still 300 people in custody, according to Amnesty International. Some were being held at the federally run Metropolitan Detention Center in New York City in unknown conditions. And there were reports of suspects being held for months without facing charges.

Criticism of the United States' treatment of terrorism suspects went international in the early days of 2002, after the Pentagon began shipping Taliban fighters captured in Afghanistan to a prison compound at Guantánamo Bay, a U.S. military base in, of all places, Cuba. It quickly became apparent that America's prisoners were being afforded little more in the way of rights than Fidel Castro's political prisoners on the same island. The Pentagon refused to grant the Taliban fighters prisoner-of-war status, which would have given them protections under international law – including the right to trial by court martial. Instead, hundreds of captives became "illegal combatants," a label that meant they would be tried, if at all, by Bush's secretive military commissions. It also made it next to impossible for the prisoners to challenge the rightfulness of their detention. Once again, justice in the United States was at odds with that of its allies, who thought America should, at the very least, respect the Geneva Conventions governing prisoners of war. It was the U.S., after all, that wanted the war on terrorism to be an international responsibility, which would imply that it would be waged under international rules; in rather typical fashion, the war on terrorism quickly became a game played under American rules only.

The American fundamentalism that incarcerates devilish enemies and dehumanizes criminals in medieval fashion glorifies, in equally extreme measures, those the country deems to be heroic and famous. Bush's black-and-white, absolutist reaction to the September 11 attacks vaulted him into the ranks of heroic American presidents, along with George Washington and Abraham Lincoln – for the first few months, anyway. A tentative, "robotic,"[46] isolationist president with a singular ability to mangle the English language before the attacks, immediately afterward Bush was transformed in the media and by the White House public-relations experts into a smooth, experienced internationalist president steeped in what many pundits referred to as a new "*gravitas.*" He came across as the kind of man Roosevelt and Truman would have turned to for advice on everything from foreign policy to dealing with difficult teenage children. *Vanity Fair*, a magazine that specializes in the deification of movie stars, rock and roll musicians, and wealthy eccentrics, was given exclusive access to the White House to photograph and lionize Bush and his cabinet in Churchillian tones in its February 2002 issue. The perfectly posed and stately pictures were taken by Annie Liebovitz, the famous photographer of celebrities. Bush's approval ratings, a survey of Americans' satisfaction with their president, had by then climbed to their highest levels and even surpassed those achieved by Ronald Reagan. A heroic president was what America needed, and the country's fundamentalist reflex was there to provide it. The public did not come to see him as having a direct line to God, in the manner of the Ayatollah Khomeini, but he did become an oracle for the American gods of Enduring Freedom and Courage.

From the White House to Las Vegas to Hollywood to the sports arenas of Chicago and New York City, American hero over-worship is a national habit, and a conflicting psychosis, too. The country both kneels before famed movie actors who make ridiculous sums ($20 million) for playing characters based on their most successful roles in previous films, and tears down the same "superstars" in lurid tabloid newspapers that invent, or at least grossly exaggerate, stories of the stars' unhappiness and weird personal lives. This American pastime has never been better satirized than in the book *A Massive Swelling: Celebrity Reexamined as a Grotesque Crippling Disease and Other Cultural Revelations*, by Cintra Wilson,[47] a book all North Americans should be encouraged, nay required, to read. Wilson writes:

> The slandering of iconage is a sport – not an act of aggression or bitterness, but an exercise. Why should these people *not* get taunted and roasted? We treat our celebrities, regardless of artistic merit, like an untouchable royal family, which causes most of us to act like dribbling serfs despite the value of our individual lives. We regard ourselves as slow-minded, vermin-infested bedwetters when presented with the gold-plated auras of media success in others. The implication of Fame, in this value-warped society, is: You've made it. You and your grand talents are so bright, you are somehow, both physically and spiritually, light-years beyond all us bone-sucking hacks.[48]

The American panorama of stars includes ridiculous hangers-on (Kato Kaelin, the idle tenant who became famous during the O. J. Simpson trial, and Chelsea Clinton, the toothsome daughter of Bill Clinton, suddenly declared to be a sex symbol by *Vanity Fair* in its June 2002 issue); the formerly talented (the pop singer Michael Jackson, whose bleached black skin is now whiter than that of Bill Clinton, who also fits in this category); the athletically gifted (Michael Jordan, the basketball player, made more money in product endorsements than the sport itself could ever throw at him; ditto for the golfer Tiger Woods); the sexually scandalous (Monica Lewinsky, Anna Nicole Smith); the criminally scandalous (O. J. Simpson, Tonya Harding); the weird crime victim (John Wayne Bobbit, whose penis was hacked off by his jealous wife and then reattached, and who now stars in pornographic films); the courageous (Neil Armstrong); the inexplicable (Gretchen Moll, Christina Aguilera); and the actually talented and hardworking, of whom there are a large number in film, music, and sports but who are suspect because they rely on their fame to enhance their value. Americans are prepared to believe the best of all these people, and the worst; one minute popular celebrities are courageously battling a minor disease or overcoming the pain of divorce, the next they are involved in sleazy love affairs or are caught being rude to their fans, an offence of heretical proportions. It is all rather unnerving when viewed from a distance, but it can be understood when put in the context of America's fundamentalist nature. Enemies are evil, American celebrities are heroic gods with all the fatal flaws inherent to such lofty status. Achilles had his vulnerable heel, Samson's godlike strength depended on the length of his hair, and Martha Stewart can be both a paragon of exemplary American womanhood and a vengeful, overweight stock manipulator, depending on the week.

Even more appalling is the fashion in which the famous develop the flighty, intemperate, and corrupt tastes of the gods. So many of them become extreme animal-rights supporters and vegan diet practitioners that it seems almost a prerequisite of their status. Hollywood is populated by herbivores who throw hissy fits when asked to sit on leather chairs. It is equally populated by substance-abusing bulimics who mimic the excesses of the final days of ancient Rome, eating then vomiting then taking drugs to forget how bad it feels to vomit, then eating again. They are gods, and so they act like gods; Americans, in turn, adopt the attitude of the pious and kneel before their idols. Cintra Wilson's wish is that, one day, Americans will renounce the fundamentalist religion that is celebrity worship:

> Celebrity is a virulent killer of fundamental human values, and unless Southern California goes up in a shiny mushroom cloud on Judgment Day, the only way to control it is to quit believing in it. Most sophisticated people don't think they do believe in Fame, but they do, in a deep, fearful, insidious way. When you *really stop* believing in the sexual comeliness of the ninety-eight-pound blonde with the saline D-cups, in the commercial earnestness of young athletes or the infantile cuteness of Goldie Hawn; when you rub the marabou from Madonna's bra out of your eyes and are no longer dazzled by Schwarzenegger's Hummer or Liberace's rhinestoned piano, the Emperor is a fat, naked freak and it all looks sick and ridiculous.[49]

The same, it should be noted at this point, applies to America's exalted devotion to democracy.

ELEVEN

DEMOCRACY'S PALACE COUP

It's not the people who vote that counts – it's the people who count the votes.

– JOSEPH STALIN

Americans worship Democracy in a rather unconvincing fashion. The voting booth is a church the people have stopped attending. By the end of the twentieth century, voter participation had fallen below 50 per cent for many elections, and even fell as low as 30 per cent in some cases. Americans seemed to feel they had little stake in the democratic process, in spite of the sycophantic bromides of their politicians about the primacy of the people and the importance of the act of voting.

The plain fact is that the very nation that demands of the rest of the world a high level of democratic activity, in exchange for entrance into the kingdom of everlasting financial aid, is one of the least healthy democracies on the planet. America has handed its political system over to special interest groups, lawyers, judges, and fundraisers, and it is now governed by a ruling class of politicians who are elected for life.

Other countries routinely get much higher voter turnout in general elections and offer voters a range of choices that start on the far left and finish on the far right, with the winner usually chosen from a party close to the safe centre. America has two centrist parties governed by the same patriotic reflexes that prevent them from challenging the status quo. The left has been marginalized into obscurity by the anti-communist hysteria of the Cold War and its own stridency, while the far right pushes its unpleasant agenda from the safe haven of the pulpit or the inside of a Ku Klux Klan robe. The Democrats and Republicans struggle for control of Congress and the White House; the Republicans have won more often lately but that does not mean the United States would be any different today had the Democrats won more elections. Both parties are merely vessels for the opinions and positions poured into them by interest groups at the national and state level.

Little enacted by an American state or federal body can be understood properly without putting on goggles that focus in on the money or lobbies behind it. The United States suddenly imposes tariffs on steel imported from overseas? That is because the Republicans need to win key seats in upcoming mid-term elections in the steel-producing state of Pennsylvania, not because the nation's economy demands it. Gigantic duties on Canadian softwood? A congressman in a lumber-producing state has been told he will lose his seat if Americans are not forced to pay more for the wood to build their homes. President Bush, a self-described free-trader, suddenly signs a bill in May 2002 that gives American agribusiness $190 billion in subsidies (a hypocritical move that deprives Third World countries of desperately needed income by depressing crop prices)? Another election-year manoeuvre.

The year 2002 offered yet another telling example of the slow death of American democracy. Every decade, the country reorganizes its political boundaries to reflect changes in population, a practice that has become an exercise in creating geographically hallucinatory districts unrelated to anything but the desire to make each district a safe seat for one of the two parties. The boundaries are redrawn by the politicians themselves, not an independent body. The result is that whichever party controls a state can rig the next election by creating Frankenstein districts: an arm and two fingers from this Republican neighbourhood sewn onto a torso from that Republican city, and a pair of legs that stretch down to two more Republican footholds that could be miles apart. The *Economist* made great fun of this shameless electoral plastic surgery in spring 2002, when the most recent gerrymandering was unveiled.[1] The British magazine singled out a district in Illinois shaped like a "crab," with its two claws reaching out to pull the appropriate voters into its Democratic maw; this was created by Republicans in order to make an adjacent seat safer by removing unwanted Democrats. Another bizarre district, this time in Florida, runs 145 kilometres (90 miles) down the east coast but spans no more than 3 miles at its widest point.

The goal, of course, is to eliminate the voter as an unknown factor in elections. American politicians cannot stand the suspense created by democracy; they like to fast-forward through the scary parts and get to the Hollywood ending without upset. As the *Economist* pointed out, this has been made easier by modern technology, which can plot voting patterns and draw corresponding maps that are accurate down to the last house. The result is a Congress – the House of Representatives and the Senate – populated by members for life. In the 2000 general election, all but six sitting congressmen were re-elected.

Such a result, which would hardly shame North Korea, is becoming the norm: the reelection rate has averaged more than 90 per cent since 1952. Not surprisingly, congressmen are reluctant to leave their warm nests. Only 28 have announced their retirement so far [in anticipation of the November 2002 congressional elections], compared with 64 in 1992.[2]

The consequence for the American democratic system is obvious. With congressmen holding impenetrable districts, there is little point in voting against the incumbent; a voter who wants to be represented by a different party is better off moving to a new district than waging a hopeless battle. The battle becomes more hopeless as the incumbent becomes more entrenched, because challengers have a difficult time raising the money required to run when their campaigns have almost no hope of being successful.

So why vote? The only remaining reason is to choose the man for the top job, the president and commander-in-chief of the United States of America. The race for president has as much impact on voter turnout as the congressional battles and could be seen as salvation from the desperate pointlessness of American politics. But even that is in doubt now.

The election of November 7, 2000, was the one that gave the world its second American president named George Bush, this one nicknamed "George W." (or simply "Dubya," as *W* is pronounced in Texas) to distinguish him from his father. George W. Bush, former governor of Texas and the son of former president George Bush, took office in January 2001 after a legal and political battle against his opponent, Al Gore, that made crooked elections in African dictatorships seem charming, even noble, by comparison.

By coincidence, while parts of this chapter were being written, the local newspapers were dutifully engrossed in the preordained re-election of one such dictator, Robert Mugabe in Zimbabwe. The election was a quaint formality designed to keep the corrupt and psychopathic Mugabe in power against the wishes of his starkly oppressed countrymen and much of the rest of the world. The voting, held over three days in the second week of March 2002, involved the usual tactics favoured by despots who suddenly find it politically expedient to bend to the wishes of international bodies like the United Nations and hold an "election": Mugabe's opponents suffered broken ribs when they carelessly threw their bodies in the path of his henchmen's feet; voters were forced to wait days in line outside polls that never opened; election "officials" carried off empty ballot boxes and returned them to polling stations miraculously stuffed with votes for Mugabe; the country's Supreme Court stepped in defiantly but to little effect; and so on. It was the usual sort of stuff that added up to yet another "poisoned" election, as one independent observer called it,[3] in another hapless post-colonial country whose welfare is at the mercy of a deranged man in control of a well-armed military.

The United States, of course, is no Zimbabwe, and only the most churlish left-wing commentator would compare the election process in the former country with that of the latter. Meet Michael Moore, the author and filmmaker whose book *Stupid White Men*[4] does pretty much just that. Moore equates George W. Bush's election in 2000 with the *coups d'état* so familiar to the citizens of South American, African, and Eastern European countries, and he is only half joking when he does it. It is Moore's opinion that Bush, the Republican candidate, conspired with a corrupt Republican Florida state government under the convenient governorship of his brother, John Ellis "Jeb" Bush, to steal the election from Al Gore, the Democratic candidate and vice president to the historically horny Bill Clinton. (Moore's take on the matter was so scathing that his publisher, HarperCollins, at first refused to release the book on its scheduled date in the weeks after the September 11 attacks.)

It is, of course, shocking to think that the president of the United States Mugabe'd the election that put him in power. In politics it is okay to buy an election, on credit or otherwise, but stealing one – that's dishonest. Americans who care about democracy can only pray that Moore is merely a ranting left-wing loony with a soft grip on the facts. Or they can read another book. At the other end of the spectrum from Moore's views is an equally glandular tome called *At Any Cost: How Al Gore Tried to Steal the Election*. Written by Bill Sammon, a *Washington Times* reporter, and published by a small Conservative house in Washington, D.C., Regnery Publishing, the book makes the contrary claim that it was Gore, not Bush, who nearly got away with electoral larceny. The book exposes "why Al Gore's wholesale assault on our democratic process will poison the air in Washington for years to come," not to mention his attempts to "blackmail GOP leaders," and how his team created Gore votes "out of thin air."[5]

Gripping stuff. On one side you have a constituency that believes an evildoing George W. Bush burgled the will of the people and debased the American democratic process, and on the other there are those who thank God every day that a righteous George W. Bush didn't let Al Gore burgle the will of the people and debase the American democratic process. The truth lies right down the middle, as so often is the case in debates of a political persuasion. The fact is that both sides in the election so enthusiastically manipulated the process and so heavily relied on partisan chicanery to get the outcome they desired that each can justifiably accuse the other of corrupting the election. The November 7, 2000, vote stands as the darkest example of what can go wrong in a political system infected with such virulent partisanship that no one, not even

Supreme Court justices, can be fully trusted. Only one thing is certain – it was not the voters who decided the outcome of the presidential election of 2000.

Actually, it is not at all clear what American voters wanted the outcome to be. When the polls had closed, they had given Gore two hundred thousand more votes than Bush but seemed to have handed the country to Bush. Although a presidential candidate with a greater portion of the popular vote has lost only once before in American history, this kind of thing can happen under the U.S. system. Voters do not choose a president directly; they vote for their candidate in their home state, and the candidate who wins the state gets that state's "electoral college votes." It takes 270 of those votes to get into the White House; some states get more electoral votes than others, so, while it is rare, it was not impossible for George W. Bush to become the forty-third president of the United States even though more Americans voted for the other guy. Not that two hundred thousand votes is a convincing majority. Americans were literally cleft in two on the question of who should be president: Bush, the semantically challenged layabout son of a former president; or Al Gore, the wooden vice president who had stood by the philandering Bill Clinton throughout the latter's impeachment trial and then about-faced during the election campaign and criticized Clinton's moral turpitude as expedience required. Neither man was all that impressive, and America seemed indifferent to who got the job. That Florida would become ground zero in an election that few seemed to care about seems oddly sad now, given that two of the terrorists who piloted those flights into the World Trade Center in New York City were in the state at the time, learning to fly commercial planes at a school in Venice, Florida.

While the popular vote was close in America as a whole, it was nothing compared to the tally in Florida. When the state's six million ballots were counted up, Bush had a majority of 1,784, a margin of victory of less than .03 per cent.[6] Because the voting had been so close across the rest of the country, the election came down to which candidate would win the state's twenty-five electoral votes. All eyes were on Florida as the night progressed. Those who watched the election results on television will recall that some networks declared Bush the winner, then took it back. Gore was watching television and conceded victory to Bush, but took that back too.

The margin of victory was so small that, under Florida state law, it triggered an automatic recount, which is why Gore un-conceded the election. The two camps quickly staked out positions: Bush called for a speedy resolution so he could get on with the organizing the transition of power from Clinton to himself, thus staking sole claim to the winner's circle. Gore, obliged to challenge the apparent outcome, called for patience; he did not want Americans to make any "rush to judgment"[7] about who had won the election based merely on poll results. And then the two sides went to work trying to wrest victory out of each other's death grip. Each quickly deduced that the outcome would depend on which votes were recounted where, and how that recount was carried out. At that historic moment, the choice of forty-third president of the United States was taken out of the hands of living, breathing voters and placed in the care of vilely partisan political workers, and, ultimately, in the hands of judges who, it now seems, were equally given to one side or the other.

It is important to mention at this point that one relatively trustworthy source believes the election was indeed stolen, although not from Gore or Bush but, rather, from black voters. That source is the United States Commission on Civil Rights, an independent, bipartisan fact-finding agency that investigates complaints that citizens are being deprived of their right to vote (among other rights) on the basis of their race, age, sex, disability, or national origin. The Commission was created under the Civil Rights Act of 1957; it was born, in other words, of black America's struggle to end segregation and discrimination.

The USCCR, acting on complaints from numerous black voters in Florida who had been turned away from polling booths on November 7, 2000, or who otherwise felt thwarted in their efforts to have their votes counted, used its power to subpoena witnesses and held three days of hearings into the election in January and February 2001. It subsequently released a damning report that was largely ignored by the American media, or media anywhere else, for that matter. On the other hand, the recount and its fallout were reported minute-by-minute, to the point where only the mentally infirm and belligerently cloistered were unaware what a "chad" was by the time the process was a week old.

The recount and its attendant media circus were legitimate news stories, settling, as they did, who would be the next president. But the Commission on Civil Rights saw a deeper problem. "Despite the closeness of the election, it was widespread voter disenfranchisement, not the dead-heat contest, that was the extraordinary feature of the Florida election," the Commission reported in its Findings and Recommendations.[8] The Commission found the disenfranchisement – the denial of the right to vote – of black voters in particular to be so widespread that it recommended that the United States Department of Justice "immediately initiate the litigation process against the governor, secretary of state, director of the Division of Elections, specific supervisors of elections and other state and local officials"[9] for their part in the systematic removal of black voters' names from registration lists, and for the fact black voters were ten times more likely to have their ballots rejected than white voters. The report also took election officials to task for intimidating voters outside polling stations in black neighbourhoods through the presence of police, and for closing polls before the vote was over in those same communities. And it recommended that the state purchase better vote-counting machinery; different counties used different systems, with reliable, modern ones found in better-off white neighbourhoods and less reliable, dated machinery that produced more rejected ballots in poorer black and Hispanic neighbourhoods.

In *Stupid White Men*, Michael Moore sees the Commission's report as evidence the Bush family compact went to work to steal the election from Al Gore long before the night of the election. The plot was simple: remove as many black voters from registration lists as possible prior to the vote, since it is the received wisdom that most blacks in America vote Democrat. Florida's governor was none other than George W.'s brother, and its secretary of state, Kathleen Harris, was George W.'s presidential Florida election campaign co-chairman, so it is at least arguable that the purge of black voters from registration lists was orchestrated.

The Commission on Civil Rights stayed out of the politics and stuck to the facts. What it discovered was that in 1997, following a mayoral election campaign in Miami that was egregiously corrupt even by Florida standards, the state undertook a cleanup of its voter lists. So many dead people had voted for the man who won the mayor's seat that the election was subsequently overturned. The Florida government subsequently gave the job of redoing the voter lists to a private company, and it asked that company not only to remove dead people but also to purge the names of all convicted felons.

In the United States, criminals convicted of committing a felony lose their right to vote until their sentence is served. In

January 2001, at the time the commission was holding its hearings, 3.9 million Americans were not allowed to vote – "disenfranchised" – because of felony convictions. Of that number, 36 per cent were black, even though blacks only make up 13 per cent of the American population, according to 2000 census figures. In Florida, one in three disenfranchised former felons is black, and it is one of only eight states that does not automatically restore a felon's voting rights once his or her sentence has been served. The felon must apply for clemency to the state cabinet, a lengthy and expensive process (the Commission heard testimony that it costs a minimum of $10,000 in legal fees and can take as long as six months). Other states restore voting rights automatically, no questions asked, no legal fees, no bureaucracy, but not Florida.

The company awarded the contract to purge the voter lists, OTB Online, went about gathering names from various state and federal databases and created new lists in 1998, 1999, and 2000. It followed explicit instructions to cast as wide a net as possible when searching for names to purge, even though it had the technology to narrow down the field. Despite its warnings to the Florida Division of Elections that its "exclusion lists" contained numerous "false positives" – that is, legitimate Florida voters who were not convicted felons and were only there because their name or circumstances were similar to that of an actual felon – the Division of Elections accepted the lists as they were and forwarded them to local election officials with instructions to verify their accuracy.

The Civil Rights Commission found that the 2000 list had an error rate of 14 per cent. Some election officials who were asked to verify the list's accuracy were so appalled by the way it was compiled that they refused to use it for the November 7 election, instead referring to lists used in elections in 1998 that had been updated. Some officials went out of their way to give the benefit of the doubt to voters who arrived at their polling station on November 7 only to discover they had been removed from the list, allowing them to vote if they swore an affidavit that they were not convicted felons; other officials refused to let the people on the list vote and were uncooperative when it came to trying to sort things out in the voter's favour. Phone lines at the office of the Supervisor of Elections were tied up for hours, computers didn't work, and voters were given misinformation on how to rectify their situation that sent them on pointless missions from one polling station to another. "The state of Florida's use of this purge list, combined with state law that places the burden on voters to remove themselves from the list, resulted in denying countless African Americans the right to vote," the Commission found. The report never gives a firm number of blacks denied their right to vote, and it acknowledges that white voters were also on the list in error, but it concluded that a disproportionate number of black voters were prevented from casting their vote on November 7. Given that George W. Bush's majority in the Florida election was a mere 154 when all was said and done, this is evidence that the will of the people was thwarted through the actions of a state government that was, by political allegiance, not sympathetic to their voting intentions. If a net total of 155 more black Democrat voters had been able to vote that day, the history of America would be on a different course today. It is a stunning thought.

Another aspect of felon disenfranchisement worth noting is that, under Florida legal precedent, a person who commits a felony in another state, serves his sentence there, and has his right to vote automatically restored by that state must be allowed to vote, no questions asked, in Florida. For reasons unexplained, under the watch of Kathleen Harris, the Republican secretary of state whose department oversaw the purging of felons, the Division of Elections told OTB Online that felons with restored voting rights from other states still needed to apply for clemency in Florida. When the issue was raised during the Commission on Civil Rights hearings, the Florida Executive Board of Clemency confirmed this was an error, a correction of the facts that came too late for anyone excluded from voting in the federal election.

And in one more striking coincidence, the Commission reported that "'miscommunication' led to approximately 8,000 persons who committed misdemeanors in Texas being incorrectly identified as felons in Florida."[10] This miscommunication occurred between the state governed by Jeb Bush and the state governed by his brother, presidential candidate George W. Bush.

There is no concrete evidence that partisan political forces were at play during the run-up to the election in Florida. The Civil Rights Commission makes no mention of it; its report points the finger at incompetence and indifference, character-istics that cross all political lines where bureaucracy is con-cerned. On the other hand, partisanship was the dominant force in the aftermath of the vote and the infamous recount.

In the United States of America, the ultimate democracy, nearly every public office is filled in an election. State comp-trollers, chief financial officers, attorneys general, local judges, prosecutors, sheriffs, you name it, they are elected. It is one of the reasons the criminal system is so tough in the U.S.; if you are a judge up for re-election and the citizenry has a taste for harsher sentencing, as it often does in most coun-tries, how do you suppose you will rule on criminal cases? As well, virtually all appointed positions are filled along party lines, including state supreme courts and the United States Supreme Court. Partisanship is the main current running through every level of American civic life. In many elections,

the ballot is a lengthy list of candidates for all kinds of different positions, ranging from sheriff to president. Voters can
pick and choose between candidates from different parties or,
in the blind faith only politics can inspire, select all the candidates from one party, regardless of their record, with a single
stroke of the pencil or pull on a lever. This remarkable display
of fealty reinforces the partisanship of American life. Almost
every mainstream voter is either a hardcore Democrat or a
hardcore Republican, with a romantically inclined minority
relegated to hopelessly marginal third parties of no consequence (e.g., the Green Party, the Reform Party, the Communist Party, the American Heritage Party, the American Nazi
Party, the Family Values Party, the American Falangist Party,
the Prohibition Party, the Pansexual Peace Party).[11] The so-
called "checks and balances" of the American political system
usually weed out the abuses of such single-mindedness: the
president can veto the Congress; within Congress, the Senate
and the House of Representatives can override each other,
control of each house passing from one party to the other on
a regular basis; and the judicial system can override both
Congress and the White House. It is rare that one party will
control the White House and both houses of Congress while
also having a majority of like-minded judges on the Supreme
Court. (Rare but not impossible. The Republicans achieved
the grand slam of American politics in the November 7, 2002,
midterm elections. Bush's party won a majority in the Senate
and the House, giving it control of Congress, the White
House, and the Supreme Court.)

It was in this context of extreme partisanship that George
W. Bush and Al Gore put teams to work on the ground in
Florida after the November 7, 2000, presidential election produced the ultimate squeaker. Because the outcome had been so
ludicrously close, every single example of voter dissatisfaction

was quickly turned into a *cause célèbre*. The incompetence and indifference unearthed by the Civil Rights Commission were, in some instances, ridiculous.

In Palm Beach, a retirement community, voters were faced with a confusing two-page "butterfly" ballot. The punch holes for choosing a candidate ran down the middle of the two pages; Gore was the second candidate on the first page but the third hole to be punched. The second hole somehow belonged to the first candidate on the right-hand page – Pat Buchanan, the right-wing Reform Party candidate known to espouse anti-Semitic rhetoric. Palm Beach County has the highest Jewish population by density in the United States. Many residents are over sixty-five and have trouble seeing and hearing. Thus, many eyebrows shot up when Buchanan received 3,407 votes in a county where he had not campaigned a single day or spent a cent on advertising, and where he was generally reviled. At the Lakes of Delray retirement community, where the residents are 95 per cent Jewish and 100 per cent Democrat, Buchanan got forty-seven votes.[12] Even Buchanan's campaign manager, his sister Bay Buchanan, admitted the outcome was laughable. "We do not believe they [the votes cast for her brother in Palm Beach County] are all ours," she said at the time. "We think there was clear confusion and we understand the confusion since we've looked at the ballot ourselves."[13] Election officials estimated that not only did Buchanan pick up more than 3,400 votes on the confusing ballot but another 19,000 ballots were spoiled because of "overvoting" – people who in their confusion voted for Gore *and* Buchanan, thus disqualifying their ballot.

Overvoting as a result of confusing ballots also occurred in other parts of the state. In Duval County, the ballot listed the ten presidential candidates on two pages along with the inexplicable instruction to "vote all pages." Many did exactly as instructed and thus spoiled their ballots. More than half of the spoiled ballots marked Gore or Bush on the first page and a second choice on the second page. An independent study of the ballots carried out by the National Opinion Research Center concluded that, based on the presumption the over-voters intended to choose either Gore or Bush, Gore lost a net total of 3,089 votes to that one confusing ballot.

But overvotes were not the issue in the recount following the November 7 election. It was "undervotes" that caught the media's attention and where Gore focused his efforts to tweak the recount in his favour. Undervotes occur when a voter fails to choose any candidate in the regulated way on a ballot. That can mean circling a candidate's name instead of marking an X beside it; with a punch-card ballot, in means failing to dis-lodge the tiny square of paper called a "chad" that must be fully removed in order for the automated counting machines to read the voter's intentions accurately. Sometimes voters only manage to give the chads a gentle prod with the voting stylus, resulting in a "dimpled chad"; sometimes they partially dislodge the thing, creating a "hanging chad." In either case, the machines reject the ballot, and an undervote occurs.

With the election in a dead heat, on the morning of November 8 Gore and Bush began assembling teams and sending them in waves to south Florida. News reports esti-mated that the two sides had in the neighbourhood of four hundred operatives each on the ground, but that may be too conservative. Mass confusion was one common denomina-tor; the other was the desire to prejudice the recount process to produce the needed results. Gore's team quickly decided not to demand a statewide recount but instead to focus on four Democrat-leaning counties: Palm Beach, Miami-Dade, Broward, and Volusia.[14] The hope was to produce, if not enough votes to overtake Bush's molecule-thin lead, then enough to make it difficult for Kathleen Harris, the Republican secretary of state who was also George W. Bush's Florida campaign co-chairman, to certify the November 7 results in favour of her boss seven days after the election, as required under Florida law. The Bush strategy amounted to gumming up whatever strategy Gore came up with by disputing recounted votes and the recount process in general, and building public sympathy for the idea that bothering with a recount was a cause of national disunity and needless upset. If they could make it to the certification deadline and still have the lead, Bush would win the election. For the same reasons, the Bush camp never called for a statewide recount.

Florida law was contradictory, however. It said the election had to be certified on November 14 but also said all recounted votes should be considered. The law did not make it clear what happened when the recounting of votes went on after the certification deadline. Harris tried and failed to certify the election on November 14 but the Florida Supreme Court, a seven-member body dominated at the time by six Democrat appointees, set that certification aside in a ruling on November 21 and made the new deadline November 26.

The partisan shenanigans were well underway long before the Florida Supreme Court made its ruling, however. Members of Gore's team later admitted that one of their tactics involved the gathering of intelligence on the members of the election review boards in each of the four chosen counties.[15] Twelve people, three per county, were subjected to the kind of file-building usually limited to the Federal Bureau of Investigation in its pursuit of political undesirables. The information would tell the Democrats who was on their side and who was a Republican, who could be pushed and who would require more subtle forms of persuasion. The strategy worked in Broward County, where the review panel agreed to recount ballots in the manner most sympathetic to the voters' "intentions"; if a ballot appeared to all three recounters to be in favour of a particular candidate, even if the chad in question was dimpled so slightly as to have been rendered so by a gentle breeze, the vote was counted. Gore picked up hundreds of votes there.

Not so in Palm Beach, where the confusing ballot and sore Jewish voters quickly turned the county into a media flashpoint. Al Lieberman, Gore's running mate, whipped up a furor over the numerous overvotes there and pressed the Democrats to file a suit demanding a new election with a fresh ballot, one that did not seem to come from the mind of Dr. Seuss; Democrat lawyers abandoned that idea as being a non-starter under Florida law.[16] Instead, the Democrats focused on the undervotes and the recount, but this time the Republican-dominated three-member review team was not interested in following Broward County's lead and reading the chads like tea leaves to determine voters' intentions. They adopted a stricter, though still Democrat-friendly, set of rules about interpreting intentions, and a county that Gore expected would yield a gold mine of new votes was ultimately a disappointment.

Miami-Dade was also a disappointment for the Democrats, even though it was a party stronghold. Two things worked against Gore. One was a demonstration, dubbed the "penny loafer riot,"[17] by a small group of well-dressed young Republicans who claimed that Democrats were stealing ballots marked in favour of Bush. They began banging on a glass partition outside the room where the ballots were being prepared for recount and ended up chasing all the Democrats out of the building. The county subsequently cancelled the recount and stuck with the results as they stood on November 7. The other problem for Gore was less concrete: there were reports the Cuban-American mayor of Miami was angered that Bill

Clinton's administration had used its might to snatch Elián González, a six-year-old Cuban refugee who had washed up on Florida's shore, from a family member's home in Miami and eventually ship him back to Cuba in June 2000.[18] Putting a quick stop to the recount in Miami-Dade and perhaps denying the Democrats more votes may have been the mayor's revenge (such intrigue is typical of Florida's politics), but this remains unproven.

Meanwhile, Volusia County came up with ninety-eight more votes for Gore. By November 15, Bush's lead had been reduced to three hundred.[19] The Republicans by then had begun raising questions about the legitimacy of the recount and repeatedly alleged that the process was open to "mischief." Hand recounts were not as reliable as machine counts, they said, and their operatives began a witch hunt for errant chads. One Republican observer began screaming and panicking at the sight of a chad lying on the floor at the site of the Broward County recount; other observers said they saw one election official using a ballot to clean her fingernails. Republicans accused Democrats of eating chads, and in one instance they called in the sheriff's office to seize seventy-five tiny bits of paper as evidence that chads were being discarded, but the evidence turned out to be exactly what it appeared to be – tiny bits of paper.

The Republicans and Democrats also organized demonstrations and counter-demonstrations in the streets of Broward County and elsewhere. At one such protest, six hundred Republicans shouted "No more chads!"[20] A battle of the placards emerged, with each side endeavouring to get its latest hand-scrawled witticism on the evening news. The Democrats quoted Stalin: "It's not the people who vote that counts – it's the people who count the votes." The Republicans made fun of senior citizens' inability to understand a ballot that the vast majority in Palm Beach had been able to navigate: "Punched the wrong hole? Hope you're not driving."[21]

The partisan behaviour was a sickening sight to many and damaging to the U.S.'s reputation as a model democracy. The *Economist* magazine in London wrote in its November 25, 2000, edition that the events "called into question the notion that, whereas other countries may burn tyres in the streets, America at least conducts its electoral process according to the rules of law."[22] In an editorial in the same edition, the magazine said:

> Ever since election night, the main participants have disgraced themselves. At times the two parties have seemed stuck in an escalating competition of hypocrisy. Consistency and integrity have been trumped by the need to say whatever might convince which court. Mr. Gore should be blamed for beginning this downward spiral. Mr. Bush, however, should be castigated for refusing to countenance what was surely the fairest possible solution – a manual recount of all the Florida ballots.[23]

But what had gone on up to that point was nothing compared to the final three rounds in court. Here partisanship became the decisive factor in the choice of the president. It was a partisanship both sides knew they could count on. The Democrats had an ace in the hole because six of the seven members of the Florida Supreme Court were their appointees, making that a reliably sympathetic institution. The November 21 decision to allow recounts seemed to confirm this. But the Republicans had a handful of aces up their sleeve, in the form of five Republican-appointed judges out of the nine on the highest court in the land.

On November 26, Kathleen Harris certified George W.

Bush as the winner of the election, by 537 votes. The Democrats immediately filed suit to overturn her decision. On December 4, Leon County Circuit Court Judge N. Sanders Saul ruled that the certification stood and Bush was the winner, based on his opinion that further recounts would not change the result. The Gore team appealed next to the friendly confines of the Florida Supreme Court, which on December 8 overturned the certified result, did its own count, and cut Bush's lead to 154 votes.[24] The court ruled 6-1 that the recounts must be completed in order to protect the right of voters to be heard, even though the recounts went past the very deadline the court had set. "This election should be determined by a careful examination of the votes of Florida's citizens and not by strategies extraneous to the voting process," the judges said in the majority opinion. The lone dissenting opinion came from the Republican appointee, who criticized the court for not setting the rules for the recount and warned the ruling would plunge the nation into an "unprecedented and unnecessary constitutional crisis."[25]

The Bush team immediately asked the Supreme Court in Washington to overturn the decision, which is exactly what the justices did in a 5-4 vote divided along party lines on December 12. Actually there were two decisions: a 7-2 ruling sending the case back to Florida Supreme Court to sort out the question of setting rules for the recount; and the 5-4 vote setting the deadline for certification of the election exactly two hours after the Supreme Court decision was handed down, making any more recounts a moot point. Gore graciously conceded at that point, paving the way for George W. Bush to assume the presidency by a majority of a single electoral college vote.

The decision, hailed by Republicans for lifting the country out of crisis, is seen by Democrats and liberal thinkers as blatant hypocrisy on the part of conservative justices who had to wring themselves with a hard twist to the left in order to concoct Bush's election victory. Michael Moore in *Stupid White Men* says two of the Republican-appointed justices, Chief Justice William Rehnquist and Sandra Day O'Connor, both in their seventies, wanted to retire but felt they had to do so under a Republican president so that their replacements would be like-minded conservatives. "On election night," Moore writes, "O'Connor was heard lamenting at a party in [Washington, D.C.] that she couldn't hold out another four – or eight – years. Junior Bush was their only hope for securing a contented retirement."[26] Moore also wrote that the son of another of the Republican justices was a lawyer with the firm representing the Bush team before the Supreme Court, which Moore called a conflict of interest.[27]

Whatever their private reasoning, the justices' public thinking, once revealed in their unsigned majority decision, suggested, as an article in the *Los Angeles Times* put it, "that the conservatives, though united on the result, struggled mightily to find a federal violation that justified overruling the Florida courts."[28] The decision maintained that because Florida had no precise standards for deciding which votes were legal and which were invalid, the various recounts up to that point violated the Constitution's guarantee of "equal protection under the law."

> In the past, the conservative justices have preached against using such vague constitutional phrases as "equal protection" and "due process of law" as reasons for second-guessing the states. The conservatives also say that the court should look to the intent of the framers of the Constitution. The equal protection clause, part of the 14th Amendment, was added to the

Constitution after the Civil War to protect blacks from discrimination in the South. Nonetheless, faced with the most important case of their careers, the conservatives turned to the equal protection clause as a basis for stopping the hand recounts in Florida.[29]

In other words, the justices turned to an amendment they had repeatedly disdained in previous rulings, particularly rulings involving the disproportionate number of black men awaiting death sentences in the United States, to justify putting an end to recounts that might have sent the wrong man to the White House. Alan Dershowitz, a Harvard law professor and civil rights activist, published a book in 2001 called *Supreme Injustice*, in which he called the ruling "the single most corrupt decision in Supreme Court history, because it is the only one that I know of where the majority justices decided as they did because of the personal identity and political affiliation of the litigants."[30] Another writer called the justices "criminal,"[31] and even some conservatives admitted that they struggled to find a justification for the ruling.

There were also intelligent conservative writers who saw it as the correct legal decision and who argued the conservative justices' past interpretation of the equal-protection amendment was consistent with the recount decision. The decision is now a much-studied precedent at law schools across the United States, needless to say.

Still, a significant number of critics felt that, had it been Bush trailing on election day, the same five justices would have allowed the recounts to continue. But that ignores the central point about partisan politics in the United States. It now appears beyond argument that, had the Supreme Court been dominated by Democrat appointees, Gore would have won the day. This was the most important decision the court ever made, the one time its nine men and woman, each of them a political appointee, were in a position to deliver to their appointers a victory of crucial significance. There is no reason to believe a Democrat majority would have acted differently; one only needs to look to the Florida Supreme Court's earlier decision for proof of that.

One Supreme Court justice wrote in his dissenting opinion, "Although we may never know with complete certainty the identity of the winner of this year's presidential election, the identity of the loser is perfectly clear. It is the nation's confidence in the judge as an impartial guardian of the law."

POSTSCRIPT

A year after the election, a study of the ballots determined that, had the Supreme Court allowed the recount to continue under existing standards, George W. Bush would likely still have won the election by a tiny margin. The same study also found that if the recount had been done under subsequently adopted Florida rules designed to give voters the benefit of the doubt when they make innocent mistakes on their ballots, Al Gore would have won, again by a margin as thin as a chad turned on its side. The study did not address the findings of the Commission on Civil Rights that a large but undetermined number of black voters were scurrilously removed from voter registration lists and never got to cast a ballot, spoiled or otherwise.

The U.S. Justice Department and the Florida government never took action on the United States Commission on Civil Rights's recommendations. Jeb Bush, the governor of Florida, and other Republicans in the state dismissed the report as biased on the grounds that six of the eight members of the Commission were Democratic appointees. Many other sources, including the *New York Times*, took the report at face value because the Commission's past work had been consistently non-partisan and the report's conclusions were based on recorded testimony. Two former presidents, Democrat Jimmy Carter and Republican Gerald Ford, who together head the U.S. National Commission on Election Reform, wrote in the *Atlanta Journal-Constitution* in 2001 that the voter registration system in Peru is "far superior" to those in use in America's various states. The *Economist* said, "America's voting system has been shown to be not just technologically incompetent but structurally flawed, with far too many overseer roles given to partisans."[32]

Despite Jeb Bush's claims of bias in the USCCR report, he spearheaded a reform of Florida election laws in 2001.[33] The new law bans punch-hole vote-counting machinery, thereby eliminating chads; it outlaws the confusing "butterfly" ballot that baffled the voters of Palm Beach; and it calls for hand recounts in close races, something the Republicans were opposed to throughout the recount process on the grounds such things could lead to "mischief." The law does not, however, make it any easier for a felon who has served his time to have his voting rights restored, nor does it create an impartial body to oversee elections. Most of the reforms mirror the recommendations made in the USCCR report. A similar federal package passed in April 2002 focused on eliminating out-of-date voting machinery and made it easier for voters to correct mistakes on their ballots.

Robert Mugabe was declared the winner of the election in Zimbabwe and immediately began rounding up opponents and jailing them.

Finally, Americans, even those in Florida who were so aggrieved in the days after the election, never seemed to care that the voting process was taken away from the people and handed to two wild competing packs of partisan wolves. Al

Gore, who grew a beard (a sure sign of a guilty conscience, some would say) and became a journalism-school lecturer, just does not inspire the loyalty required to make his loss an issue. And George W. Bush so masterfully acquitted himself with his handling of the terrorist attacks of September 11, 2001, that many Americans are glad that he fell into, or stole, or whatever, the job of president. Newspaper reports prepared on the anniversary of the election demonstrated that Americans cannot imagine another man in charge; Bush's approval ratings were in the 90-per-cent range throughout most of the months following the attacks, although they began to fall in the spring of 2002. Given the losses the nation suffered in the attacks, it is a forgivable reaction; still, it is troublesome that a nation determined to govern itself through the will of the people has failed to investigate events that hijacked so vital an American principle.

The Commission on Civil Rights understands this American tendency to resist self-examination. In its report on the November 7, 2000, election, it quotes Martin Luther King at the top of the chapter on "Findings and Recommendations": "The great majority of Americans . . . are uneasy with injustice but unwilling yet to pay a significant price to eradicate it."

TWELVE

THE EMPTY CULTURE

I wonder why we listen to poets, when nobody gives a fuck.
- "ASHES OF AMERICAN FLAGS," WILCO

America's foreign intervention and presence abroad have dominated and shaped the world since the end of the Second World War. Institutions as sacred as foreign boundaries and even governments have been United States inventions; many of the current tensions between the U.S. and other countries have their source in covert CIA or overt military operations carried out for political ends over the past twenty-five to fifty years. But unwanted American influence on other countries, and the consequent backlash, does not begin and end with spies and missiles. It also extends to movie stars and hamburgers.

The ubiquitous presence of American clothing and lifestyle products, movies, music, and television has long been a sore spot in foreign countries, creating a tension that is dismissed by Americans as jealousy at best, and tribalism at worst. Arab countries were the hot spots for anti-Americanism in 2002, but it is France that has had the quintessential love/hate relationship with the United States, one that goes back to the earliest days of American history. France was America's first European ally; it supported the winning side in the Revolutionary War, and French political thought of the day contributed to the drafting of the American Constitution. France also settled much of the eastern and southern parts of what came to be the United States; France's holdings were sold by Napoleon to the American government in the Louisiana Purchase in 1803, a seminal moment in the United States' dominance of North America. The Statue of Liberty in New York was a gift of the French government in 1886. A free exchange of styles and attitudes continued between France and the United States throughout the twentieth century. Writers such as Ernest Hemingway and Ezra Pound spent years in Paris in the century's First Quarter, when the city was a mecca for non-conformist artists of all stripes and nationalities. The French ate up American styles and attitudes, from blue jeans to James Dean, while Americans seeking artistic liberty and cheap wine and, later, a place to see grand European culture and feel a little Bohemian for a while, turned France into a major holiday destination. That is the love side of the relationship.

But as much as the French have always been pulled toward America, they are also repelled by the country's rootless and vulgar popular culture. "United States" is a metaphor in France for cheap quality, bigness for its own sake, violence, arrogance, mass production, pushiness, haste, and lack of refinement. This anti-Americanism was made concrete in a book published in 1980 entitled *La France colonisée*, which became a bestseller. Among other controversial exposés, the author, Jacques Thibau, revealed to his countrymen how their politicians began to hire American public-relations firms to run their campaigns in the 1970s, turning French elections, a previously sober and well-considered Gallic undertaking, into popularity contests in which the candidates were marketed in a fashion similar to orange juice and automobiles.

Thibau was also among the first to show how American movies had taken over the theatres of European cities by the early 1970s, reducing the once-grand cinema cultures of France, Great Britain, and Italy to marginal, art-house status. American cinema has since come to dominate the world, and the world's view of itself. Between the end of the Second World War and 1970, for instance, France made ten films about the war while the U.S. churned out 311,[1] promoting America's image as the conquering and liberating hero nation at the expense of the contributions of other Allied forces.

Conservative commentators and politicians in the United States argue that the displacement of French films by American movies is simply the cultural market at work. If more French people had a taste for their own cinema, there would be more local films for them to choose from; and if American films were not so popular, there would be less demand for them. This is a disingenuous argument. There is still a relatively strong French film industry; in spring 2002 at a multiplex cinema on boulevard Montparnasse in Paris, six of twelve films on offer were French, while the other six were American. Compared to Canada, where virtually every film in every theatre is American, that is an astounding percentage of locally produced cinema. Clearly there is an appetite in France for the works of its sons and daughters, more than enough to keep moviegoers happy. There is another truth at play here, Thibau revealed, and that is if American film is popular in France, it is because that's the way the American government wanted it after the end of the Second World War.

When the French government, broke and exhausted in 1945, negotiated refinancing with Washington, the American negotiators insisted that, in return for more credit, France open its market to U.S. films. The French had, up to that point, limited the number of foreign films allowed into the country each year. The American film studios had a large backlog of films that had not been shown in Europe, and they had co-operated throughout the war with the U.S. government by lending their stars to the War Department for propaganda reels and morale-boosting USO tours. Now they wanted payback. They got it, and more. Under pressure from American negotiators and desperate for financial aid, the French relented and agreed to lift their country's quotas on foreign film. Before the agreement, in 1945, France issued visas to forty-six American films. In the first six months alone of 1947, that number increased to 338.[2] The French were permitted to set a quota obliging theatres to show four weeks' worth of French films out of every thirteen weeks, but that did little to satisfy critics. "Condemning French film to disappear," wrote an editorialist in Le Monde, "amounts to submitting the French public to an unchecked propaganda in favour of American tastes and American spirit. . . . It will not be a joyous thing to see our people absorb unlimited quantities of this stupefying substance."[3] Absorb they did, and today French cinema and culture have a strong strain of Americanism running through them.

French television is littered with American fare.[4] A tourist in a Paris hotel can watch dubbed versions of popular U.S. shows like *JAG*, *All My Children*, and *The Simpsons* (also on the German channels available in Paris; it is worth the trip across the ocean just to hear Homer Simpson speaking Sergeant Schultz's mother tongue). The French can also watch French soap operas that have a distinctly American style, which is evident when the action cuts from a talky scene in a wealthy home to a teary interchange in a hospital bedroom involving a hunky doctor, and then goes to a badly staged car accident followed by the credits; the same goes for game shows, right down to the host whose relentless cheeriness is so un-French that the only thing that suggests he is from France is the language he is speaking.

Again, Americans see this as the free market at work, and to the extent that television networks seek ratings by broadcasting shows that will attract the most viewers at the lowest possible cost, they are right. Still, that point of view overlooks two important facts. First, America is the world's dominant producer of films and TV shows,[5] which means it is the default creator of the mountains of filler required to complete a twenty-four-hour broadcast schedule. America's dominance of television sets around the world is less a testament to the quality of its productions than to the fact there are a lot of them to go around. That said, a nation that also dominates the world arms market with a complete lack of concern for who buys what is not going to preoccupy itself with worries over the inherent artistic value of *The Dukes of Hazzard*.

Second, the free-market point of view rather blithely ignores how people in other countries feel about being bombarded with a culture, and the values portrayed in that culture, that is not their own. America holds its values dearly but seems unable or unwilling to understand that other countries, however small and poor, do the same for their own. It would seem strange for an American to think that someone would watch *Dallas* or *JAG* for anything other than the inherent entertainment value of those shows, but that's because the presumptions about the characters' attitudes and achievements are native to an American viewer. An unemployed young man in Bulgaria who watches *Dallas* sees obscenely wealthy people being treated like royalty and living like kings on the strength of their ability to steal and stab friends in the back; he has a difficult time separating that impression from his impression of American people as a whole. Why wouldn't he resent the United States for rewarding such despicable low-lifes while he lives in a one-room basement apartment in Sofia? Why shouldn't he resent people so in love with their ability to buy things when he can barely stitch together the means to buy a light bulb and a can of coffee? Why do Americans get to be such profligate consumers just because they live in Boise, Idaho, instead of Eastern Europe?

The omnipotence of American culture around the world and the conflicted feelings it creates in the people of other countries is something the United States has ignored at its peril. It is also a phenomenon that was well-documented before September 11 in a book every bit as prescient at Chalmers Johnson's *Blowback*. Even the title was startlingly clairvoyant – *Jihad vs. McWorld: How Globalism and Tribalism Are Reshaping the World*. Written by Benjamin R. Barber, the book's cover image is of a woman whose only visible features are her eyes, through the slit of her Arab-style veil, and her right hand, in which she holds a can of Pepsi. The jacket alone probably resulted in the book, first published in 1995, becoming a bestseller after September 11, and Barber becoming a darling of the seminar circuit.

Barber, a professor at Rutgers University in New Jersey and a prodigious author, uses "McWorld" and "Jihad" as generic terms (although "jihad" has since become a loaded word) to identify two competing world views: globalization and nationalism. He considers both to be a threat to democracy, making his thesis more popular with the left than the right; still, what he says has an obvious clarity to it, one that holds up better than a simplistic division of the world into good and evil.

The first scenario [jihad] rooted in race holds out the grim prospect of a retribalization of large swaths of humankind by war and bloodshed: a threatened balkanization of nation-states in which culture is pitted against culture, people against people, tribe against tribe, a Jihad in the name of a hundred narrowly conceived faiths against every kind of interdependence, against every kind of artificial social cooperation and mutuality: against technology, against pop culture, and against integrated markets; against modernity itself as well as the future in which modernity issues. The second [McWorld] paints that future in shimmering pastels, a busy portrait of onrushing economic, technological, and ecological forces that demand integration and uniformity and that mesmerize peoples everywhere with fast music, fast computers, and fast food – MTV, Macintosh, and McDonald's – pressing nations into one homogenous global theme park, one McWorld tied together by communications, information, entertainment, and commerce.[6]

What we have is a world taken over by (mostly American) entertainment and lifestyle companies that wish to expand their markets in every corner of the world, the way the U.S. film industry did in France in 1945. The only defence against this cultural imperialism is nationalism, which expresses itself in the benign and slightly hypocritical anti-Americanism of France or, more dangerously, in the rabid fanaticism of Osama bin Laden and the unregretted Taliban government in Afghanistan. In George W. Bush's world, the only two choices are between McDonald's and bin Laden; between the goodness of capitalism and globalization, and the evil of terrorism; between uncontrolled access by American media giants to foreign television stations and movie theatres, and the Taliban ministry of vice and virtue. Bush's supporters did not for nothing associate anti-globalization protesters in Seattle with the Al-Qaeda operatives who hijacked a plane and flew it into my sister's office building.[7] The American government's predominant responsibility is to protect the country's interests, commercial and otherwise, which means expanding the American economy, which in turn means opening markets for American products. Using the September 11 attacks to do so was, as the French say, very American.

Of course, the Bushian view of things is simplistic. There are more choices than merely opening your country to globalization or succumbing to violent disintegration. Every country in the world imposes regulations to protect its national and cultural institutions, and the United States would too if its television networks were in danger of being overrun with an influx of vulgar Russian television shows dubbed into English. That is not about to happen. If it were – and if a midterm election required it – America would immediately find a way around its Constitutional amendment guaranteeing free speech and limit the presence of non-American productions on its airwaves. As it is, America is much more concerned with getting its films onto more screens overseas. The State Department regularly includes the limits on foreign film importation in its reports on the economies and trade practices of other countries; how many American films and TV shows can be sold where each year is of vital national interest, apparently. This telling bit comes from the State Department's report on Taiwan dated March 2000:

> Taiwan eased import restrictions on foreign film prints from 38 to 58 per title in late 1997. The number of theaters in any municipality allowed to show the same foreign film simultaneously also increased from 11 to 18. Effective August 1997, multi-screen theaters are

allowed to show a film on up to three screens simulta-
neously, up from the previous limit of one. Taiwan has
pledged to abolish these restrictions upon accession to
the WTO. In the cable TV market, concerns remain
that the island's two dominant Multi-System Operators
(MSOs) occasionally collude to inhibit fair competition.
Control by the two MSOs of upstream program distribution, for example, has made it difficult for U.S.
providers of popular channels to negotiate reasonable
fees for their programs.[8]

Another similar State Department trade-practices report
on India detailed how the U.S. government, on behalf of the
American film industry, has lobbied the Indian government to
ease restrictions on the importation of foreign films and on
foreign ownership of local broadcast companies. India is the
world's biggest producer of feature films in terms of sheer
quantity (as opposed to film budgets), churning out more than
eight hundred a year, compared with about five hundred a year
in the U.S. It is one market the United States entertainment
industry has yet to crack, as opposed to, say Canada, where the
top-ten-grossing films the week of May 17-23, 2002, were all
American blockbusters; or Japan, where nine out of ten were
American.[9] The selling of American entertainment abroad is
clearly as much of a preoccupation for the government as the
selling of arms and computers. Governments around the
world are under constant pressure to make sure U.S. film and
TV companies are allowed in unfettered by nationalistic
worries about culture and identity. In the American view of
things, there can be no freedom until people everywhere are
able to watch *Married . . . With Children* every night and their
multiplexes are showing *Spider-Man* on all ten of their screens
on the movie's opening weekend.

This insensitivity is aggravated by the fact that half of the five hundred American movies that get churned out each year are bad, if not terrible. U.S. films are no longer, for the most part, works of art. They do not even aspire to that lofty goal – they are product, pure and simple. The *Economist* reported in its issue of May 11, 2002, that major releases such as *Spider-Man* rely on theatre-ticket sales for only 20 per cent of their total revenues. Four-fifths of a blockbuster's income is now generated by video, DVD, and pay-TV sales; from product placements in the movie (Spider-Man prefers Dr. Pepper when he works up a thirst battling crime); and from the sales of games, action figures, school bags, fast-food meals, and other related spinoffs.[10] American movies are merely the tip of a gigantic marketing iceberg; all they are required to do is create excitement that will result in big ticket sales on the first weekend of their release, and induce children to pressure their parents to buy the spinoff junk. Few producers of these films even have the courage of their convictions; before their release, the movies are shown to focus groups that judge whether the characters are adequately appealing and the ending satisfyingly uplifting. Endings are changed and characters are dropped, or given more prominence, based on the focus groups' reactions.[11] Judging by the films being released, Americans require movies that finish with the so-called Hollywood ending – hero saves the day and gets girl, and all moral quandaries are resolved. Better yet if the film is based on a book, comic book, television show, or original film that has already proven itself to be popular, and whose pre-established saleability makes it all that much easier to market the rip-off version. The most heavily marketed films of 2001 and 2002 were those that came from the world of bestselling books, comics, and Saturday-morning television cartoons: *Lord of the Rings: The Fellowship of the Ring, Harry Potter and the Philosopher's Stone, Spider-Man, Scooby-Doo, Bridget Jones's Diary,* and *About a Boy* were among them. Another huge film of 2002 was the fifth installment of the well-established *Star Wars* saga, *Attack of the Clones.* Entirely original films with morally ambiguous or depressing endings that are allowed to get to the theatre do not make money, for the most part, or are relegated to art-house screens. Meanwhile, reliably upbeat and pro-American films such as *The Majestic* (2001) and *A Beautiful Mind* (2001) are trumpeted as Academy Award–winning classics, even though they are remarkable only for the amount of gossip their stars can generate and the banality of their dialogue.

In the last ten years or so, the most unrelentingly bad American movies were the so-called comedies. These disturbingly poor efforts were not comedies but in fact charmless exercises in puerile humour that relied heavily on bodily discharges to generate laughs. The success of *There's Something About Mary,* which was at least original to some degree, was understood by Hollywood to be encouragement to make even grosser movies in which lengthy close-ups of people in mid-bowel-movement were merely a tame foreshadowing of the really bad things to come later.

Again, marketing was the key to the success of such films, a fact that became even more apparent in June 2001 when one studio, Sony, was caught faking positive movie reviews on its newspaper advertisements and posters. The giant corporation invented a reviewer named David Manning of the *Ridgefield Press,* which happened to be a real newspaper in Connecticut. When the paper said it had no reviewer by that name, Sony admitted it had invented David Manning, as well as his praise for the film *A Knight's Tale* and at least three other films. In its defence, Sony claimed such things were standard practice in the industry, as indeed they were. Other companies were subsequently caught faking newspaper reviews, as well as getting employees to pose as the enthusiastic "fans" of their movies for television commercials, and then yet more companies admitted to doing the same thing. In March 2002, Sony agreed to pay a $326,000 fine to the state of Connecticut and to ban the practice.

And this is the film industry to which the people of other countries, at the expense of their own cultural identities, must grant unlimited access to their theatres in order to ensure freedom and prevent terrorism. They are not even getting American culture in exchange, at least not in the sense that the films represent day-to-day life in the United States. What they are getting is the cinematic equivalent of rice cakes – a mass-produced generic product that, because of its basic blandness, relies on marketing and special effects to generate any appeal. Do you prefer yours with caramel, cheese flavouring, or plain?

The same criticism applies to the American popular-music industry, which also relies on marketing, not talent, to make money. The country that created jazz, blues, and rock and roll still produces music of terrific originality and beauty – the band Wilco immediately comes to mind – but most people will never know that. Instead, American music is dominated by manufactured "artists" who must produce immediate hits, or die trying. Britney Spears, *NSYNC, the Backstreet Boys – these are the people who win the awards for their songs and videos. To be fair, they are not altogether terrible, but, like American studio-made movies, they don't represent any kind of living culture; they are a prefabricated image that has been tested with, and approved by, the necessary focus groups. The music is empty of everything except noisy clichés about love, sex, and violence; the accompanying videos are a series of poses (pouty close-up; defiant stance in the rain; heartfelt casting downwards of eyes; wide-shot dance sequence; rebellious moment of indifference to fact singer is in a video) that are edited to flash by at such a quick pace that trying to interpret them is pointless. They exist only to be quickly fired into the brains of teenagers without causing thought.

Wilco, meanwhile, is a very thought-provoking band led by a singer, Jeff Tweedy, determined to pay tribute to the best in American folk music and poetry while experimenting with contemporary sounds and textures. For that, and for the sin of completing a new album that did not contain a marketable radio hit, Wilco was coldly dropped by its label in 2001. This came on the heels of a previous work, *Summerteeth*, that is considered by critics to be a modern American masterpiece and that sold well for the label, Reprise Records. That previous success, as well as the efforts by Wilco to be true to its vision, meant nothing, however, in an American music industry that puts much more emphasis on "industry" than on "music." As *Rolling Stone* magazine reported about the Wilco saga:

> Consolidation in the music industry has forced executives to think even more about instant success and less about long-term growth. Patience for artists to develop was running thin at Reprise. The label had been folded into the AOL Time Warner empire, which was cutting overhead in recent years, laying off more than 600 employees and dropping bands that weren't selling. [David] Kahne, a veteran producer who has worked with Sublime, Romeo Void and Paul McCartney, considered each act song by song rather than taking the long-term view. "Records with songs on the radio sell

better as a rule," he says. "The flavor of the record company has a lot to do with its heritage, but at the same time it's a changing company." And that means hits, now.[12]

Wilco eventually signed with another label after the new album, called *Yankee Hotel Foxtrot*, drew tremendous response on the Internet. The new label, Nonesuch, was also owned by AOL Time Warner. This indecision and poor management is symptomatic of a nation that does not know how to celebrate talent that is not attached to celebrity. Until someone is famous, or causes a scandal, their worth as an American artist, actor, singer, or writer remains unnoticed by the mass market.

Railing against the paucity of artistic integrity in the American entertainment industry and its ubiquitous influence on the rest of the world can seem rather pointless, of course. All imperial nations throughout history, from Greece to Rome to France and England, have sown their values in foreign soil. The received wisdom has always been that imperialism brought with it prosperity and peace. Globalization, a non-nation-specific form of imperialism – the imperious spread of multinational, stateless capitalism – is similarly seen as a magic pill whose soothing properties are known to cause an outbreak of democracy. Who would not want that? But because of the United States' domination of the entertainment and lifestyles industries, "globalization" is barely distinguishable from "Americanization." It feels to many not like a two-way street but a one-way path to the American values that can be seen every night on *Mork & Mindy*, *Magnum P.I.*, *Batman*, *Beverly Hills 90210*, *Scooby-Doo*, and professional wrestling, all shows that a correspondent for the *Atlantic Monthly* magazine watched in Kazan, the capital city of Tatarstan, a Russian republic located about eight hundred kilometres (five hundred miles) east of Moscow, in early 2002.[13] The writer also discovered a Reebok running-shoe store and a McDonald's restaurant in Kazan, and went to a theatre where three American movies were playing, along with one French one. He visited strip clubs and bars with names like The Manhattan Club. The writer was pleased to report on the presence of what he called "Western pleasures," although, other than the French movie, all the "Western" pleasures he mentioned were, in fact, American. He did not spot anyone playing pétanque and drinking Ricard; there was no one drinking Molson Canadian beer and playing road hockey; there is no description of a German beer hall or English pub. All we find in Kazan that is out of the ordinary is American television, American fast food, American cigarettes, and American soft drinks. "It is exactly this sort of market-driven secularism," the writer concludes triumphantly, "that many Muslim clerics fear – and with good reason."

Muslim clerics may rightly fear it but, in the hands of the right Muslim reactionary or terrorist leader, McDonald's and its ilk are useful tools in the cultivation of anti-American sentiment. Bad-tasting food prepared in haste and indifference is hardly a sign of cultural superiority; the same goes for soulless, violent, unfunny films. These things can be more aptly interpreted as a testament to the weakness of a culture. The same goes for expensive running shoes sold with the endorsement of sports celebrities whose annual incomes are beyond the imaginations of the people who stitch the shoes together in poor countries. In Saudi Arabia in May 2002, citizens began to boycott American outlets such as McDonald's to protest the U.S. government's support of Israel in its war with Palestine. In Iran in March 2002, a government agency began selling a boy-and-girl doll set called Dara and Sara to counter the high sales of Ken and Barbie dolls in that country. The traditionally robed dolls were developed by the Institute for the

Intellectual Development of Children and Young Adults, a branch of the Education Ministry. Toy-store owners were quoted as saying they welcomed the dolls because Barbie's clothes were revealing and therefore "wanton." "I think every Barbie doll is more harmful than an American missile," one store owner told the BBC.[14]

Exported American culture is as much an irritant as a sign of modernity in foreign countries, and the United States' indifference to that fact, and to the difficulties it causes the governments of those countries, only makes it worse. America pushes and pushes against foreign trade barriers until they are removed, while all the while hypocritically maintaining its own barriers. It insists on the liberalization of markets in developing countries, which can lead to sudden influxes of speculative "hot" money that disappears as quickly as it appears, leaving countries in financial crisis and more impoverished than before.[15] It unabashedly uses its lone veto on the International Monetary Fund to turn the IMF's agenda in favour of American interests. Other nations' tastes, values, and culture are irrelevant to this arrangement, and thus are not given enough time to adjust to the effects of American-led globalization. Countries that protest against globalization are lectured about democracy; Americans who protest are, since September 11, 2001, apt to be equated with terrorists. It has become un-American, and thus undemocratic, to believe in a developing nation's right to manage its economic destiny, or even to progress at a slower pace than globalization's advocates insist upon.

The first thing Afghans living under the Taliban regime did when that regime fell was go to the movies and listen to music in public, activities that had been banned until then. People everywhere want the same freedoms; the hunger for popular culture is not limited to one nation. But the culture satisfying that hunger has to match the appetite. People are not wrong to insist on the primacy of their culture within their own borders – especially when the culture trying the hardest to invade those borders can be so unappetizing, and even toxic.

THIRTEEN

THE SUPERSIZING
OF AMERICA

You want fries with that?
  – A FAST-FOOD CATCH-PHRASE

Americans are a corpulent lot. It is not so noticeable in the better neighbourhoods of big cities like New York and Los Angeles, where urban chic requires a uniform thinness, but step into the poorer quarters, the countryside, and smaller cities and it immediately becomes apparent that the people of the United States are as fleshy as a force-fed goose in France, their livers as unhealthy as that of the doomed bird. Statistics bear out this impression: the U.S. Surgeon General estimated that 61 per cent of adults in the country were overweight or medically obese[1] in 1999, while 13 per cent of children and 14 per cent of adolescents were in the same overloaded boat.[2] There are an estimated 51,000,000 obese American adults.[3] The population figure for the U.S. (287,042,660[4]) does not do justice to the mass of humanity jiggling across the country; in terms of weight alone, Americans are more likely equal to a population of 400,000,000. The sheer yardage of Spandex, denim, and sweatpant material required to hide that much skin boggles the mind.

But this is the land where the majority rules, and the majority is overweight. America, in its inimitable fashion, has consequently declared fatness to be beautiful – sexy, even – a marked change from the country's obsession with thinness, jogging, and well-being during the 1970s. There are television sitcoms and talk-shows that feature large men and women in starring roles (*The Drew Carey Show, The View*); the stars often develop and market clothing lines for overweight people and become spokesmen for the tubby majority. There is a National Association to Advance Fat Acceptance (NAAFA), whose "Hall of Fame" includes Babe Ruth, Louis Armstrong, Miss Piggy, and Buddha. There is an American Obesity Association, whose Web site declares that, "Obesity is not a simple condition of eating too much. It is now recognized that obesity is a serious, chronic disease. No human condition – not race, religion, gender, ethnicity or disease state – compares to obesity in prevalence and prejudice, mortality and morbidity, sickness and stigma."[5]

There are magazines, such as *Dimensions*, dedicated to the virtues of "BBWs" – an apparently well-understood acronym for "big, beautiful women." There is even a BBW magazine, whose motto is "The Power of Plus." There are Web sites with names like livinglargeinc.com that offer modelling jobs to overweight women and urge them to be proud of their size. There are pornographic Web pages where extremely fat women perform all the same graphic sex acts reserved for the svelte and saline-enhanced on mainstream porn sites. With more than half American women wearing size twelve and up, stores dedicated to "plus-size" shoppers are becoming as ubiquitous as regular clothing stores; mainstream designers including Liz Claiborne and Ralph Lauren have jumped on board and now produce fashions specifically for larger men and women.[6]

And then there are the lawsuits, twenty-one listed on the NAAFA Web site alone, brought by overweight Americans against employers, transportation companies, and governments deemed to have discriminated against BBWs and fat men. Many of the cases outlined on the NAAFA Web site pertain to men and women, some of whom clock in at more than 135 kilos (300 pounds), who have been fired from jobs or refused employment on the basis of their size. Employers in the United States often provide health insurance to employees, a highly prized and expensive benefit in a country that does not have socialized medicine, which explains companies' reluctance to add extremely overweight (and often unhealthy) people to their group policies. It is a losing battle for employers, though; there are now a number of states that have ruled that obesity is a disability, making it an offence to discriminate on that basis. In California, there are law firms that handle nothing but cases brought by the morbidly obese, cases that often deal with the denial of health-insurance coverage for bariatric surgery, the complicated but usually successful operations to shrink patients' stomachs so that they feel fuller more quickly and consequently eat less.[7]

In short, being overweight in America has become so routine that its non-acceptance has become a civil rights issue. It is officially recognized as a disease by the federal government, which pays out $77 million a month in social security payments to some 137,000 obese people whose condition prevents them from working.[8] In some states, a firefighting department can no sooner refuse a job tryout to a slow-moving man of 160 kilograms (350 pounds) than it can to a healthy, capable one on the basis of his religion or sexual orientation. Some welcome this development, as in some small way it is a refreshing counterpoint to the fashion and film industries' obsessions with women who are so skinny their bony shoulders, as Cintra Wilson once described them in an article on Salon.com, look like the knuckles of a hand. Who wants to eat a vegan diet, free of all the gastronomic pleasures available to mankind, just so they can wear size-one dresses that reveal every single tendon under their skin? And anyway, how can anyone maintain a fat-free, well-conditioned physique, given the working hours North Americans impose upon themselves?

What this overlooks, as the American Obesity Association puts it, is that obesity is a "major epidemic"[9] in the United States. Obesity leads directly to more than three hundred thousand deaths a year and perhaps as many as four hundred thousand – a mortality rate similar to or greater than that caused by tobacco-related diseases. Put another way, obesity kills as many as one out of every six or seven Americans who die each year, including the ones brought down by old age, accident, and foul play.[10] Only in this case the killer is not a recognized and vilified poison, like cigarettes, but something considered to be virtuous – the American diet.

Americans have forgotten how to eat. Worse, they have destroyed food, rendering it not a provider of life but an agent of destruction. During the 2002 Winter Olympics in Salt Lake City, Utah, the deputy sports minister of Belarus found himself obliged to complain about the steady diet of hamburgers and prefabricated sandwiches the organizers had made available to his country's athletes. "Our sportsmen . . . need normal meat, fresh fruit juices, hot soup," the minister told Reuters. His disgust at the American diet is understandable: there is an argument to be made that a large percentage of the products on sale in American supermarkets and restaurants should be labelled the way cigarettes are – with warnings that their unchecked consumption can cause disease and death. In the United States, processed food kills.

A book published in 2002 made plain the extent to which diet has changed the way people die in the United States. Marion Nestle's *Food Politics: How the Food Industry Influences Nutrition and Health* outlines the evolution of death in America between 1900 and 2000. A table of the ten chief causes of death in 1900 lists, in descending order, tuberculosis, pneumonia, diarrheal diseases, heart disease, liver disease, injuries, stroke, cancer, bronchitis, and diphtheria.[11] Many of these were poorly understood communicable diseases brought about by, among other things, harsh working conditions, lack of treatment, and poor nutrition. The United States Department of Agriculture, created in 1862 to ensure a stable food supply for America, took it upon itself at the end of the nineteenth century to provide dietary advice thought to prolong the lives of Americans, a role it has maintained ever since. Combined with better sanitation, medicine, and housing, the improved diets recommended by the USDA increased the average life expectancy of Americans from forty-seven years in 1900 to seventy-seven in 2000.

Now, it seems, the American diet is undoing those other advances. One hundred years later, after the introduction of processed foods – and, in the last twenty-five years, the proliferation of fast-food restaurants – the top-ten American killers, in order, are heart disease, cancer, stroke, lung disease, accidents, pneumonia and influenza, diabetes, suicide, kidney disease, and liver disease. Seven of the top-ten modern causes of death are now directly relatable to diet and nutrition, Nestle writes. These are diseases that can be prevented, or whose genetically predetermined onset can be delayed, through proper nutrition and, more significantly, by eating less. The problem is that, as Nestle says, "Advice to eat less . . . runs counter to the interests of food producers."[12]

The United States food industry is a behemoth. Seven of

the world's ten largest food companies are American (the largest is the Swiss company Nestlé, to which Marion Nestle has no connection).[13] They compete fiercely for customers and churn out masses of products that rely on marketing, pricing, taste, and convenience – not nutritional value – as selling points. A trip to an American grocery store can stagger people from other countries. There are dozens of brands of peanut butter alone; the choice of breads can take an entire aisle to itself; the same goes for soda pop and potato chips. In 1998 alone, American companies came out with eleven thousand new products,[14] the vast majority of which were snacks and baked goods. The president, George W. Bush, nearly choked to death on a pretzel while watching a football game at the White House in January 2002, a much-reported event that most likely further increased the respect average Americans had for him in the months after September 11. More than ever, he was one of them.

In 2001, America's total production of hamburgers, frozen pizzas, cake, meats, eggs, soft drinks, snacks, chocolate bars, cereals – of all the stuff lining grocery store shelves and available at restaurants and fast-food outlets – was roughly the equivalent of twice as many calories as required for its citizens to carry out "normal human activity."[15] The U.S. population could have doubled overnight and no one would have gone hungry. More significantly, this glut forces competition, Nestle points out. With supply outstripping demand, or at least need, food companies must do everything they can to win customers. Coca-Cola and Taco Bell are in American public high schools, selling nutritionless, high-caloric soft drinks to students, and producing their high-fat fast-food lunches. The companies' advertisements are all over the television, flogging their fatty and sugar-laden products during children's shows and in prime time.[16] Their lobbyists were in

Washington pushing Congress for more subsidies and using the image of the struggling family farmer, an American icon, to sway public opinion, even though most products sold in supermarkets come from giant factory farms that bear no resemblance to the traditional family operation. The election-oriented farm subsidy bill that Bush signed in May 2002, a bill whose pretzel logic infuriated the rest of the world and seemed an act of hypocrisy on the part of a leader who had vowed to push for freer global trade, was merely another acknowledgment of the food industry's influence.

Nestle writes that the food industry's lobbying extends beyond the demand for subsidies and into the realm of regulations that allow them to present their products in the best possible light. She lays out in detail how pressure from the meat industry prompted the USDA to change its perfectly good advice to "eat less meat" to the more positive-sounding "choose lean meats."[17] Meats in general, many of which are high in saturated fats that can cause heart disease and other problems, are now billed as "lean" products. Breakfast cereals are allowed to say they are "part of a nutritious breakfast" because their otherwise minimal nutritional content is enhanced with a half-dozen "essential" vitamins and are meant to be served with orange juice and toast, both of which are actually nutritious. Thanks to the fact it contains calcium, an important mineral found in many other food products, milk is sold as an indispensable health food, even though it is not essential to a nutritious diet and can actually cause health problems in people over the age of five.[18] Juice manufacturers are permitted to make the claim their products contain "real fruit" when in fact they merely contain added sugars made from fruit sources. Perhaps the most ridiculous of all, soft drinks, which contain not a single redeeming nutritional quality, now boast that they are "fat-free." Gasoline is fat-free, too, but you wouldn't drink it.

Marion Nestle's book leaves the reader with the impression that food in America is no longer food at all. It is a series of branded products designed to make life convenient for a society in which people are both too busy to prepare meals at home and are misinformed about the nutritional value of the prepared foods and restaurant meals they rely on for more than half of their diet. The constant regulatory lobbying of the food industry has created confusion about what is good for you and what is bad. One decade, eggs are a deadly source of cholesterol and to be avoided; the next, they are a sexily marketed source of protein. One minute, fat is bad for you; the next, only some fats are bad while others are essential to health. What has been lost is the ability and desire to produce home-cooked meals containing fresh and healthy products that follow the seasons, along with an understanding of how much food should be eaten.

As a result, Americans simply eat far too much for the amount of activity they undertake. Nestle, in a research paper co-authored with Lisa Young, demonstrates that restaurant portions, in particular those served by fast-food outlets, as well as the portions of prepared foods, have grown steadily in America since the 1970s, "in parallel with increasing body weights."[19]

> In contrast to practices that were common just 15 to 25 years ago, food companies now use larger sizes as selling points (e.g., Double Gulp, Supersize); fast-food companies promote larger items with signs, staff pins, and placemats; manufacturers of diet meals such as Lean Cuisine and Weight Watchers frozen dinners

advertise larger meal sizes; restaurant reviews refer to larger portions; and national chain restaurants promote large-sized items directly on menus. Restaurants are using larger dinner plates, bakers are selling larger muffin tins, pizzerias are using larger pans, and fast-food companies are using larger drink and french-fry containers. Identical recipes for cookies and desserts in old and new editions of classic cookbooks such as *Joy of Cooking* specify fewer servings, meaning that portions are expected to be larger. Another indicator of the trend toward larger portions is that automobile manufacturers have installed larger cup holders in new models to accommodate the larger sizes of drink cups.[20]

The proportions are staggering. 7-Eleven, a corner-store chain, sells a sixty-four-ounce (nearly two-litre) soft-drink container – a half-gallon pail of sugar water that alone provides one-third of the daily calories (800) a human needs to survive. The largest size of fast-food french fries contains 610 calories; there are giant chocolate bars with 680 calories. A "Supersized" fast-food meal can easily contain almost all the calories a person needs for one day's worth of activity; add to that breakfast and another meal, not to mention snacks, and there are Americans who consume the equivalent of three days' worth of food in a single day, each and every day.

Store-bought processed foods are also larger, cookies in particular. In 2002, the average biscuit serving was seven times heftier than the size recommended by the USDA.[21] American meal and snack portions have become obscene, a reality that complicates another worrisome trend – the relentless use of trans fatty acids in almost all processed foods. Trans fats are vegetable oils that have been chemically altered through a process of hydrogenation to become more solid and stable; in the process they produce trans fatty acids. These fats were designed to be an alternative to saturated fats, which are well-known to cause health problems. Products now boast of being "low in saturated fats," but they are not obliged under U.S. law to reveal how much trans fat they contain. Margarine is the best known trans fat, which is also known as "partially hydrogenated" and "hydrogenated" oil; trans fats are also prevalent in most manufactured baked goods, crackers, cereals, snacks, and frozen meals. The hydrogenation process is something about which scientists still knew very little in 2002, but there were by then a number of studies linking hydrogenated oils to heart attacks, obesity, cancer, and other diet-related problems. One study estimated that trans fatty acids are responsible for thirty thousand premature deaths in America every year. There were some scientists who were saying the human consumption of trans fats should be stopped entirely; at the very least, they said, food products that contain them should carry warnings about their dangers, an idea supported by the U.S. Food and Drug Administration but still not implemented in spring 2002.

The final complicating factor is the sedentary lifestyle of a large percentage of the American population. The Surgeon General reports that fewer than one-third of American adults engages in the minimal amount of physical activity required to prevent weight gain, and 40 per cent get no exercise at all.[22] Children and adults in the United States spend an average of three to fours hours a day watching television, according to a number of studies on the subject. Television is considered so vital a part of American life that when a judge in New York sentenced a sixty-year-old fraud artist to ten months of home detention without television, his lawyers appealed on Constitutional grounds.[23] The Surgeon General's recommendations for battling obesity include watching less television, a pastime that induces snacking and idleness and exposes children to advertising for junk food; there are studies that show watching less TV – even thirty minutes less a day – and doing something active instead will result in weight loss.

Americans also sit and stare at computer screens both at home and at work. In poorer areas, where obesity is more prevalent, there are few if any organized sports activities for children. Anyone with children knows that, short of a genetic disposition to portliness, it is very difficult to fatten up a child, let alone make them obese, because they are so active and their metabolism is on fire as they grow. But Americans somehow do it to one in six of their children.

This American abundance of corpulence would be less noteworthy were it not spreading to other countries around the globe at a frightening pace. Canada, the country most familiar with the American diet, has been hit with its own child-obesity epidemic. The *Canadian Medical Association Journal* reported in November 2000 that the percentage of boys who were overweight jumped from 15 in 1981 to 35.4 in 1996, while the percentage of overweight girls went from 15 to 29.2; the rate of childhood obesity tripled in the same period, from 5 per cent to 16.6 per cent for boys, and from 5 per cent to 14.6 per cent for girls.[24]

France, noted for its people's ability to consume vast quantities of pastries and cheeses without gaining weight, has been hit with a similar epidemic since the arrival of American fast-food chains in the 1980s. There is now a French knockoff of McDonald's called Quick on every corner, from which issue tired parents chasing children hopped up on grease and sugar, and who carry the plastic trinkets such chains use to lure families in. A study released in 2002 revealed that the number of medically obese people in France had tripled in three years, to 17 per cent of the population.[25] Researchers blamed the weight gain on a increased consumption of animal fats and a decrease in healthier foods served in traditional French fare. They also blamed a decline in the quality and freshness of food served in restaurants as owners cut corners to compete with fast-food chains – in short, an Americanization of eating habits and trends. Today, every pharmacy in Paris advertises weight-reduction products and dubious anti-cellulite creams in their windows where once they pitched suntan lotions and perfumes.

The American Obesity Association has identified obesity as an international epidemic[26] that is transmitted through globalization, or at least through the prosperity and modernization brought by freer trade. The World Health Organization has identified the same troubling development and provides a name for it – "globesity."[27] It reports that, "In 1995, there were an estimated 200-million obese adults worldwide and another 18-million under-five children classified as overweight. As of 2000, the number of obese adults has increased to over 300-million." In some developing countries, obesity now coexists with terrible malnutrition, as the upper classes adjust to a more sedentary way of life, start driving cars, and forgo their traditional diets in favour of faster and faster foods, while the poorer sectors of the economy continue to struggle with too much work and not enough calories. Some native populations in developing countries suddenly display genetic dispositions to obesity after being exposed to American diets, resulting in serious health problems for people with little or no access to good medical care.

Once again, globalization means Americanization. The people in developing countries in Southeast Asia are not being exposed to a French diet or Italian diet. What they are getting is the American diet – oversized fast-food meals and processed foods high in trans fats; meals of low nutritional value that offer convenience in exchange for health, a loss of touch with the rhythm of the seasons and local produce, and the destruction of whatever relationship exists between their culture and their food.

The people suffering the most from this, though, are Americans themselves, who have become confounded by the contradictory nutrition and diet advice coming from every corner of the food industry. At times it seems like the only thing to do is throw in the towel and supersize one's life. We are all going to die anyway, so why worry? But if that is the case, why die eating bad food? In the end, that is the worst part of the American diet – its joylessness. Cramming over-salted potato chips or french fries cooked in lard into one's mouth and washing them down with an 800-calorie pail of Coke seems a rather dull way to go; a stroke induced by a steady intake of fresh butter, well-aged meats, and fine wines seems much preferable. The American diet does not send the message to other countries that they are dealing with a superior intellect. Rather, it reinforces the notion that all the United States of America has going for it is its substantial weight and its willingness to throw it around.

FOURTEEN

A NATION OF
ACTION FIGURES

Who doubts that America is strong? But that's not all America has to be.
– SUSAN SONTAG, *THE NEW YORKER*, SEPTEMBER 24, 2001

On May 11, 2002, the Paris edition of the *International Herald Tribune* reported that George W. Bush, president of the United States of America and resolute commander of the war on terrorism, was going to spend the rest of the spring and summer focusing on domestic issues. This qualified as big news, even in Paris. In January, Bush's top advisers had told him his Manichaean handling of the war on terrorism would be enough to bring the Republican Party victory in critical midterm elections in November 2002. Then an internal Republican poll was telling these same advisers that Americans were now more concerned with mundane issues like the economy and education. "We need more than just taxes/terrorism to win," Republicans were told in a confidential briefing report that accompanied the poll. The *Herald Tribune* quoted the person who conducted the poll as saying, "American memories last a nanosecond. We are moving beyond a world shaped by September 11 into the world of a much more characteristic off-year election. Which means you have to address issues of concern here at home."[1]

A week later, the White House shifted direction again after media reports revealed President Bush had been briefed by his intelligence agencies on August 6, 2001, about the likelihood of hijackings in the United States by Al-Qaeda operatives. Washington officials were "in a funk over ominous warnings of an imminent, major terrorist attack" in July and August, according to one newspaper article.[2] The FBI had arrested Zacarias Moussaoui, a French citizen of Moroccan descent, on August 16, 2001, after he paid $6,800 in cash for flight-simulator training, but the Bureau failed to link his activities to a report dated July 10 from an agent in Arizona in which the agent warned that Al-Qaeda operatives appeared to have enrolled in flights schools across the U.S.[3]

After the attacks, it also came to light in the American media, which apparently now felt safe questioning a president they had shielded from examination only months earlier, that U.S. intelligence officials knew that hijackers might use commercial planes as missiles against American targets, including the White House and the Pentagon. The atrocities of September 11 had not been unimaginable after all, despite claims to the contrary by the Bush administration.

Faced with bad press about his country's disastrous intelligence failures and the possibility his Republican Party would be held to account in the November midterm elections, Bush and his advisers went on the counterattack. They jogged Americans' weak memories about September 11, and the dangerous new world America now inhabited, in an overt attempt to prevent the government's pre-attack complacency from becoming a political liability. In a series of interviews and press conferences, Bush's officials, including the vice president and high-ranking military personnel, announced solemnly that more terrorist attacks on U.S. continental soil were inevitable. It was not a question of *if*, but *when*, they said. One official even raised the spectre of Palestinian-style suicide bombings in crowded American malls and streets. Bush himself travelled to Europe to remind allies of their stake in the war on terrorism. "In this war we defend not just America or Europe," he told the German parliament. "We are defending civilization itself."[4]

Thus, the world was different after September 11, but American politics were ever the same. Seven months after what had been described as a nation-altering, historic moment, the attacks were just another political football being punted around Washington, D.C. The Democrats pushed for and got congressional hearings into the failings of the American intelligence community. The FBI, so disorganized before the attacks, pre-emptively announced it was reorganizing its priorities. Priority number one would be fighting terrorism.

In the background of this political noise was the most obvious evidence that life had returned to normal in the United States – self-serving hypocrisy. President Bush's high-minded declarations about good and evil, and his calls to the nobler purpose of defending civilization, masked much baser American goals: securing oil routes in the Caspian Sea and South America, increasing the nation's already gigantic military budget, establishing new military bases in key regions, strengthening its military presence in the Pacific and East Asia, continuing its hegemony in the Middle East, and further reducing resistance to free trade in untapped foreign markets.

If the year were 1942, it might have been easy to support the president when he spoke of good versus evil. But in the twenty-first century, it is hard to preserve one's faith in the United States' claims to honourable intentions, or to its insistence that it is "defending civilization." Even a brief examination of the past fifty years of U.S. history has made it clear to me that the American government used the events that nearly robbed me of my sister to further its overseas agenda, expand its influence, and prevent criticism of its plans to launch retaliatory strikes. It has failed to address the issues that created Osama bin Laden in the first place. It has more than failed on that score: it has made it impossible for others of good faith to do so without being equated with the terrorists, thereby inflicting a painful silence on the global majority. As a consequence, the world was a safer place in the spring of 2002 only to the extent that American military retaliation had disrupted the activities of Al-Qaeda. In all other ways, the world was less safe. America's self-interested, hypocritical reaction to the attacks was destined to aggravate the tensions that produced the terrorism in the first place. The war on terrorism might capture more Al-Qaeda members, but the expansion of American bases in the Middle East, Southeast Asia, East Asia, and elsewhere will inevitably create new recruits. There may well be suicide bombings in shopping malls and more hijackings and other atrocities in New York, in Los Angeles, in Chicago, because America is still blithely feeding the frustration and anger against itself.

If I am angry with the United States government, I still feel sorrow for what Americans went through that day. In addition to the personal loss of their loved ones, Americans, who have all the right instincts about life and liberty, have been forced to question every assumption they ever had about their security. It is perhaps impossible for anyone but an American citizen to understand just how unsettling this is. America is a country that, to a pathological degree, has long considered itself to be invulnerable and heroic. Americans don't just love their country, they see it as a modern Mount

Olympus, the official address of the gods, and they cannot understand why others don't see it that way, too. Much of this stems from the religious fundamentalism discussed in an earlier chapter. But even moderate Americans who are aware of all the atrocities and all the betrayals of democracy committed in their name will, at some point in any conversation about their country, fall back on the notion that theirs is history's greatest and noblest nation. It is a fascinating aspect of American life.

Henry Kissinger, in his book *Diplomacy*, traces this blind faith back to the beginnings of the United States of America. People who don't understand why the U.S. thinks itself superior to its European forerunners (rather than remaining respectfully subservient, as Canada does) should remember that the America was meant from the start to be the anti-Europe – a nation where the people, not kings, ruled. Its founders were also determined to live on a part of the planet where war was not a regular event created by the necessity to balance the powers of suspicious, tightly packed neighbours. Alone on its side of the world, with a continent all to itself and gigantic oceans serving as moats on either side, the U.S. always wanted to follow its own course. Its leaders decided early on that their new nation would not, in George Washington's words, "implicate ourselves, by artificial ties, in the ordinary vicissitudes of [European] politics, or the ordinary combinations and collisions of her friendships and enmities. Our detached and distant situation invites and enables us to pursue a different course."[5] Kissinger, a geopolitical pragmatist who believes nations should pursue their interests without shame, sentiment, or conscience, explains in bemused tones how Washington's vision of a "detached and distant" stance turned into a quasi-religious calling complete with missionary undertones.

As a repository of the principle of liberty, America found it natural to interpret the security conferred on it by great oceans as a sign of divine providence, and to attribute its actions to superior moral insight instead of to a margin of security not shared by any other nation.[6]

Using that as a starting point, successive American leaders came to the conclusion that the greatest contribution their country could make to the rest of the world would be to spread its democratic values, an ambition no less grandiose than that of any imperial power that came before it. America considered its expansion across the entire continental U.S.A. as its "manifest destiny," a divine inevitability that extended into Mexico, Central America, and its island protectorates. Believing itself morally superior to the European nations, it considered its actions in other countries to be above criticism, "turning itself into a Great Power without being required to practice power politics. America's desire for expansion and its belief that it was a more pure and principled country than any other in Europe never clashed."[7]

The greatest test of this dogma came at the start of the First World War, Kissinger writes. Americans felt no desire to go to war on behalf of their distant European motherland, even if their interests were at stake. Sending soldiers to Europe did not hold any missionary appeal. Woodrow Wilson, the president, was aware that it was in his country's interests to prevent the rise of a single European power, but also knew he could not stir the American public into battle with that argument alone.

Wilson grasped that America's instinctive isolationism could be overcome only by an appeal to its belief in the exceptional nature of its ideals. Step by step, he took an isolationist country into war, after he had first demonstrated his Administration's devotion to peace by a passionate advocacy of neutrality. And he did so while abjuring any selfish national interests, and by affirming that America sought no other benefit than vindication of its principles.[8]

In his next leap of logic, Wilson came to the conclusion that "the security of America was inseparable from the security of *all* the rest of mankind,"[9] an extraordinary conceit, which, in Wilson's view, meant "there was no essential difference between freedom for America and freedom for the world."[10] To further persuade his countrymen to go to war, Wilson demonized the German empire and insisted that peace could only come with total victory,[11] a good-versus-evil approach that has since become the major rhetorical characteristic of American foreign policy.

This, then, is the positive, pro-American way of looking at the country's role in the world – America as a nation that serves only the interests of democracy, national sovereignty, and freedom, never its own mercenary interests; a Great Power that would never inflict on another state that which it did not wish to have inflicted upon itself; one that is ready to sacrifice itself whenever a new evil arises. It is America as the Heroic Nation, the superpower as Superman.

A more accurate description, one construed in the U.S. as anti-Americanism, is that of the United States as an imperial power ruled by an aggressive business class whose interests the government protects mercilessly under the guise of higher callings, such as international security, the spread of democracy, the expansion of free markets, and the protection of human rights. Under this description, the United States is just another nineteenth-century colonial power, scheming to protect its borders and expand its commercial interests while insisting to itself and the world that its presence on foreign soils is the result of a divinely imposed moral obligation to bring civilization to the dark and savage natives of the planet's undemocratized corners.

This is not the way Americans have ever wanted to see themselves, or ever will. Americans need to believe their actions are selfless, their leaders heroic, their nation great, and their values universal. Otherwise, their very existence comes into doubt. Woodrow Wilson exposed his country's self-image when he boasted, "America is the only idealistic nation in the world."[12]

The rest of the world is grateful that there is a nation out there founded on ideals that are universally admired. The United States is not the world's oldest democracy, and certainly not the world's best-working one, but its existence has inspired downtrodden peoples around the globe and created an international consensus that countries are better off when their populations are not repressed. In that sense, Americans are deservedly proud, and their country's imperialism, like that of Europe before it, has brought some good to the world.

But, like the European powers that came before them, Americans are afflicted by a blindness that is a symptom of their elevated view of themselves. Like church leaders who ignore the sexual abuses committed by their clergy and weaken the credibility of organized religion, American leaders fail to see that they cannot preach democratic values and betray them at the same time without damaging the very idea of democracy. Hypocrisy is the most corrosive substance on earth; it can eat through the patina of a nation's ideals faster than rust can go through the floor of an old Buick. When the United States betrays democracy and freedom in Nicaragua, Chile, Guatemala, Iran, and North Korea, or in countless developing nations ruled by brutal despots who use anti-communism or anti-terrorism as plastic bait to lure in American support and weaponry, it corrodes the very notion of U.S.-style democracy as a superior way of life. You cannot sell the idea that liberty is precious and mock it at the same time. We live in a post-modern world, but not that post-modern. The devaluation of the currency of democracy by the United States is perhaps the darkest stain on that country's history. Democracy is no longer a secure investment when its most self-righteous supporter is prepared to subvert it on behalf of a fruit company. Under those circumstances, a strong, preferably benign, monarch may be a safer bet.

People always want solutions at the ends of books, but I have none to offer. The clichéd answer would be to say that America begins and ends with its people, and therefore it is up to them to demand better behaviour of their government. But Americans, judging by their voting habits, have lost confidence in their ability to change their government's course.

Another option might be to appeal to Americans' ingrained and admirable idealism, but that, too, seems to be waning. If America were truly a nation of idealists, it would stop selling arms to repressive regimes. If it were truly idealistic, then reporters who made fun of the president would be revered, not fired. A country built on ideals would never allow suspects – even possible terrorists – to be held for months without trial; its leaders' spokesmen would not warn people to watch what they say but, rather, encourage them to speak out. In an ideal country, the wealthy son of a former president would not be able to come to power in a dubious election with the help of a powerful brother and a partisan Supreme Court. Ideal republics do not give way to thinly disguised fiefdoms of the rich and powerful.

Given this, perhaps the solution is not a reinvigoration of American ideals, but their removal from the international conversation that September 11 created. My sister and her family, and the rest of us on the planet, are no safer now that the United States has declared a war on terrorism. It is more likely that we are more in danger of indiscriminate acts of violence than ever before, because if we are at war with terrorism, terrorism will fight back. It's an obvious equation and a frightening one for every country that allies itself with the United States. In November 2002, an audiotape recording said by American officials to be the voice of Osama bin Laden carried a direct threat of retaliation against Canada, Italy, Britain, and other countries that fought with the U.S. in Afghanistan. And we know this is no ordinary threat – the September 11 attacks were a clear warning of how cruel Al-Qaeda is willing to be, and how far it can reach.

Then again, the menace is just terrorism. The world is not threatened, as the United States insists, by an exterior force trying to bring an end to earthly civilization. Terrorism has reared its head before, and it has been defeated before by the concerted efforts of international intelligence services and police departments. It is a horror the nations of the world must deal with vigorously, but it is not something they should let dominate their relations or guide all their decision-making. In terms of strict self-interest – of national security policies that are not infected by American rhetoric – the rest of the world would be wise to examine the grievances behind the terrorists' actions, even if that were to go against the American government's agenda. It would be more realistic, and more useful, to frame the debate in unsentimental geopolitical terms, rather than in heroic American terms of good versus evil. It might not be ideal, but it just might work.

One might hope that if the United States were isolated in

this manner, it would abandon its juvenile pretensions to moral superiority. If Americans recognized that their country was just one more imperial power – if they abandoned the conceit that they represent political perfection – perhaps they would become more engaged in the world around them and less apt to look down upon it.

But how do you get a nation to show maturity when an event as massive as September 11 provokes a reinforcement of its misguided and abstract idealism, rather than a re-examination of its misguided and concrete behaviour? What can be done with a country that thinks it was attacked by terrorists because Muslim countries have not been adequately informed of how great the United States really is, and all that is required to rectify this is to pump more Britney Spears over Middle East airwaves, as a Senate hearing was told by an official in the State Department in June 2002?[13]

This is why I have no answers, and why I feel at a loss.

FIFTEEN

EPILOGUE:
THE "BULLY ON THE BLOCK"

There is no future in trying to challenge the armed forces of the United States.
    – COLIN POWELL, SPEAKING IN 1992

December 16, 2002, Toronto
The post–September 11 world continued to take shape in the weeks before Christmas 2002. As Christians prepared for one of their most important religious holidays and Muslims ended one of theirs, Ramadan, America's "war on terror" shifted its focus to Iraq. At the time, no one could say for certain whether Osama bin Laden was dead or alive; experts in voice recognition debated whether a taped message said to be that of the Al-Qaeda leader was real or faked, while the United States government insisted the recording was authentic. Several terrorist acts outside the U.S. were linked to Al-Qaeda, including the bombing of a nightclub in Bali that killed hundreds of people and a bombing and missile attack in Kenya that targeted Israelis. But the world's attention was focused on Iraq, where United Nations inspectors were searching for weapons of mass destruction in factories and palaces. The U.N. had adopted a resolution calling on Iraq to

disarm and submit to inspections, or face invasion. Saddam Hussein, seeking to expose weaknesses in the U.S.-led coalition behind the resolution, played along but drew out the process as long as possible. Every day brought news of another fruitless search, and the Iraqi government sent a twelve-thousand-page report on its arms production to the United Nations that it claimed was proof the country was not hiding biological, chemical, or nuclear weapons. There was a growing skepticism in international circles that the U.N. would find what it was looking for, but there was also a growing concern that the U.S. was going to invade Iraq regardless of the outcome of the inspections. You could feel it in the air; the United States was about to go to war again.

This time, though, it would be a war led by an America that officially intended to wield its vast armed forces to rule the world. President George W. Bush's rhetoric about the "axis of evil" and leaks to the media during the early part of 2002 by his administration officials that hinted at a new American foreign policy had become by the fall a co-ordinated effort to turn the September 11 tragedies to the advantage of the government's hawks. There can be little doubt any more that although the American people were not prepared for the arrival of terrorism on their shores, the Bush administration was.

The concrete proof came one year and ten days after the attacks, when the Bush administration released "The National Security Strategy of the United States," a policy document the president is required to submit to the American Congress.[1] The document renounced diplomacy as America's chief means of relating to the other nations of the world and replaced it with a monologue about absolute military dominance. The trial balloons floated in the *New Yorker* in April 2002 by Condoleezza Rice, Bush's national security adviser, and Richard Haass, the director of policy planning for the State

Department, to the effect that America was concerned with preventing the rise of a competing superpower, and that it would usurp the sovereignty of countries that did not show enough enthusiasm for America's war on terrorism, were the set-up for the new policy.[2] The punchline was delivered with the document's arrival in Congress: America told the world it would send its soldiers into any country or region it deemed to be a threat to its interests, both commercial and military. And, above all, the United States was determined to expand its military capabilities to such an extent it would be pointless for any other country, or group of countries acting in concert, to try to match it.

The strategy document is crystal clear about the United States' right to use its military might when and where the government of the day chooses. America, the document states, will "disrupt and destroy terrorist organizations," with a focus on "those terrorist organizations of global reach and any terrorist or state sponsor of terrorism which attempts to gain or use weapons of mass destruction or their precursors." As well, the government will defend "the United States, the American people and our interests at home and abroad by identifying and destroying the threat before it reaches our borders. While the United States will constantly strive to enlist the support of the international community, we will not hesitate to act alone, if necessary, to exercise our right to self-defense by acting pre-emptively: ... and denying further sponsorship, support and sanctuary to terrorists by convincing or compelling states to accept their sovereign responsibilities."[3]

The strategy document is equally clear about America's intention to remain absolutely, not relatively but absolutely, dominant in military terms: "The United States must and will maintain the capability to defeat any attempt by an enemy – whether a state or a non-state actor – to impose its will on the

United States, our allies, or our friends. We will maintain the forces sufficient to support our obligations, and to defend freedom. Our forces will be strong enough to dissuade potential adversaries from pursuing a military buildup in hopes of surpassing, or equaling, the power of the United States. . . ."[4]

The policy was backed by hard cash. The U.S. defence budget for 2003 was set at $380 billion, though it was sure to increase if the country invaded Iraq. The base amount was more than six times greater than that of Russia's defence budget and more than eight times that of China's.

The Bush administration's allies praised the strategy as bold and new; some were so blasé as to point out that America was merely making overt the policies it had carried out covertly in Iran, Nicaragua, Chile, and other unfortunate countries, and therefore no one should be alarmed. Critics saw the strategy the same way but with a different spin: as confirmation of the United States' hypocritical habit of acting underhandedly while claiming it respects the will of the international community and the values of democracy and freedom. What was ignored by virtually everyone who commented on the strategy document was the fact that this was not a new policy at all; it was, in fact, the culmination of efforts by leading members of Bush's administration who had worked with his father, George Bush Sr., during the latter's presidency from 1988 to 1992 to reinvigorate the American military following the collapse of the Soviet Union in 1991.

The end of the Cold War was a difficult moment for American hawks. They felt their country's interests were best served by the maintenance of massive military superiority over the rest of the world, but with the Soviet regime no longer a threat, public support for expensive weaponry began to wane. Taxpayers, emboldened by the prospect of living in a peaceful era, were not easily convinced their country needed to expand its muscle. This was a source of consternation for key Republican officials, most notably Dick Cheney, the senior Bush's secretary of defence, wrote David Armstrong in the October 2002 issue of *Harper's* magazine. Armstrong appears to have been the only American journalist who noticed that the language of the September 21, 2002, strategy document was a lightly diluted version of similar documents prepared by Cheney and other principal Bush officials, including Colin Powell, during the 1990s but never acted upon. What was written in that period was the precursor of the argument the second Bush administration would put forward ten years later.

Armstrong recounted how Powell and Cheney teamed up at the beginning of the 1990s to try to convince Congress of the need for the United States to maintain its armed forces at Cold War levels, and even to expand them. Armstrong wrote:

> In early 1992 . . . a new logic entered into their appeals. The United States, Powell told members of the House Armed Services Committee, required "sufficient power" to "deter any challenger from ever dreaming of challenging us on the world stage." To emphasize the point, he cast the United States in the role of street thug. "I want to be the bully on the block," he said, implanting in the mind of potential opponents that "there is no future in trying to challenge the armed forces of the United States."[5]

A classified Pentagon policy statement from 1992 known as the Defense Planning Guidance (DPG) reiterated the idea that the United States should "prevent any hostile power from dominating a region," Armstrong also reported. It urged the U.S. government to convince its allies that they did not need to expand their militaries because American combatants would be there to protect their interests for them.[6] The policy statement furthermore developed the notion of pre-emptive strikes against groups or nations building weapons of mass destruction; the strikes would punish aggressors "through a variety of means."[7] And it outlined America's determination to go it alone when its allies failed to support its incursions onto foreign soil to protect its interests. Armstrong continued:

> While coalitions – such as the one formed during the Gulf War – held "considerable promise for promoting collective action," the draft DPG stated, the United States should expect future alliances to be "ad hoc assemblies, often not lasting beyond the crisis being confronted, and in many cases carrying only general agreement over the objectives to be accomplished." It was essential to create "the sense that the world order is ultimately backed by the U.S." and essential that American position itself "to act independently when collective action cannot be orchestrated."[8]

Armstrong noted that among the interests the U.S. would be prepared to defend unilaterally were, as stated in the DPG, "access to vital raw materials, primarily Persian Gulf oil."

The policy Cheney and Powell developed in the early 1990s was shelved during the presidency of Bill Clinton, a Democrat, from 1992 to 2000. Clinton sought to turn the end of the Cold War into a new era of global peace and prosperity, a noble goal undermined both by his credibility problems and, in hindsight, by his failure to recognize the militant Islamic terrorist attacks against American interests overseas during his tenure for what they were, i.e., a growing and real threat. When George W. Bush was elected in 2000 with

Cheney as vice president, Cheney's hawkish outlook moved to the forefront of the administration's thinking but remained hindered by the lack of a compelling threat that would sell it to the American public. Early in his mandate, Bush pulled the U.S. out of international ballistic missile treaties that he said prevented his country from properly protecting itself; he also made it clear the United States would never submit to the International Criminal Court, a new tribunal that investigates war crimes.[9] The moves were upsetting to American allies, but neither was seen as anything more than the parochialism of a rookie Texan president who had zero experience in foreign relations. No one detected a larger scheme. Then came September 11, 2001, followed by Bush's immediate pronouncement that the rest of the world must be with America or with the terrorists. Then came the Reaganesque "axis of evil," followed by warnings that the U.S. was prepared to invade Iraq even if such an action went against the will of the United Nations and the rest of the international community. And then came "The National Security Strategy of the United States," the final act in a Republican political drama that had lasted more than a decade.

It is hard to imagine Dick Cheney's policy being presented to the American public in an official manner had the September 11 tragedies never occurred. If a wacky conspiracy theorist believed the widespread American intelligence failures that allowed the attacks to happen were deliberate, and he was looking for a motive to support his accusation, the policy and its enthusiastic public acceptance by the American public might stand up in court.[10] Americans went, in the space of one morning, from facing no exterior threat to believing they faced the most grave danger since Pearl Harbor. The country's role in the world as global policeman was rejuvenated, just as Bush and Cheney wanted. Terrorism was the new communism, and Americans were once again scared into supporting a massive military buildup to the tune of close to $50 billion for 2002 alone.

In this context, it is difficult not to see the United States' renewed determination to remove Saddam Hussein from office in Iraq, with or without the support of allies, as the test case for the Cheney Doctrine. Invading Iraq meets all the criteria: America's security and commercial interests are threatened by Hussein's regime; it would test the notion of creating ad hoc coalitions that exist only for the duration of the crisis at hand; and any U.S. attack would underscore the unbridgeable gap between American military power and that of all other nations combined. If anything, an American invasion of the country would be even more of a mismatch of enemies than was the Gulf War. The lesson to the world would be obvious.

Bush's approach to building support for an American invasion was, during the summer and fall of 2002, torn straight from the Cheney playbook. The day before the National Security Strategy of the United States was delivered to Congress, Bush asked Congress for the authority to use "all means he determines to be appropriate, including force," to remove Hussein from office. And he had this message for his nation's allies: "If the United Nations Security Council won't deal with the problem, the United States and some of our friends will."[11] In other words, as the policy stated, *we will not hesitate to act alone, if necessary, to exercise our right to self-defense by acting pre-emptively.* America could have gone after North Korea in the fall of 2002, as it had restarted its nuclear weapons program, but the Bush administration instead chose to deal with that crisis through diplomatic channels. The conclusion one draws from that is that North Korea does not meet all the criteria of the Cheney Doctrine. There are no raw materials worth going to war over in that country, and the tiny, beleaguered nation has no hope of expanding its influence in the region to the detriment of America's interests.

Thus, the United Nations Security Council's eventual and inevitable acquiescence to America's demands for a resolution calling on Iraq to disarm or face invasion was hardly a diplomatic victory, and it certainly was not a triumph of good over evil. It was merely a deliberate and determined bully following its game plan and getting its way. No one likes a bully, especially one who hides behind empty claims of moral superiority. But that is the United States of America in the twenty-first century. The rest of the world faces difficult choices in this new era of U.S. dominance. In the fight between international terrorism and the international community, smaller countries like Canada and France have little alternative but to side with the U.S. In doing so they will have to hand their sovereignty to the American military and hope for the best. Nations such as Russia, China, and India can hold talks, as they have done more than once, about forming an alliance to contain the United States, but they will risk the wrath of an America bent on never having to compete for power again.

The tragedy of the United States' craving to be absolutely powerful is that it will feed on itself. If regions form alliances to serve as a counter-balance to American supremacy, America will have little choice but to launch a cold war to enforce its doctrine. As for small countries, it means those that oppose the United States' interests and incur its military wrath in future will never be able to mount a conventional counter-attack. Hammered into submission, they will only be able to fight back with clandestine attacks carried out by small groups of suicidal zealots fuelled by a hatred of their enemy. Innocent American citizens will once again be in the line of fire, and their government will call it terrorism.

APPENDIX:
THE INTERVIEW WITH AMY

The following is an edited transcript of the telephone interview the author recorded with his sister on September 11, 2001. It was first published in the *National Post* on September 12. Amy was not identified and was referred to as an office worker who was on the fifty-fourth floor of the south tower of the World Trade Center when the first plane struck the north tower.

Witness: I got to work probably at 8:30 a.m. I was getting a cup of tea and there was a shudder in the building and the lights blinked on and off and then we heard a noise. I looked out the windows and there was paper flying everywhere, and then I looked over at One World Trade and it was on fire on the top of it.

So we all ran out to the elevator, got partway down and then had to go the rest of the way down in the stairwell. Probably halfway down the stairwell, the second plane hit our building.

That was not a good moment.

It felt like the building was going to fall over. It was swaying back and forth, shuddering . . .

NP: Was there a loud explosion?

W: I can't remember. Everybody said, "Walk faster" and everyone was . . . calm, cool, and collected. We got down into the basement of the building and they pointed us through the mall. We had to walk a long way. Then we had to go down another level and came out and saw the buildings were in flames. From then on in, we were in shock. We just started walking really slowly, not realizing what had happened. We felt like we needed to get out of the area, and um, what happened? I was somewhere downtown on a phone when the first building collapsed. And, um . . .

I can't really remember everything.

We walked quite a ways. There were no cars in the street. Lots of ambulances. Um, people really dazed and, uh . . .

NP: When you were standing there making tea and you saw the fire in the other building, did you automatically assume another bomb had gone off in the World Trade Center?

W: No, no. We saw the fire, and then someone said a plane hit the building and we, you know, thought it was just a plane accident. An accident. So we were somewhat calm until we were in the stairwell . . . and we felt the shudder, and that was a terrible moment.

NP: Was it the kind of shudder that threw you off your feet?

W: Yeah.

NP: People fell down?

W: Uh, I don't think so. We all kept going.

NP: Who organized the evacuation?

W: No one. No one. There was no organization.

NP: You just decided to get out of the building because the other one was on fire?

W: Yup.

NP: That was a good decision.

W: It was an unbelievable decision.

NP: Once you were out, were the streets filled with soot and smoke? Could you see?

W: Where we were, it was pretty clear but then we were in . . . Oh I know what happened. We got to a gallery in Soho because we were trying to call and none of the cellphones were working. We got into the gallery and they had a TV on and we could start to see what had happened. And that's when the first building [the one the worker had escaped from] fell.

And then we were walking up Broadway and went into a store to get a battery for our cellphones and we heard a radio broadcaster describe how she had been at the base of the building when a huge fireball exploded out of the basement of the building. She was implying there was a bomb in the basement of the World Trade Center, as well.

NP: Did you notice the building leaning or being off-kilter after the plane hit?

W: I don't know. I was so disoriented. I was really off-kilter myself. I don't know if it was the building or me. . . .

NP: After that, how did you get back to Brooklyn [where the worker lives]?

W: Um, we heard on the street that we needed to get away from downtown so we just started walking north.

We also heard that everything was shut down. We got to a friend's in [Greenwich] Village for a glass of wine and saw everything on TV and realized what we'd escaped. It was just devastating.

Then, oh, I know what we did! We decided we would go and give blood and walked over to the hospital. It was quiet but in a state of shock. There were people outside waiting to find people. They turned us away.

There had been a call on TV for blood but that hospital couldn't take us so we started walking further north.

We got to a subway where they said there was a train running that could get me home. So I got on the train, and that was not fun. Being down below, packed with people, what the terrorists had targeted . . .

NP: How do you feel about New York City now?

W: I don't know what I think about New York right now. I'm totally stunned. And, you know . . . there are people lost and missing. It's bigger than New York. It's huge. It's a huge, huge thing that has happened here in the U.S.

It's not just New York.

ENDNOTES

CHAPTER ONE

1 Transcript of Bush's remarks upon his arrival at the White House on September 16.

2 Roosevelt's exact words on December 8, 1941, were: "Yesterday, December 7, 1941 – a date which will live in infamy – the United States of America was suddenly and deliberately attacked by naval and air forces of the Empire of Japan."

3 Sherry Cooper, "Unholy Judgments: Critics Who Imply That the United States Got What It Deserved Are Ignoring the Harsh Realities, Especially For," *National Post*, September 28, 2001, all ed., sec. Business.

4 John Powers, "Media Fundamentalism," *LA Weekly*, September 21-27, 2001.

5 The issue, the first one subsequent to the attacks, was dated September 24, 2001.

6 David Talbot, "The 'Traitor' Fires Back," Salon.com, October 16, 2001.

7 Ibid.

8 Ibid.

9 Charles Krauthammer, "This Is No Time for Agonized Relativism," *National Post*, September 22, 2001, all ed., sec. Opinion: p. A14.

10 David Talbot, "The 'Traitor' Fires Back," Salon.com, October 16, 2001.

11 Ibid.

[12] Ibid.

[13] FedEx did more than $211 million in business with the Department of Defense in the fiscal year 2001, according to the Federation of American Scientists. The FAS monitors all arms sales in the United States. See <www.fas.org>.

[14] Steve Sebelius, "Free Speech Isn't Free," *Las Vegas Review-Journal*, October 2, 2001, all ed., sec. Opinion.

[15] Kera Bolonik, "Marian and Me," Salon.com, January 7, 2002.

[16] Jerry L. Martin and Anne D. Neal, "Defending Civilization: How Our Universities Are Failing America and What Can Be Done About It," *American Council of Trustees and Alumni Web site*, <www.goacta.org>, February 2002.

[17] Ibid., pp. 12-30.

[18] Unsigned editorial, "Blaming the U.S., whitewashing terrorism," *National Post*, September 19, 2001, all ed., sec. Opinion.

[19] Aaron Lukas, "America Still the Villain: Protesters Are Still Planning to Demonstrate Against the U.S. Even Though the IMF and World Bank Meet," *National Post*, September 18, 2001, all ed., sec. Opinion. Lukas is an analyst at the Cato Institute's Center for Trade Policy Studies; the Cato Institute is a libertarian American think-tank.

[20] Martin and Neal, "Defending Civilization," *American Council of Trustees and Alumni Web site*, p. 34.

[21] Ibid., p. 33.

[22] Edited by B. Silvers and Barbara Epstein, *Striking Terror: America's New War* (New York: The New York Review of Books, 2002), p. 20.

[23] Ibid.

CHAPTER TWO

[1] James Astil, "Strike One," *Guardian*, October 2, 2001, Web site, <www.guardian.co.uk>.

[2] Reported by Noam Chomsky in *9-11* (New York: Seven Stories Press, 2001).

[3] James Risen and David Johnston, "Experts Find No Arms Chemicals at Bombed Sudan Plant," *New York Times*, February 9, 1999, all ed., sec. Foreign.

[4] Ibid.

5   James Risen, "Question of Evidence: A Special Report; To Bomb Sudan Plant, Or Not: A Year Later, Debates Rankle," *New York Times*, October 27, 1999, all ed., sec. Foreign.

6   Ibid.

7   Ibid.

8   Ibid.

9   According to testimony in the court transcripts of *U.S.A. v. Usama bin Laden, et al.*, the Sudanese government gave the tannery to Al-Qaeda in 1993 as payment for the construction of a road. The testimony was given February 7, 2001. The transcript can be read at <http://cryptome2.org/usa-v-ubl-03.htm>.

10 Astil, "Strike One," *Guardian*, October 2, 2001.

11 Quoted from "Confused, Inconclusive and Contradictory: An Assessment and Analysis of the American Government's 'Evidence' for the Cruise Missile Attacks on Sudan," published September 1998 by the European Sudanese Public Affairs Council. The report was found on the Council's Web site at <www.espac.org>.

12 Christopher S. Wren, "Sudanese Foes Give Consent for Relief Aid for Civilians," *New York Times*, March 17, 2002, final ed., sec. Foreign: p. 13.

13 Jonathan Broder, "How to Turn a Criminal into a Hero," Salon.com, August 26, 1998.

14 The article entitled "Clinton's scandals root cause of missile strikes at Sudan and Afghanistan" by Zafar Bangash was found at <www.muslimedia.com>. The Web site is the Internet arm of the radical Islamic newspaper *The Crescent*.

15 Loren Jenkins, "Is bin Laden a Terrorist Mastermind – Or a Fall Guy?" Salon.com, August 27, 1998.

16 Tim Weiner and James Risen, "Decision to Strike Factory in Sudan Based on Surmise Inferred from Evidence," *New York Times*, September 21, 1998, final ed., sec. Foreign.

17 Chomsky, *9-11*, p. 46.

CHAPTER THREE

1   Robert Jay Lifton and Greg Mitchell, *Hiroshima in America: A Half Century of Denial* (New York: Avon Books, 1995), p. 24.

2   Ibid., p. 23.

3 Taken from a War Department press release entitled "Eye Witness Account, Atomic Mission Over Nagasaki," dated August 9, 1945. It was found on the Internet (e.g. at <nuketesting.enviroweb.org/hiroshim/laurenc1.htm>).

4 Ibid., p. 28.

5 "Forgetting the Bomb; The Assault on History," *The Nation*, May 15, 1995.

6 Robert H. Ferrell, *Off the Record: The Private Papers of Harry S. Truman* (New York: Harper & Row, 1980).

7 Lifton and Mitchell, *Hiroshima in America*, pp. 15-16.

8 Taken from a report from the U.S. National Archives, Record Group 77, Records of the Office of the Chief of Engineers, Manhattan Engineer District, T.S. Manhattan Project Files, and found on the Internet at <www.dannen.com/decision/trin-rad.html>.

9 Lifton and Mitchell, *Hiroshima in America*.

10 Ibid.

11 Ibid., Chapter 4, Part 1.

12 Ibid., p. 133.

13 Taken from the so-called Franck Report of June 11, 1945. It was officially called the Report of the Committee of Political and Social Problems, Manhattan Project. It was found on the Internet at <www.dannen.com/decision/franck.html>.

14 Lifton and Mitchell, *Hiroshima in America*, pp. 154-55.

15 Ibid., p. 155.

16 Ibid., p. 134.

17 Gar Alperovitz, *The Decision to Use the Atomic Bomb and the Architecture of an American Myth* (New York: Albert A. Knopf, 1995), pp. 18-22.

18 Ibid., p. 17.

19 Ibid., p. 23.

20 Quoted by Janet Bloomfield, chair of the Campaign for Nuclear Disarmament, at <www.oneworld.org/news/world/bloomfield.html>.

21 Ibid.

22 Ibid.

23 Ibid.

24 Lifton and Mitchell, *Hiroshima in America*, p. 129.

25 Taken from an article entitled "President Truman Did Not Understand," *U.S. News and World Report*, August 15, 1960.
26 Lifton and Mitchell, *Hiroshima in America*, p. 160.
27 The official bombing order can be found at <www.dannen.com/decision/handy.html>.
28 This excerpt from Truman's speech on August 9, 1945, can be found at <www.dannen.com/decision/hst-ag09.html>.
29 Lifton and Mitchell, *Hiroshima in America*, p. 58.
30 Ibid., p. 428.
31 Ibid., Chapter 2, Part 1.
32 Ibid.
33 Ibid., p. 37.
34 *Nagasaki Journey: The Photographs of Yosuke Yamahata, August 10, 1945* (San Francisco: Pomegranate Artbooks, 1995).
35 Lifton and Mitchell, *Hiroshima in America*, p. 162.
36 Taken from an article entitled "President Truman Did Not Understand," *U.S. News and World Report*, August 15, 1960.
37 "Finding Russia's Lost Radioactive Luggage," *National Post*, December 21, 1999.

CHAPTER FOUR

1 James D. Delk, *Fires & Furies: The L.A. Riots* (Palm Springs, California: ETC Publications, 1995), pp. 221-22. This anecdote was quoted in "Lessons in Command and Control from the Los Angeles Riot," an article by Christopher M. Schnaubelt in the Summer 1997 issue of *Parameters, the U.S. Army War College Quarterly*. It was found via a link on the FAS Web site.
2 See <www.fas.org./man/dod-101/ops/urgent_fury.htm>.
3 Jeffrey Goldberg, "A Great Terror," *New Yorker*, March 25, 2002: 55-56.
4 Chalmers Johnson, *Blowback: The Cost and Consequences of American Empire* (New York: Henry Holt and Co., 2000), p. 4.
5 See <www.fas.org.>.
6 Johnson, *Blowback*, pp. 3-4.
7 Ibid., pp. 4-5.
8 Ibid., p. 15.

9 See <www.fas.org/asmp/profiles/turkey.htm>.

10 Marjorie Miller, "Britain Illegally Expelled Chagos Islanders for U.S. Base, Court Rules," *Los Angeles Times*, November 4, 2000.

11 Ibid.

12 The plight of the Ilois natives is well documented in "Diego Garcia: A Contrast to the Falklands," by John Madeley. Madeley wrote the report for the Minority Rights Group, a London-based human-rights group of the day. It was found on the Internet.

13 Ibid.

14 Miller, "Britain Illegally Expelled Chagos Islanders," *Los Angeles Times*, November 4, 2000.

15 Johnson, *Blowback*, p. 35.

16 Ibid., p. 55.

17 The figure comes from the database in the Arms Sales Monitoring Project at <www.fas.org>.

18 Johnson, *Blowback*, p. 64.

19 Ibid., pp. 5-6.

20 Edited by Robert B. Silvers and Barbara Epstein, *Striking Terror: America's New War* (New York: New York Review of Books, 2002), p. 22.

21 In a radio address on September 15, George W. Bush said, "Our response must be sweeping, sustained and effective. We have much to do and much to ask of the American people. You will be asked for your patience, for the conflict will not be short. You will be asked for your resolve, for the conflict will not be easy."

22 Nicholas Lemann, "The Next World Order," *New Yorker*, April 1, 2002: 42-48.

23 Ibid., p. 44.

24 Ibid., pp. 44-45.

25 James Baker is quoted from newspaper sources on the Web site <www.brianwillson.com>, a site operated by a Vietnam war veteran, S. Brian Willson, whose disillusionment with his government's foreign policies prompted him to become an outspoken peace activist.

26 Ed. Silvers and Epstein, *Striking Terror*, p. 20.

27 Steven Erlanger, "Europe Seethes as the U.S. Flies Solo in World Affairs," *New York Times*, February 23, 2002, all ed., sec. Foreign.

28 Ed. Silvers and Epstein, *Striking Terror*, pp. 27-28.

29 Erlanger, "Europe Seethes," *New York Times*, February 23, 2002, all ed., sec. Foreign.

30 Johnson, *Blowback*, p. 93.

31 Turner promised $100 million a year for ten years for programs approved by the U.N., as he could not donate the money directly to the organization.

32 Johnson, *Blowback*, p. 88.

33 Ibid., p. 87.

34 Tamar Gabelnick, "Security Assistance After September 11," May 2002. A summary of the report, from which this and subsequent citations were taken, is available on the Internet at <www.fas.org/asmp/library/articles/fpif-911.htm>.

35 Ibid. According to the report, "Overall, the Bush administration has increased military aid and training by significant amounts relative to past levels [since September 11]. Foreign Military Financing (FMF), which provides grants for countries to buy U.S. military equipment and services, rose from $3.57-billion in FY [fiscal year] 2001 to a requested $4.12-billion for FY 2003. The administration's FY 2002 supplemental appropriation request included another $372.5-million in counter-terrorism FMF funds for a wide range of countries including Oman, Nepal, Ethiopia, and Djibouti. Funding for International Military Education and Training (IMET), one of many foreign military training programs, rose from $58-million in FY 2001 to a requested $80-million for FY 2003, a jump of 38%."

36 Ibid.

37 Ibid.

38 Ibid.

CHAPTER FIVE

1 Chalmers Johnson, *Blowback: The Costs and Consequences of American Empire* (New York: Henry Holt and Co., 2000), p. 12.

2 Andrew A. Reding, "The Evolution of Governmental Institutions," Chapter 2 of *Revolution and Counterrevolution in Nicaragua*, Thomas Walker, editor (Boulder, Col.: Westview, 1991), pp. 15-47. Found at the Web site <www.worldpolicy.org/americas/nicaragua/walker.html>.

3 Ibid.
4 Ibid.
5 Ibid.
6 Ibid.
7 Ibid.
8 Ibid.
9 Ibid.
10 Ibid.
11 Ibid.
12 Noam Chomksy, *Necessary Illusions* (1989). Chomsky's writings appear at <www.zmag.org/chomsky>.
13 Reding, "The Evolution of Governmental Institutions," in *Revolution and Counterrevolution in Nicaragua*, (ed. Thomas Walker), pp. 15-47. Found at the Web site <www.worldpolicy.org>.
14 See <http://pbs.org/frontline>. The Frontline Web site documents terrorist attacks on Americans, 1979-88. According to the site, the U.S., through Israel, supplied Iran with one hundred anti-tank missiles in August 1985 and another 408 anti-tank missiles the next month. The shipments resulted in the release of three American hostages. A total of thirty foreigners were kidnapped in Lebanon from 1982-92, many of them Americans, including the journalist Terry Anderson. He spent a total of 2,454 days in captivity.
15 Selection from the Senate Committee Report on Drugs, Law Enforcement and Foreign Policy chaired by Senator John F. Kerry.
16 James Risen, "CIA Says It Used Nicaraguan Rebels Accused of Drug Ties," *New York Times*, July 17, 1998, all ed., sec. Foreign.
17 Johnson, *Blowback*, p. 8.
18 Gary Cohn and Ginger Thompson, "Unearthed: Fatal Secrets," *Baltimore Sun*, June 11, 1985, national ed., sec. Front: A-1. The entire history of Battalion 316 was unearthed by the *Baltimore Sun* in a four-part series. The reports led to investigations and the release of classified documents that corroborated the stories. The series is referred to constantly by other sources investigating America's role in Nicaragua, and it has never been refuted.
19 Ibid.

[20] Ginger Thompson and Gary Cohn, "A Carefully Crafted Deception," *Baltimore Sun*, June 18, 1995, all ed., sec. National.

[21] Ibid.

[22] Ibid.

[23] Ibid.

[24] Ibid.

[25] Ibid.

[26] Ibid.

[27] Gary Cohn and Ginger Thompson, "Former Envoy to Honduras Says He Did What He Could," *Baltimore Sun*, December 15, 1995, all ed., sec. National.

[28] Ginger Thompson and Gary Cohn, "Honduras Charges Soldier," *Baltimore Sun*, July 26, 1995, all ed., sec. National.

[29] Gary Cohn and Ginger Thompson, "Unearthed: Fatal Secrets."

[30] Gary Cohn, Ginger Thompson, and Mark Matthews, "Torture Was Taught by CIA," *Baltimore Sun*, January 27, 1997, all ed., sec. National.

[31] The KUBARK manual is available on the Internet at a number of sites, including <http://heart7.net/mcf/kubark.htm>. Some of the contents of the manual have been deleted by government officials. What remains makes it clear that, under KUBARK, U.S. agents can inflict physical and psychological torture, including "medical, chemical or electric methods," if prior approval is given by "Headquarters."

[32] Ibid.

[33] Ginger Thompson and Gary Cohn, "Torturers' Confessions," *Baltimore Sun*, June 13, 1995, all ed., sec. National.

[34] Mark Matthews, "Republicans Kill Bill to Open Files on Rights Abuses," *Baltimore Sun*, September 3, 1998, all ed., sec. National.

[35] Tim Golden, "Honduran Army's Abuses Were Known to CIA," *New York Times*, October 24, 1998, all ed., sec. Foreign.

[36] Ibid.

[37] Gary Cohn and Ginger Thompson, "Unearthed: Fatal Secrets."

[38] "Tales from a Failed Coup," *Economist*, April 27, 2002, p. 31.

CHAPTER SIX

1. Chalmers Johnson, *Blowback: The Costs and Consequences of American Empire* (New York: Henry Holt & Co., 2000), pp. 13-14.
2. Tim Weiner, "CIA Plotted Killing of 58 in Guatemala," *New York Times,* May 28, 1997, all ed., sec. Foreign.
3. Ibid.
4. Ibid.
5. U.S. Department of State background notes on Guatemala <www.state.gov/r/pa/ei/bgn/2045.htm>.
6. Johnson, *Blowback*, p. 14.
7. Christopher Hitchens, *The Trial of Henry Kissinger* (New York: Verso, 2002), p. 56.
8. The "CIA Activities in Chile" report, p. 13. Available on the Internet at the National Security Archive <www.gwu.edu/~nsarchiv/news/20000919/index.html>. According to its introductory paragraph, it was based on "extensive Congressional reports regarding U.S. activities in Chile in the late 1960s and 1970s; . . . the memoirs of key figures, including Richard Nixon and Henry Kissinger; . . . [the] CIA's oral history collection at the Center for the Study of Intelligence; and [consultations] with retired intelligence officers who were directly involved."
9. Ibid., p. 6.
10. Ibid., p. 2.
11. Ibid., p. 4.
12. Ibid., p. 7.
13. Ibid., p. 10.
14. Ibid., p. 4.
15. Ibid., p. 11.
16. Ibid., p. 20.
17. Ibid., p. 17.
18. Ibid., p. 17.
19. Ibid., p. 21.
20. Ibid., p. 7.
21. Ibid., p. 21.
22. Henry Kissinger, *Diplomacy* (New York: Simon & Schuster, 1995), p. 767.

23 "Teaching Nicaragua a Lesson," by Noam Chomsky, found at <www.thirdworldtraveler.com>. Chomksy is quoting Julie Preston, the *Boston Globe*'s Central American correspondent at the time.

24 Available at <www.brianwillson.com/awolvpat1.html>.

25 Reported in the *Boston Phoenix*, a left-wing alternative newspaper in Boston, Mass., on April 24, 1987. The article was found on-line at <www.cia-on-campus.org/umass.edu/trial.html>.

26 Kissinger, *Diplomacy*, p. 763.

27 Ibid., p. 767.

28 Hugh Brogan, *The Penguin History of the U.S.A.* (second edition), (London, New York: Penguin Books, 2001), p. 691.

29 The speech "Remarks at a Fundraising Dinner for the Nicaragua Refugee Fund, April 15, 1985," can be found at <www.reagan.utexas.edu/resource/speeches/1985>.

30 Ibid.

31 Sam Dillon, "A Decade of Obsession," *New York Times*, March 3, 1996, all ed., sec. Book reviews. The quote was in the words of the writer who reviewed *A Twilight Struggle: American Power and Nicaragua, 1977-1990* (New York: The Free Press, 1996) by Robert Kagan. Kagan was a deputy to Assistant Secretary of State Elliott Abrams during the Reagan administration.

32 Brogan, *The Penguin History of the U.S.A.*, p. 690.

33 Henry Kissinger, *Diplomacy*, p. 764.

34 Brogan, *The Penguin History of the U.S.A.*, pp. 690-91.

35 Quoted at <www.anet.net/~upstart/gorby.html>.

36 The decision, from which the following citations are taken, can be found at the International Court of Justice's Web site at <www.icj-cij.org>.

37 Kissinger, *Diplomacy*, p. 767. The full quotation is: "Like Woodrow Wilson, Reagan understood that the American people, having marched throughout their history to the drumbeat of exceptionalism, would find their ultimate inspiration in historic ideals, not in geopolitical analysis."

38 The U.S. government's meddling with the 2001 election in Nicaragua was well-documented in the *Guardian* by Duncan Campbell in "Getting the Right Result: Nicaragua's Election Showed U.S. Still Won't Allow a Free Vote," November 6, 2001.

39 Mirta Ojito, "Conversations/Zoilamérica Narváez: A Victim of Sexual Abuse in a Prison of Political Ideals," *New York Times*, March 29, 1998, all ed., sec. Week in Review.

40 Nicholas Lemann, "The Next World Order," *New Yorker*, April 1, 2002: 44-45.

CHAPTER SEVEN

1 Bush's State of the Union address is available at <www.white-house.gov>.

2 Steven Erlanger, "German Joins Europe's Cry That the U.S. Won't Consult," *New York Times*, February 13, 2002, all ed., sec. Foreign.

3 Elisabeth Bumiller, "Damage Control," *New York Times*, February 24, 2002, all ed., sec. Foreign.

4 See <www.state.gov/r/pa/ei/bgn/2792.htm>.

5 William Stueck, "Korean War," *The Oxford Companion to United States History*, 2001 ed., p. 423.

6 Ibid.

7 Anna Kasten Nelson, "National Security Council Document #68," *The Oxford Companion to United States History*, 2001 ed., p. 541.

8 Figures from the U.S. Department of State Web site at <www.state.gov>.

9 Chalmers Johnson, *Blowback: The Costs and Consequences of American Empire* (New York: Henry Holt and Company, 2000), p. 120.

10 Ibid., p. 128.

11 Ibid., p. 130.

12 BBC World News, November 18, 2002, see <www.news.bbc.co.uk/2/hi/asia-pacific/2487737.stm>.

13 Johnson, *Blowback*, p. 133.

14 <www.fas.org/asmp/index.html>. The FAS says delivery figures are often higher than reported because the State Department tends to understate the actual value of the weapons and equipment transferred.

CHAPTER EIGHT

1 At <www.state.gov/r/pa/ei/bgn/5314.htm>.

2 The reference is in *Time's* 1979 "Man of the Year" essay on Ayatollah

Khomeini. It can be found on the Internet at <www.time.com/time/special/moy/1979.html>.

3   <www.nytimes.com/library/world/mideast/041600iran-cia-index.html>.

4   <www.gwu.edu/~nsarchiv/NSAEBB/NSAEBB28>.

5   "Historian's note," Dr. Donald N. Wilber, *Overthrow of Premier Mossadeq of Iran, November 1952–August 1953.*

6   Ibid., p. 77.

7   James Risen, "Secrets of History: The CIA in Iran," *New York Times,* April 2000, Web ed.

8   <www.iranian.com/Opinion/2000/January/Century/index.html>. Not a scientific survey, but telling nonetheless.

9   <www.time.com/time/special/moy/1951.html>. *Time* names as Man of the Year the person who has most affected the news for better or worse. Other Men of the Year have included Hitler (1938), Stalin (1939), and, in 1979, Ayatollah Khomeini.

10 "Mohammed Mossadegh: Challenge of the East," *Time,* January 7, 1952, taken from the Internet at <www.time.com/time/special/moy/1951.html>. This was *Time*'s "Man of the Year" article on Mossadegh.

11 Ibid.

12 Wilber, *Overthrow of Premier Mossadeq of Iran, November 1952– August 1953,* p. 82.

13 James Risen, "Secrets of History: The CIA in Iran," *New York Times,* April 2000, Web ed.

14 Wilber, *Overthrow of Premier Mossadeq of Iran, November 1952– August 1953,* p. 29.

15 Ibid., p. 30.

16 Ibid., p. 34.

17 From an appendix to Donald N. Wilber's report entitled *Military Critique: Lessons Learned from TPAJAX re Military Planning Aspects of Coup d'Etat,* p. 5.

18 In Chapter 10 of Donald Wilber's case history, he laments that the CIA "lacked contacts capable of placing material so that the American publisher was unwitting as to its source, as well as being able to see that no changes in theme or emphasis were made. In

contrast to this relatively ineffective venture, the Iran desk of the State Department was able to place a CIA study in *Newsweek*, using the normal channel of desk officer to journalist. Recognizing the fact that the Agency is not able to employ such a channel as just described, it does appear that some improvement of capabilities might be desirable. Either these contacts used to secure the unwitting publication of material should be expanded and improved, or else there should be a provision made for passing material directly to cleared editors and owners of press media."

[19] Wilber, *Overthrow of Premier Mossadeq of Iran, November 1952– August 1953*, p. 29.

[20] Ibid., p. 34.

[21] Ibid., p. 37.

[22] Ibid., p. 46.

[23] Ibid., p. 65.

[24] Ibid., p. 66.

[25] Ibid., p. 67.

[26] "Mohammed Mossadegh: Challenge of the East," *Time*, January 7, 1952. Taken from the Internet at <www.time.com/time/special/ moy/1951.html>.

[27] Risen, "Secrets of History: The CIA in Iran," *New York Times*, April 2000, Web ed.

[28] "Ayatullah [*sic*] Khomeini: The Mystic Who Lit the Fires of Hatred," *Time*, January 7, 1980. Available on the Internet at <www.time.com/time/special/moy/1979.html>.

[29] Neil MacFarquhar, "Bush's Comments Bolster Old Guard in Tehran," *New York Times*, February 8, 2002, all ed., sec. Foreign.

CHAPTER NINE

[1] Declassified State Department documents in this section were found on the Internet at <www.foia.state.gov>, the department's Freedom of Information Act Electronic Reading Room. The document "Saddam Hussein: The Cult of Personality" is the source for the information about Hussein's style of government. Another source is the department's 1990 human-rights report for Iraq.

[2] A State Department document from November 1974 strongly urged that two U.S. army officers not undertake a planned visit to

Iraq because "accusations of U.S. involvement with Kurds and Iranians are widespread," and if the regime caught wind of the visit, or became suspicious of its motives, they would have risked an "occurrence of 'incident' from which it would be difficult to extricate ourselves."

3 From a declassified State Department document sent from Baghdad to Washington dated December 1974, and whose subject was "U.S. Policy on Iraqi-Iran Conflict."

4 Ibid.

5 Ibid.

6 From a declassified "U.S. Interests" cable from Baghdad to Washington and other points, dated September 1980, and whose subject was "Next Steps in the Iraq-Iran Confrontation."

7 From an undated State Department document most likely written in late 1981.

8 From a declassified cable dated July 1988 that recounted George Bush Sr.'s statement to the U.N. Security Council on the July 14 IranAir incident.

9 This was outlined in a letter from the United States–Iraq Business Forum to George Shultz, the secretary of state, on November 20, 1986.

10 The visits by the businessmen and the bankers are outlined in two State Department documents dated June 1989, one of which was titled "The Iraqi Debt and U.S. Business Opportunities."

11 The letter was dated August 4, 1989.

12 Paul Walker, *The Myth of Surgical Bombing in the Gulf War*. Document found at <http://deoxy.org/wc/wc-myth.htm>. Walker was the director of the Institute for Peace and International Security at the Massachusetts Institute of Technology at the time he wrote the document.

13 Ibid.

14 Quoted by Joyce Chediac in "The Massacre of Withdrawing Soldiers on 'The Highway of Death.'" The report can be found on the Internet at <http://deoxy.org/wc/wc-death.htm>.

15 Laurie Mylroie, *The War Against America: Saddam Hussein and the World Trade Center Attacks: A Study of Revenge* (New York: HarperCollins, 2001).

[16] Ibid., p. 253.

[17] Ibid., p. 252.

CHAPTER TEN

[1] The transcript of ABC News' December 22, 1998, broadcast can be found at <ABCnews.com>.

[2] Robert Jay Lifton and Greg Mitchell, *Hiroshima in America: A Half Century of Denial* (New York: Avon Books, 1995) p. 28.

[3] Andrew Reding, "Quid Pro Quo: Europe Needs U.S. to Recognize EU Power," worldpolicy.org, October 3, 2001. Article found at <www.worldpolicy.org/americas/usa/01-1003-pns-usa-europe.html>.

[4] The U.S. Supreme Court banned the death penalty for mentally retarded people in a split decision on June 20, 2002. The court said any prisoner on death row with an IQ of less than seventy should have their sentence commuted to a life in prison. There were an estimated one hundred retarded people on death row at the time of the ruling.

[5] *Scientific American* reports on the Web page <www.sciam.com/1999/0799issue/0799numbers.html> entitled "Christian Differences" that the percentage of Americans who attended church once a month in the 1990s was 55, compared to a 25 per cent in England, 17 per cent in France, 38 per cent in Spain, 8 per cent in Russia, 47 per cent in Italy, and 25 per cent in Australia. The big European exception was Ireland, where the number is 88 per cent; in Northern Ireland it is 69 per cent.

[6] The Gallup Organization produces an annual Index of Leading Religious Indicators for the United States. It is based on eight questions. The findings in 2001 were: 95 per cent said they believed in God; 91.7 per cent stated a religious preference; 65.6 per cent were members of a church; 41.1 per cent had attended church in the last seven days; 57.7 per cent said religion was very important in life; 61.7 per cent said religion answers their problems; 59.7 per cent had "high confidence" in organized religions; and 63.9 per cent gave high ratings to the ethical standards of clergy. This produced a Religious Indicator of 671 in 2001, compared to 653

in 1992. The highest recorded Index was 746, in 1956, and the lowest was 651, in 1989.

7 Rodger Doyle, "Christian Differences," *Scientific American* Web site <www.sciam.com/1999/0799issue/0799numbers.html>.

8 Ibid.

9 Cited in Mark A. Noll, "Religion," *The Oxford Companion to United States History*, 2001 ed., p. 658.

10 See <www.wfu.edu/~matthetl/perspectives/twentyone.html>.

11 William Vance Trollinger Jr., "Fundamentalist Movement," *The Oxford Companion to United States History*, 2001 ed., p. 295.

12 Ibid.

13 Trollinger, "Moral Majority," *The Oxford Companion to United States History*, 2001 ed., p. 514.

14 Trollinger, "Christian Coalition," *The Oxford Companion to United States History*, 2001 ed., p. 118.

15 Michael Lind, "The Right Still Has Religion," *New York Times*, December 9, 2001, all ed., sec. Op-Ed.

16 *The New World Order* (1991), p. 227. This quotation and those accompanying it were found on the Internet at <www.sullivan-county.com/news/pat_quotes/index.htm>.

17 *The 700 Club*, 1992.

18 *Washington Post*, August 23, 1993.

19 Michael Lind, "The Right Still Has Religion," *New York Times*, December 9, 2001, all ed., sec. Op-Ed.

20 Ibid. Ashcroft is so pro-gun that, even in the weeks after the September 11 attacks, he refused to allow the FBI to use gun registration documents to find out whether suspected Al-Qaeda members living in the United States had purchased weapons.

21 Noted in a May 21, 2002, Gallup Organization briefing entitled "Keeping the Faith: George W. Bush and Religion." The poll revealed that half of Americans say Bush's "frequent discussion of his religious beliefs in public does not affect their opinion of him, while more than a third (37%) say it makes them view the president more favorably, and just 12% say it causes them to view him less favorably." Clearly, Bush has much to gain by wearing his Christ-loving heart on his sleeve.

22 Bush is quoted in an April 22, 2002, article in the *New York Times* by Elisabeth Bumiller as saying, "Government can write checks, but it can't put hope in people's hearts or a sense of purpose in people's lives. That is done by people who have heard a call and who act on faith and are willing to share in that faith. And I'm not talking about a particular religion – I'm talking about all religions under the Almighty God."

23 Elizabeth Bumiller, "Talk of Religion Provokes Amens as Well as Anxiety," *New York Times*, April 22, 2002, all ed., sec. National.

24 See Chapter 3 of this book, on the atomic bombing of Hiroshima and Nagasaki.

25 Robert F. Worth, "Truth, Right and the American Way: A Nation Defines Itself by Its Evil Enemies," *New York Times*, February 24, 2002, all ed., sec. Week in Review.

26 Ibid.

27 Human Rights Watch released *No Escape: Male Rape in U.S. Prisons* in April 2001. This quotation is taken from a press release related to the launch of the report's findings. The release can be found in the Internet at <www.hrw.org/press/2001/04/usrape0419.htm>.

28 Ibid.

29 "USA: Amnesty International Condemns Housing Minors in Wisconsin Supermax Prison." Found on the Internet at <web.amnesty.org/ai.nsf/Index/AMR511082001?OpenDocument &of=COUNTRIES\USA>.

30 From Human Rights Watch on the Internet at <www.hrw.org/campaigns/drugs>.

31 Ibid.

32 Twelve states out of the fifty in the U.S. had banned the death penalty in 2002.

33 "Worldwide Executions Doubled in 2001," an Amnesty International report dated April 4, 2002, and found on the Internet at <web.amnesty.org/ai.nsf/Index/ACT500052002?OpenDocument& of=THEMES\DEATH+PENALTY>.

34 Ibid.

35 Richard Moran, "Capital Punishment," *The Oxford Companion to United States History*, 2001 ed., p. 104.

[36] Kris Axtman, "U.S. Milestone: 100th Death-Row Inmate Exonerated," *Christian Science Monitor*, April 11, 2002.

[37] Moran, "Capital Punishment," *The Oxford Companion to United States History*, p. 104.

[38] Article 3(1) reads, "In all actions concerning children, whether undertaken by public or private social welfare institutions, courts of law, administrative authorities or legislative bodies, the best interests of the child shall be a primary consideration."

[39] Article 6(5) reads, "Sentence of death shall not be imposed for crimes committed by persons below eighteen years of age and shall not be carried out on pregnant women."

[40] "In Whose Interests?", an Amnesty International document dated April 24, 2002, and found on the Internet at <web.amnesty.org/ai.nsf/recent/AMR510632002!Open>.

[41] From an Amnesty International press release dated October 23, 2001, and entitled "Amnesty International Calls for Respect of Detainees' Rights in Wake of 11 September."

[42] William Glaberson, "The Law; Tribunal v. Court-martial: Matter of Perception," *New York Times*, December 2, 2001, all ed., sec. National.

[43] "President Issues Military Order," <www.whitehouse.gov/news/releases/2001/11/20011113-27.html>.

[44] "Justice Deformed: War and the Constitution," *New York Times*, December 2, 2001, all ed., sec. Editorial.

[45] "John Ashcroft Misses the Point," *New York Times*, December 7, 2001, all ed., sec. Editorial.

[46] Susan Sontag's term – see Chapter 1.

[47] Cintra Wilson, *Massive Swelling: Celebrity Reexamined as a Grotesque Crippling Disease and Other Cultural Revelations* (New York: Viking/Penguin, 2000).

[48] Ibid., p. xix.

[49] Ibid., p. 226-27.

CHAPTER ELEVEN

[1] "How to rig an election," *Economist*, April 27, 2002, pp. 29-30.

[2] Ibid.

3 Jan Cienski, "Mugabe Has Early Lead in What Monitors Call a Poisoned Election," *National Post*, March 13, 2002, final ed., sec. Foreign: p. A16.

4 Michael Moore, *Stupid White Men . . . And Other Sorry Excuses for the State of the Nation* (New York: HarperCollins, 2001).

5 Quotes taken from Regnery Publishing Web site at <www.regnery.com/regnery010403_atanycost.html>.

6 Mark Z. Barabak and Richard A. Serrano, "America Waits: Florida Justices OK Hand Recount," *Los Angeles Times*, November 17, 2000, final ed., sec. National: p. A1.

7 Barabak and Mike Clary, "America Waits: Florida Recount Underway," *Los Angeles Times*, November 9, 2000, final ed., sec. National: p. A1.

8 *Voting Irregularities in Florida During the 2000 Presidential Election*, a report by the United States Commission on Civil Rights, Chapter 9, p. 1. The entire report is available on the Commission's Web site at <www.usccr.gov>. (N.B. The report page numbers referred to in these footnotes correspond to the page numbers assigned to the pages when the author printed the report from the USCCR's Web site. They may not reflect the page numbering of an original hard copy of the report.)

9 Ibid., Chapter 9, p. 2.

10 Ibid., Chapter 5, p. 12.

11 These marginal parties found at <www.politics1.com/parties.htm>.

12 Mark Fineman, "America Waits: Where Balloting for Buchanan Surged, Outrage Among Voters Who Detest Him," *Los Angeles Times*, November 10, 2000, final ed., sec. National: p. A1.

13 Megan Garvey, "America Waits: Bay Buchanan Sees Something Peculiar in Palm Beach Voting," *Los Angeles Times*, November 10, 2000, final ed., sec. National: p. A26.

14 Bob Drogin, Lisa Getter, and Stephen Braun, "America Waits; Sunday Report; A Political War to End All Waged over Recount Votes," *Los Angeles Times*, December 10, 2000, final ed., sec. National: p. A1.

15 Ibid.

16 Ibid.

17 Ibid.

18 Ibid.

[19] Barabak and Serrano, "America Waits," *Los Angeles Times*, November 17, 2000, final ed., sec. National: p. A1.

[20] Ibid.

[21] Ian Brodie, "Florida Basks in Spotlight: U.S. Election 2000," *The Times*, (London, England), November 15, 2000, final ed., sec. Overseas: p. 19.

[22] "Whatever Will They Think of Next?", *Economist*, November 25, 2000, p. 29.

[23] "In the Mire," *Economist*, November 25, 2000, p. 17.

[24] Barabak and Serrano, "America Waits: Fla. High Court Backs Gore," *Los Angeles Times*, December 9, 2000, final ed., sec. National: p. A1.

[25] Ibid.

[26] Moore, *Stupid White Men*, p. 11.

[27] Ibid., pp. 11-12.

[28] David G. Savage and Henry Weinstein, "Decision 2000; 'Right to Vote' Led Justices to a 5-4 Ruling," *Los Angeles Times*, December 14, 2000, final ed., sec. National: p. A1.

[29] Ibid.

[30] Cited in David G. Savage, "The Nation; Court Scrutinized for Supreme Intervention," *Los Angeles Times*, August 26, 2001, final ed., sec. National: p. A18.

[31] Ibid.

[32] "In the Mire," *Economist*, November 25, 2000, p. 17.

[33] Dana Canedy, "Florida Leaders Sign Agreement for Overhaul of Election System," *New York Times*, May, 4, 2001, final ed., sec. National.

CHAPTER TWELVE

[1] Jacques Thibau, *La France colonisée* (Paris: Flammarion, 1980), p. 74.

[2] Ibid., pp. 68-69.

[3] Ibid., p. 69.

[4] There are more than two hundred American television shows in syndication around the world and in the United States, according to Variety.com.

[5] According to Variety.com, seven of the ten largest entertainment companies in 2001 were American, nine out of ten if Sony and

Vivendi-Universal were included. As well, twenty-five of the top fifty were American.

6 Benjamin R. Barber, *Jihad vs. McWorld: How Globalism and Tribalism Are Reshaping the World* (New York: Ballantine Books, 1995), p. 4.

7 See Chapter 1, where a columnist is quoted as writing, "In the struggle between civilization and barbarism, those who torch a McDonald's and those who ram airplanes through skyscrapers are releasing their destructive energies in a common cause."

8 Found on the Internet at <www.state.gov/www/issues/economic/trade_reports/1999/taiwan.html>.

9 Variety.com keeps track of the weekly film grosses in a variety of North American, South American, European, and Asian countries. In the week of May 17-23, 2002, the top-ten list in every country covered by *Variety* was dominated by American fare, notably *Star Wars II: Attack of the Clones* and *Spider-Man*. Few countries even had a local film on the list; the big exception was France, where five out of ten were homegrown.

10 "The Spider's Bite," *Economist*, May 11, 2002, p. 65.

11 A report on CNN.com dated September 28, 1988, revealed that in the original version of Steven Spielberg's *E.T. The Extraterrestrial*, the alien dies. Test audiences hated that dark ending and it was changed to one where the alien is reunited with his family. The same article says the endings of *Pretty Women* and *Fatal Attraction* were altered on the basis of test audience reaction. And in the film *My Best Friend's Wedding*, the gay character played by Rupert Everett was a minor role but was made a more important one when audiences clicked with Everett's performance. Sometimes test audiences have a positive effect, letting directors know the plots of their films, as edited, are incomprehensible, but most changes are commercial ones to increase the film's appeal to the widest possible number of viewers. The CNN.com story was found on the Internet at <www.cnn.com/SHOWBIZ/Movies/9809/28/screen.test>. CBSNews.com, meanwhile, reported on November 6, 2001, that reactions from test audiences to the film *Black Hawk Down*, about a courageous mission by American soldiers in Somalia, prompted the studio to release the film in December of that year instead of on its planned release date in

March 2002. The test audiences, still emotionally raw from September 11, ate up the tale of American heroism.

12 Greg Kot, "The Classic Album That Almost Wasn't," *Rolling Stone*, May 23, 2002.

13 Jeffrey Tayler, "Islam versus the Pleasure Principle," *Atlantic Monthly*, March 2002, pp. 35-37.

14 "Muslim Dolls Tackle 'Wanton' Barbie," BBC News Web site, March 5, 2002.

15 An excellent book on the good and bad sides of globalization is *Globalization and Its Discontents* by Joseph E. Stiglitz (New York: W.W. Norton & Company, 2002). Stiglitz won the 2001 Nobel Prize for economics; he served in the Clinton cabinet as an adviser on global economic policy and as chief economist for the World Bank.

CHAPTER THIRTEEN

1 Medical obesity should not be confused with morbid obesity or "superobesity," terms that apply to exceptionally fat people who can often weigh more than 400 pounds. (The world's fattest man was an American who weighed 1,400 pounds when he died of heart failure, according to the *Guinness Book of World Records*.) Under the guidelines set out by the U.S. Surgeon General, a man of six feet and average build is considered overweight at 190 pounds and obese at 220 pounds. The guidelines do not apply to well-muscled people or pregnant women. Critics of the system used for determining medical obesity, which is based on a ratio of body weight to height called body mass index, say it is too stringent and therefore produces an overestimation of the problem.

2 Statistics taken from *The Surgeon General's Call to Action to Prevent and Decrease Overweight and Obesity*. The report was released December 13, 2001. It can be viewed on the Internet at <www.surgeongeneral.gov/topics/obesity>.

3 The American Obesity Association at <www.obesity.org/subs/fastfacts/obesity_US.shtml>.

4 According to the U.S. Census Bureau's U.S. POPClock for May 14, 2002. The "clock" is located on the Internet at <www.census.gov/cgi-bin/popclock>.

5 The American Obesity Association is a non-profit organization whose sponsors include pharmaceutical companies and weight-control companies that would have an interest in overstating the obesity problem in order to sell more diet-control drugs, equipment for stomach stapling, and memberships in weight-reducing clubs. Its Web-site address is <www.obesity.org>.

6 Kevin Cowan, "Big Is Beautiful: Designers Catching On," Scripps Howard News Service, February 19, 2002.

7 The American Society for Bariatric Surgery's Web site describes in detail the various kids of stomach-stapling and bypass procedures performed on morbidly obese and "superobese" men and women. Bypass surgeries originally involved shunting digested food directly from the stomach to the lower intestine so that its calories could not be absorbed by the upper intestines. The procedure has proven to be fraught with complications, including severe liver problems, and is no longer recommended by the ASBS. The currently favoured technique is stomach stapling with a bypass around the unused part of the stomach to the intestines. A newer technique is gastric banding, wherein a band is placed around the upper part of the stomach to create a smaller "stomach" that still allows the digested food to pass to the rest of the stomach and through the intestines. There are now inflatable bands that can be enlarged or shrunk, increasing or decreasing the size of the new, smaller stomach at the discretion of the doctor and patient. All the surgeries require discipline on the part of the patient, who must chew carefully and avoid certain foods such as ice cream and gassy sodas in order to prevent acid reflux and persistent vomiting.

8 Information taken from <www.obesity.org/subs/disability>.

9 See <www.obesity.org/subs/advocacy>.

10 According to the U.S. POPClock, about 2,500,000 Americans die each year of all causes.

11 Marion Nestle, *Food Politics: How the Food Industry Influences Nutrition and Health* (Berkeley and Los Angeles: University of California Press, 2002), p. 32.

12 Ibid., p. 31.

13 Ibid., p. 12.

14 Ibid., p. 25.

[15] Ibid., p. 13. Nestle writes, "The U.S. food supply – plus imports minus exports – provides a daily average of 3,800 calories per capita. This level is nearly twice the amount needed to meet the energy requirements of most women, one-third more than that needed by most men, and much higher than that needed by babies, young children, and the sedentary elderly."

[16] According to Nestle (*Food Politics*, p. 22), in 1999, food companies spent $33 billion on advertising, 70 per cent of it on convenience foods, candy and snacks, alcohol, soft drinks, and desserts. Just 2.2 per cent was for vegetables, fruits, grains, or beans. Most of their advertising is for the things people should eat the least of in a healthy diet: fats, oils, and sweets.

[17] Ibid., p. 44.

[18] Ibid., p. 78. Milk contains lactose, a sugar that is basically indigestible by people over five. Whole milk is also high in fat.

[19] Lisa R. Young and Marion Nestle, "The Contribution of Expanding Portion Sizes to the U.S. Obesity Epidemic," New York University, June 3, 2001.

[20] Ibid.

[21] Ibid.

[22] *The Surgeon General's Call to Action to Prevent and Decrease Overweight and Obesity.*

[23] Benjamin Weiser, "Grounded for 10 Months (And No TV!), A Convict Pleads for Mercy," *New York Times*, March 6, 2002, all ed., sec. National.

[24] Mark S. Tremblay and J. Douglas Willms, "Secular Trends in the Body Mass Index of Canadian Children," *Canadian Medical Association Journal*, November 28, 2000.

[25] David Graham, "The Fat Revolution," *Toronto Star*, March 22, 2002, all ed., sec. Life.

[26] See <www.obesity.org/subs/fastfacts/obesity_global_epidemic.shtml>.

[27] "Controlling the Global Obesity Epidemic," <www.who.int/nut/obs.htm>.

CHAPTER FOURTEEN

[1] Elisabeth Bumiller, "Polls Drive Bush Shift to Domestic Concerns; Terror Fight Isn't Key to Midterm Voting," *International Herald*

Tribune, May 11-12, 2002, Paris ed., sec. World News: p. 2. The *International Herald Tribune* is an overseas publication owned jointly by the *New York Times* and *Washington Post*. The article quoted here was originally written for the *Times*.

2   Tu Thanh Ha, "Big Picture Missed in Run-up to Terror," *Globe and Mail*, May 25, 2002, final ed., sec. World: p. A4.

3   Ibid.

4   Toby Helm, "Bush Urges Europe to Join War on Terror," *National Post*, May 24, 2002, final ed., sec. World: p. A12.

5   George Washington is quoted in Henry Kissinger's *Diplomacy* (New York, Toronto: Simon & Schuster, 1994), p. 32. Of all the books I read during the course of writing this, *Diplomacy* was the one I found to be the most telling and instructive. Every American should read at least chapters 2 and 31.

6   Ibid., p. 32.

7   Ibid., p. 36.

8   Ibid., p. 44.

9   Ibid., p. 47.

10 Ibid. Kissinger quotes Woodrow Wilson's State of the Union address in 1915: "Because we demand unmolested development and the undisturbed government of our own lives upon our own principles of right and liberty, we resent, from whatever quarter it may come, the aggression we ourselves will not practice. We insist upon security in prosecuting our self-chosen lines of national development. We do more than that. We demand it also for others. We do not confine our enthusiasm for individual liberty and free national development to the incidents and movements of affairs which affect only ourselves. We feel it wherever there is a people that tries to walk in these difficult paths of independence and right."

11 Ibid., p. 49.

12 Quotation taken from *The Spirit of America: Favourite American Quotes, Poems, Songs, and Recipes* (New York: Clarkson Potter, 2002), p. 4.

13 "U.S. Must Step up Public Diplomacy, Officials and Senators Agree," Washington File, June 11, 2002. The Washington File is a reporting service of the U.S. State Department. The report in question was of testimony to the Senate Foreign Relations Panel given by Charlotte

Beers, undersecretary for public diplomacy and public affairs, and Norman Pattiz, chairman of Westwood One, the largest U.S. radio network. Beers reported that, based on polls, three-quarters of Muslims in the Middle East have an "unfavourable opinion" of the U.S. "There are many lessons that we are still learning from [September 11], and certainly one of the most important is that we can and should do more to educate, and influence the attitudes of, foreign audiences toward our country," Beers told the hearing. "No longer is it acceptable to let others define America, our beliefs, tenets, and values. It is in our collective national security interest that we do a better job defining ourselves to the world." Pattiz subsequently played a sample of the programming American broadcasters plan to use in the Middle East on an American network called Radio Sawa (Sawa means "together" in Arabic). The broadcast featured a song by Britney Spears.

EPILOGUE

1 David E. Sanger, "Bush to Outline Doctrine of Striking Foes First," *New York Times*, September 20, 2002, all ed., front page. The *Times* received a final draft of the document a day before its official release on September 21, 2002.

2 See Chapter 4 for the original reference to the *New Yorker* article.

3 Excerpt from *New York Times*, September 20, 2002, all ed., p. A10.

4 Ibid.

5 David Armstrong, "Dick Cheney's Song of America: Drafting a Plan for Global Dominance," *Harper's*, October 2002, p. 78.

6 Ibid.

7 Ibid.

8 Ibid, p. 79.

9 The ICC, based in The Hague, came into force on July 1, 2002, after sixty signatory states ratified the original statute, which came out of an international conference in Rome in the summer of 1998. One hundred and twenty countries voted for the creation of the court, while seven voted against it: the U.S., China, Iraq, Libya, Yemen, Qatar, and Israel. Human Rights Watch has accused the United States of trying to "undermine" the ICC by signing treaties with states to exempt U.S. servicemen and women from the ICC in

those countries, and by adopting the American Servicemembers' Protection Act on August 3, 2002. The law includes provisions for the punishment of states that sign the ICC treaty and an "invasion of The Hague" provision that authorizes the American president to "use all means necessary and appropriate" to free U.S. personnel detained by the ICC. See <www.hrw.org/campaigns/iss/us.htm>.

10 As late as November 2, 2002, the Bush administration was being accused by the families of the victims of September 11 of stalling the creation of an independent commission to look into the intelligence failures leading up to the attacks. Various intelligence agencies, including the CIA and the FBI, were aware of suspected terrorists taking flying lessons in the U.S. in the summer before September 11 but failed to put the pieces together. This was in spite of the fact that it was known that terrorists had plotted to smash planes into targets in the past; the most recent threat had come at the G7 summit in Italy earlier that year. The impasse was suddenly ended in December 2002, when Bush named Henry Kissinger to lead the inquest into the intelligence failure. Kissinger accepted the job but backed out two weeks later when he learned he would have to reveal who his clients are at his blue-chip consulting firm. This was a relief to some of the victims' families, who recognized Kissinger as a man more loyal to the people who hire him than to the American Constitution.

11 Todd S. Purdum and Elisabeth Bumiller, "Bush Seeks Power to Use 'All Means' to Oust Hussein," *New York Times*, September 20, 2002, all ed., front page.

INDEX